Virtual Homelands

THE ASIAN AMERICAN EXPERIENCE

Series Editors
Eiichiro Azuma
Jigna Desai
Martin F. Manalansan IV
Lisa Sun-Hee Park
David K. Yoo

Roger Daniels, Founding Series Editor

A list of books in the series appears at the end of this book.

Virtual Homelands

Indian Immigrants and Online Cultures in the United States

MADHAVI MALLAPRAGADA

UNIVERSITY OF ILLINOIS PRESS
Urbana, Chicago, and Springfield

© 2014 by the Board of Trustees
of the University of Illinois
All rights reserved
Manufactured in the United States of America
1 2 3 4 5 C P 5 4 3 2 1
♾ This book is printed on acid-free paper.

Library of Congress Control Number: 2014940417
ISBN 978-0-252-03863-1 (hardcover)
ISBN 978-0-252-08022-7 (paperback)
ISBN 978-0-252-09656-3 (e-book)

Contents

List of Illustrations — vii

Acknowledgments — ix

Introduction: Recasting Home — 1

1. Homepage Nationalisms: Silicon Indians and Curry Codes — 21

2. Out of Place in the Domestic Space: H4 Indian Ladies Negotiating Belonging — 46

3. The Wired Home: Commodified Belonging for the Transnational Family — 82

4. Desi Networks: Linking Race, Class, and Immigration to Homeland — 115

Conclusion: Home Matters in the Age of Networks — 143

Notes — 153

Index — 181

Illustrations

Figure 1.	Photo montage using guns, explosions, and combat gear to depict Indian immigrant men on the warpath to India's IT development	33
Figure 2.	Brown muscular bodies of Indian American men reconstructing Texas into a high-tech state	36
Figure 3.	Advertisement for Namaste.com reproducing an ideal image of Indian women in the immigrant setting of the United States	94
Figure 4.	DRUM members at a press conference and rally outside of City Hall demanding the passage of the Inspector General Bill for oversight of the New York Police Department in 2013	121
Figure 5.	DRUM Youth Power! members at the 2011 Open Mic on "Desi: Undocumented and Unafraid"	135

Acknowledgments

This book would not have been possible without the support of my family, friends, and colleagues, to whom I am profoundly indebted. I thank Julie D'Acci, Michele Hilmes, Hemant Shah, Michael Curtin, and Lisa Nakamura for their constructive criticism and enthusiastic support at the University of Wisconsin–Madison, where the early ideas for this book were generated. Julie D'Acci is an inspiring role model; I am grateful to her for constantly challenging me to think more deeply and write with greater clarity. The innumerable conversations I had with Hemant Shah about diasporic life not only were a source of comfort for me as I was getting used to life in a new country but also greatly enriched my intellectual training and understanding. I am grateful to Michele Hilmes and Michael Curtin for affection, support, and conversations over the years. They are my mentors in every way possible, and their ways of thinking and being in this profession inspire me. Lisa Nakamura's brilliant scholarship has indelibly influenced my research and writing. She is a friend, mentor, and ally who guides my writing with her insights and supports me with her love and kindness.

Mobina Hashmi, Jennifer Fuller, and Shazia Iftkhar enrich my life and work through their friendship, humor, wisdom, and brilliant scholarship. They patiently listen to my ideas, willingly read drafts, give honest feedback, and above all enthusiastically motivate me. I thank Bill Kirkpatrick, Josh Heuman, Ron Becker, Norma Coates, Elana Levine, Michael Newman, Kevin French, Paddy Rourke, Vera Crowell, Vinu Sampath, Melissa Curtin, Venkat Dhulipala, Chris Chekuri, Himadeep Muppidi, and Aswin Punathambekar for their friendship. My gratitude also goes to Kirin Narayan, V. N. Rao, Sunaina Maira, Purnima

Mankekar, Yeidy Rivero, Sangita Gopal, Srivi Ramasubramanium, Mary Gray, Kamran Ali, Pauline Strong, and Simone Browne. Radhika Gajjala mentors me in her inimitable style—warm, witty, and no-nonsense all at the same time. Paddy Enjeti, thank you for predicting that I would write a book, way before I had any idea that I would go down this path!

I thank my colleagues in the Radio-TV-Film Department at the University of Texas–Austin for their support and encouragement. Special thanks to Karin Wilkins, Joe Straubhaar, Lalitha Gopalan, Nancy Schiesari, Sharon Strover, Laura Stein, Jennifer Brundidge, Janet Staiger, Charles Ramirez Berg, and Paul Stekler. Tom Schatz has been an incredible mentor and guide; I am grateful to him for helping me navigate professional challenges and for reminding me to keep my focus on research and writing. For their integrity, friendship, and unflinching support I thank Mary Kearney, Michael Kackman, Mary Beltrán, and Wenhong Chen. At UT's Center for Asian American Studies, I have an amazing intellectual and political community that sustains me. My heartfelt thanks to Madeline Hsu, Nhi Lieu, Julia Lee, Naomi Paik, kt shorb, Kim Alidio, Kamala Visweswaran, Sharmila Rudrappa, Eric Tang, and Snehal Shingavi. My students have influenced my thinking and writing over the years; I thank them all. In particular, I thank Alex Cho, Caitlin McClune, Jacob Hustedt, Manuel Avila Santiago, Ali Sengul, Suzanne Schulz, Ricky Hill, and Natasha Raheja for engaging me in incredibly productive ways. The research and writing for this book were supported by fellowships and grants from the Center for Asian American Studies, the South Asia Institute, the Office of Graduate Studies, the College of Communication, and the Humanities Institute at UT-Austin. Their generous support provided me with the time and funds that I needed to complete this project.

At the University of Illinois Press, I am grateful to Vijay Shah, my editor, for his enthusiastic commitment to my project from the beginning. My sincere appreciation goes to Laurie Matheson, Jennifer Comeau, and Dawn Durante for all their help and support. Many thanks to the anonymous reviewers of the manuscript for their insightful comments and helpful suggestions. Thanks to David Lobenstine and Jane Curran for their expert copyediting and to Sheila Bodell for compiling the index.

I am indebted to series editor Jigna Desai for her sustained investment in my project and for being my friend, mentor, and advocate. She encouraged me to keep writing when I thought I could not, kept me on track through her gentle yet firm guidance, read drafts of chapters, provided incisive feedback, and, perhaps most importantly, trusted my voice.

Acknowledgments

I am grateful for my wonderful family in Hyderabad, Mumbai, Austin, and Chapel Hill. Radha and Vijay, thank you for always being there for me. Your love, encouragement, and steady support, combined with a tactful questioning of my work life, provided the emotional cushion I needed to write this book. Vasu, thank you for being the quiet inspiration behind this project. Your pathbreaking e-commerce company and your pioneering vision for networked Indian homes in the digital age influenced me tremendously. Shreya, Aniket, Sangita, and Sanskrita, you bring joy to my life. PCji and Radha, thank you for everything. Thank you, Heidi Siegenthaler, for being a part of our family. You lovingly take care of my daughter so that I can work, think, and write. I cannot thank you enough.

My deepest debt of gratitude is to my partner and the love of my life, Shanti Kumar. I undertook the daunting task of embarking on this project and conducting new research in the same year that I became a mother. I had no idea how difficult it would be! If it weren't for Shanti's unflinching faith in my ability to overcome challenges, I would not have been able to finish this book. Thank you, Shanti, for nurturing me with your love, sparkling wit, and delicious recipes and for single-handedly running the household during my intense writing sessions. Priya, there is no one more precious than you. Thank you for showing me how to live in the moment! Your love and my desire to play with you motivated me to get to the finish line as soon as possible. I am indebted to my father-in-law and mother-in-law for showing me how to live life fully and fearlessly through the practice of meditation. Their guidance has been invaluable to me during the ups and downs of writing this book. My parents are a constant source of love and inspiration in my life. I could not have started this book without their blessings and support, let alone finish it. I dedicate this book to them.

Virtual Homelands

Introduction

Recasting Home

Virtual Homelands: Indian Immigrants and Online Cultures in the United States is a study of the textual, institutional, and discursive politics of online media that target, speak to, and are shaped by Indian immigrant cultures. The book's main emphasis is on the idea of home, and its many reconfigurations online through the concept of the *homepage*. It critically evaluates how homepages anchor the ideals and ideologies of belonging online in relation to two dominant imaginaries traditionally associated with the time-space of the home—namely, the domestic, familial household and the public, national homeland.

The central contention of this study is that the development and popularization of online media as technologies of digital capital, virtual communication, and transnational e-commerce have engendered the homepage as a crucial site for Indian immigrants living in the United States to reimagine their identities, desires, and politics around self, community, citizenship, and transnational belonging. Therefore, the book argues that online media play a crucial role in the ongoing struggles over belonging and citizenship for diverse groups within the Indian American community by representing, reconstructing, and reimagining the Indian immigrant household and homeland (which include India and/or the United States).[1]

While the idea of a monolithic Indian American community is a hegemonic and an idealized construct, it continues to be reinforced in many mainstream narratives of online media industries and cultures in the United States and in India. However, there are multiple other narratives thriving online that point to the diverse political, social, and cultural realities of immigrant subjects. Hence online media spaces offer critical perspectives into the continuing circulation of categories that historically have been associated with Indian immigrants in the United States—including Indian Americans (U.S. citizens of Indian ethnicity), but also nonresident Indians (NRIs; Indian citizens living abroad), persons of Indian origin (PIOs; not legal citizens of India, but they maintain cultural affiliation), and South Asian Americans (a larger collective of U.S. citizens and residents from the South Asian region). Important to note here is that while these categories might have been embedded within state discourses and legal policies, their usage and circulation within community discourses have always blurred the lines between the officially demarcated categories. For instance, using the terms *NRI*, *Indian American*, and *Indian immigrant* interchangeably is very common online, thereby suggesting tensions between state agendas and public imaginations of community as well as the prescribed and lived realities of the everyday.

Hegemonic ideologies about the family and citizenship are being increasingly reconfigured online to make them interoperable with the transnational contexts of media and immigration. At the same time, alternative imaginations of the private home as a site of un-belonging and of the public nation as a site for struggles over cultural citizenship reveal the constructed nature of idealized representations of Indian immigrants as "wired" nonresident Indians.[2] As Indian immigrants recast household and homeland online, they testify to the imbrication of public agents—such as the state, the law, and the immigration system—in cultures of the domestic, the private, the familial.

For example, there are many websites, blogs, social media spaces, and mobile media platforms that claim to represent the interests of the global Indian community at large, while others target the interests of a specific subgroup, such as H-1B Indian professionals living in the United States. While the latter represent a specific, and often elite, section of the Indian immigrant community in the United States, their hegemonic location within dominant discourses about Indian immigrants' sense of belonging is foregrounded through the alternative but critical representations of gender, class, and labor relations in the community at large. Similarly, the meanings of Indian American cultural locations imagined online are recast by South Asian American activist organizations such as DRUM (Desis Rising up and Moving), SAWNET (South Asian Women's NETwork), and SAALT (South Asian Americans Leading Together), which use new media technologies to provide alternative narratives of belonging based on coalitions across race, gender, class, age, region, and religion or nationality.

These online reconfigurations of who or what is included within the Indian immigrant community point to a larger argument that underpins this book; namely, that online media offer an unprecedented space for Indian immigrants to represent themselves, establish their visibility, and help set their own cultural agendas. More importantly, online media become the very sites where the politics and cultural struggles over representation, visibility, and power relations are engendered, mediated, and contingently played out. It is precisely at this intersection—of the politics of Indian immigrant belonging and the new modalities of being and becoming at home in the network era—that this book seeks to make its contribution.

Specifically, through a series of case studies, this book investigates how the homepage, a primary unit of identification in online media, emerges as a powerful metaphor for transnational belonging for Indian immigrants. While the literal and symbolic meanings attached to the notion of being "at home" in the immigrant landscape have been addressed within studies of the Indian and the South Asian diasporic communities, this study explores how homepages illuminate the dynamic and shifting nature of immigrant politics and cultural citizenship. With the emergence of networking technologies, e-commerce, and online communications since the 1990s, the technological literacy of Indian immigrants has increasingly crystallized around the idea of being "at home" online. Similarly, in current media discussions in the United States about the role of social media platforms like Facebook, Twitter, and YouTube—and the way they are transforming long-standing distinctions between inside and outside, public and private, the home and the world, the domestic and the foreign—the tech-savvy Indian immigrant remains a very powerful force.[3]

These narratives span Indian American media and the Indian and U.S. mainstream press and are built around several recurring themes: the Indian immigrant presence in Silicon Valley, their investment in e-commerce start-ups, their creative use of online media to connect with their Indian homeland, and their resourceful creation of websites, blogs, search engines, and apps to make themselves more comfortable in their new homeland (and more able to remain connected to India).[4] The stereotype of the "wired" Indian is, of course, unique to the network era, and yet it is also the latest incarnation of a stereotype that has existed since the 1970s: the Indian immigrant as technological migrant who enters the United States by virtue of the flows of capital, labor, and knowledge across the scientific, medical, and engineering sectors between India and the United States following the immigration reforms of 1965. Similarly, the frameworks of old and new homelands, country of origin and present residence, and participation in the American economy and investment in the Indian cultural economy were never far from such hegemonic visions of the community.

What such narratives reveal is that the emergence of the homepage as an anchoring metaphor for the network age does not take us away from older imaginaries of belonging mobilized around the private household or the national homeland. At the same time, newer imaginations of mediated mobility and digital dislocation driven by the rise of Web 2.0 platforms, social media, and mobile networks do not make the question of home, domesticity, and location irrelevant. It is worth noting that social media networks such as Facebook, LinkedIn, Twitter, Tumblr, and YouTube all have homepages to firmly anchor them online. Moreover, when Facebook launched its "Home" app for android phones in April 2013, it was a clear signal that the social media giant recognizes the tremendous market potential for being the default "home screen" for mobile phones in the same way as Google, Yahoo, and Bing dominate the "homepage" market on the Web.[5] At the same time, the acquisition of the video-sharing website YouTube by Google in October 2006, Microsoft's strategic partnership with the mobile company Nokia in February 2011, and Yahoo's announcement of its plans to buy the microblogging and video-sharing website Tumblr in May 2013 are three of the more prominent examples of many acquisitions, mergers, and collaborations between pioneering Internet companies and the newer mobile and social media companies.[6] Internet pioneers realize that the aggressive pursuit of social media and mobile platforms is essential to continue their dominance of homepages and home screens; and social media and mobile platforms realize that the homepage or home screen remains as salient as ever, no matter how mobile we may be.

There are some important differences between homepages on the Web and home screens on mobile media, like smart phones and smart tablets, in terms of their interface design and technological architecture. But more significant is the way in which "home" remains the most powerful concept for media industries—new and old alike—to tether themselves to the everyday ways that customers imagine and live their lives through familiar and familial categories of domesticity, locality, and community.

Indeed, the continued salience on the concept of "home" in homepages—whether on websites or in social media or mobile media—signals the ongoing opportunity and challenge for us to construct as well as contest the many meanings associated with belonging online. To that end, this study interrogates the idea of home, specifically its expression in homepages through ideologies of the private, domestic household and the public national homeland. In doing so, the book also illuminates how questions of gender and nation, which inform existing debates on home and belonging, continue to be pressing and urgent concerns in online media. At the same time, by making questions of immigration, race, and class more central to the conversation about belonging online, this study argues for situating macro-tropes of belonging (such as nationalism and citizenship) within the micro-sites of the everyday shaped by factors such as one's migrant status, class location, racial identity, and political affiliation.

Belonging in Homepage Cultures

The homepage is the designated main, or first, page of any website. It is accessed through the site's Uniform Resource Locator (URL), the addressing scheme that begins typically with "http" or "www" and identifies and retrieves (through the help of one's browser) the desired document on the World Wide Web.[7] The symbolism of the designation "*the* homepage" for the main page that loads up when one types in a given URL address is not lost on either the designers or the users of online media. Tim Berners-Lee, also known as the inventor of the Web since he wrote the codes for the Hypertext Markup Language (HTML), Hypertext Transfer Protocol (HTTP), and World Wide Web (WWW) programs that are foundational to the medium, has described the homepage as the "destination document" at which the user or client computer arrives following network protocols.[8] Although the necessary architecture of the Internet—the Transmission Control Protocols/Internet Protocols known as TCP/IP—was ready by the mid-1970s, and the language of the Web—Hypertext Markup Language, or HTML—was written by 1990, what we think of in popular parlance as "the Web" didn't emerge until 1993, when Netscape Navigator made its mark as a graphical interface to the Web.[9] During the period between 1994 and 2001, there was a very rapid proliferation of websites, some driven by commerce and others oriented toward community, that creatively embraced the concept of the homepage to craft their online identities and participate in the creation of what is now retrospectively called *Web 1.0* (following the introduction of the term *Web 2.0* in the early 2000s, and more recent debates about *Web 3.0* or the "semantic Web" technologies).[10]

As web interfaces have evolved over the last two decades, and websites have embraced ever-newer designs and technologies to craft their online identities, the concept of the homepage continues to be the key locus for negotiating the changing spaces of the public and the private. The homepage continues to be emotionally resonant, as well as practically important, triggering associations of a home space that is familiar and therefore comforting. As the content, aesthetics, and organization of a main page likely shifts over time and across the various incarnations of websites, the designation of the homepage confers a sense of familiarity to the users of online media—a site once visited, a space once accessed. As Martin Lister points out, "even in large-scale commercial websites this reassuringly domestic terminology offers the lost browser a return to a familiar page."[11] Implicit in the link between the familiarity of the homepages with the familiarity of the home space is a nostalgic idea of home as always and already a stable, unchanging place that one could (or perhaps should) return to.

Therefore, when the homepage is strategically mobilized in online media—by community groups to online businesses to bloggers—to reproduce conservative narratives of an unchanging homeland for Indian immigrants in the United States, the political, economic, cultural, and technological investments of the sites in question go beyond their textual and hypertextual elements; just as important are the institutional cultures shaping them. Unlike traditional media and communication technologies such as television or film, whose institutional cultures have historically been framed within a nationalist optic, online media and technologies have always been viewed as transnational. Moreover, as Lisa Nakamura has argued, Asian Americans' relationship with online media, including their roles as consumers and active users, can signal how the shifting platforms of technology and media shape and in turn are shaped by ideologies of race, difference, and cultural citizenship.[12]

For instance, while Indian Americans have rarely found visibility in mainstream American television and film (although there has been a spate of South Asian American characters since the mid-2000s), they have been making their presence felt online since the earliest years of the Web. So even as *Time* magazine ran a cover headline in July 1994 about "The Strange New World of the Internet," in the dominant discourse about Indian immigrants (especially narratives from within the community), the Internet was neither strange nor was its underlying technology of networks, code, and software new.[13]

In the two decades since—a period in which the relations between (new) media, migration, and mobility have grown in both intensity and complexity—online media have borne testimony to the overlapping contours of identification and politics as well as distinctions within and across groups such as nonresident Indians, Indian Americans, and South Asian Americans. In 1994, amid the spectacular debut of Yahoo, the company that gave us its eponymous search engine, a California-based start-up funded by Indian American venture capitalists (VCs) inaugurated its own web portal. The site, webindia.com, was geared explicitly toward Indian immigrants in the United States. In its 1990s avatar (the site has since morphed into a financial service company operating within India), it functioned as a one-stop gateway to "all things Indian," in the domains of news, entertainment, finances, religion, food, astrology, and the like. The intent was to bring together all the things about India that immigrants were likely to miss and seek out in their new homeland—in other words, to bring the experience of India online. The inspiration for such an online service apparently came from the experiences of many in the start-up team. Having first arrived in the United States in the 1980s and early 1990s to work and to study, the creators had encountered firsthand the perks and challenges of living as immigrants.[14]

While webindia.com represented its content as the migration of India to the Internet, the early search engines indiainfo.com and indiaworld.com created an association between information pathways, search algorithms, and a virtual India that could be uploaded on computer screens. The motivation and premise behind webindia.com is relevant to note here, because it is one that has been replicated in many of the e-commerce ventures that followed, which have explicitly promoted their business as serving Indian immigrant needs. Exactly what those immigrant needs are continues to shift, slowly but surely, in relation to the cultural desires of consumers, the social context, and the emergent technological capacities of online media.

Next came the dot-com boom of the mid-1990s, which was inextricably linked to the rise of Indian immigrants in the fields of venture capital, Silicon Valley start-ups, and web entrepreneurial networks. Not surprisingly, the Web was projected as a familiar space as all things "Indian" were becoming accessible online. What made that space familiar were the daily domestic activities that were migrating online—reading an Indian newspaper on samachar.com, finding a recipe on bawarchi.com, finding a spouse on indianmatrimonials.com, ordering international phone cards on rediff.com, and getting the latest cricket statistics from cricinfo.com.

At the same time, the personal web page, a popular genre tied to the services of web-hosting companies such as GeoCities (later Yahoo! GeoCities) offered a host of new ways for immigrants to represent themselves online.[15] Indian graduate students at U.S. universities, while far from the only immigrant group to create web pages, were among the most visible and enthusiastic adopters of this genre. Part identity construction, part imagined community service, these pages often mixed the very private and personal (such as images and details about hometown, parents, siblings, and self) with the very public and collective (such as information about the Indian cricket team, a U.S. sports team, and other subjects of interest such as art, history, and religion).[16] Unfortunately, many of these web pages are no longer accessible, victim of the vagaries of capital investments and the lack of a systematic and thorough mechanism for website archiving.[17] Nevertheless the personal homepage cultures of Indian immigrants exemplified the evolving ways to enact belonging during a period marked by transformations in migration and media alike.

By the late 1990s, it was common for the growing number of websites that were based in India to target the Indian American community, typically with content that was India-centric but advertising that was U.S.-centric. For example, samachar.com regularly featured advertising for immigration firms, long-distance phone companies, matrimonial services, astrologists, shopping sites, and money remittance, all of which ostensibly met the needs of Indian immigrants. By the early 2000s, the total number of immigrant-oriented sites continued to grow, and they became more and more specific. Indian companies, and a growing number of American companies, developed shopping sites (indiaplaza.com, namaste.com), matrimonial and dating sites (h1bmarriages.com, indiandating.com, shaadi.com), community and chat sites (sulekha.com, garamchai.com); each further splintered the common address to the community along niche, targeted needs—the best evidence for the crucial role of Indian immigrants in the growing landscape of the World Wide Web.[18]

At the same time, Rediff.com, a Mumbai-based, commercially operated "community" site that was launched in 1996, created a business model that embraced more flexible notions of cultural citizenship. In 2000, Rediff began capitalizing on its U.S. base by unveiling a new U.S. version of its homepage as a parallel to its India-based site.[19] In providing a U.S. version and an Indian version of its homepage simultaneously, Rediff was one of the earliest online companies to acknowledge and profit from the transnational connections, fluid identities, and flexible economies that constitute the Indian American communities of the twenty-first century. In 2010, and again in 2013, Rediff revamped its website to capitalize on growing use of mobile media and social media by designing a new tiled interface that prominently displays applications like MobileRediff and Rediff e-commerce.[20]

Similarly, leading Indian banks such as ICICI Bank have used a variety of online media technologies not only to provide financial services for Indian immigrants but also to advertise their wares on the homepages of other popular sites like Rediff.com, samachar.com, and sify.com.[21] ICICI Bank also uses Facebook, YouTube, and Twitter extensively to connect with its growing consumer base in India and the United States. ICICI Bank's Twitter handle "ICICI Cares" and its Facebook slogan "Within Your Reach, Always" reveal how the bank uses the rhetoric of domesticity and community to connect with its Indian and Indian American customers who are far from the bank's home base in Mumbai.

The diversity in the modalities of address in online media toward Indian immigrant concerns testifies to the complexity as well as the specificity of belonging. An important trend is the focus on the local and regional location of the immigrant within the territory of the United States. For instance, a U.S.-based site like bayareaindia.com promotes the interests of immigrants in the Bay Area, while an India-based site like sulekha.com replicates the same pattern but on a grander scale. A very popular community site in the United States (and India), sulekha.com offers a series of city- and state-specific hyperlinks to streamline its content and make it relevant to local groups.

In addition, sites organized around specific elements such as religion, profession, language, or political affiliation reiterate the point that there is no singular interest or agenda that defines the community. Some examples of such sites include fiacona.org (Federation of Indian American Christian Organizations in North America), TiE.org (The Indus Entrepreneurs, an organization for Silicon Valley professionals), TANA.org (Telugu Association of North America, which promotes the interests and language of the Telugu-speaking community from the South Indian state Andhra Pradesh), and iacfpa.org (Indian American Center for Political Awareness, a nonprofit organization promoting political leadership and participation). Also visible in online media are hegemonic ideologies of nation, elitist iterations of class, and normative ideals of gendered and racial hierarchy. For example, the articulation of a middle-class Hindu-centric heteronormative Indian American identity is visible in overtly religious sites like hindunet.org but, importantly, also in commercially driven community sites like California-based indolink.com and nonprofit sites like Macungie, Pennsylvania–based agii.org (the home of the Association of Grandparents of Indian Immigrants).

However, it is important to remember that they exist alongside alternative imaginations of immigrant identity and alliance in sites like sakhi.org (Sakhi for South Asian women), salganyc.org (South Asian Gay and Lesbian Association of New York City), and Trikone.org (for Lesbian, Gay, Bisexual, and Transgender South Asians). Critiquing gender and sexual norms in the community but simultaneously advancing a transnational feminist, queer activist model of community and belonging, these sites ultimately reject a nationalist framing of the issues of identity and rights.

Indian Immigrants in the Age of Network Capitalism

Hegemonic discourses about Indian immigrants in the United States articulate a tight link across three frames—Indian culture, technology, and elite forms of mobility—to produce the idea that Indian immigrants are model minorities of the digital age, wired, techno-experts who, as a recent PEW report concludes, are also the wealthiest of all Asian American groups.[22] The 2012 PEW report, titled "The Rise of Asian Americans," in turn feeds into the market discourse of Asian Americans as premium consumers and, in effect, as the new frontier for the expansion of capitalism in multicultural America. Indian immigrants, in this narrative, are right at home with digital capitalist cultures and neoliberal ideologies of individual choice and consumptive citizenship.[23]

The PEW report begins with the following celebratory but misleading overview: "Asian Americans are the highest-income, best-educated and fastest-growing racial group in the United States. They are more satisfied than the general public with their lives, finances and the direction of the country, and they place more value than other Americans do on marriage, parenthood, hard work and career success."[24] The headline that was used in the official press release for the report was no less dramatic or problematic; it read, "Asians Overtake Hispanics in New Immigrant Arrivals; Surpass US Public in Valuing Marriage, Parenthood, Hard Work."[25] In a critique of the report's reliance on the image of Asian Americans as a model minority, Karthick Ramakrishnan, an adviser for the research team that produced the report, rightfully notes that the headline is disturbing for "the invidious comparisons it seemed to invite of a racial group that is overtaking Hispanics and other Americans in a metaphorical race for national supremacy."[26]

The model minority stereotype, first developed in the 1960s, reproduces the idea that Asian immigrants are successful because of their focus on individual responsibility, hard work, and family values, without getting entangled in political and social issues. In addition to being reductive, the stereotype is also dangerous for how it has too often been used: to ignore the structurally determined inequities among Asian Americans, on the one hand, and, on the other, to delegitimize racialized critiques of the state and neoliberal capitalist system by pointing to the self-reliant, complying, and idealized figure of the Asian minority subjects, whose success lies in part in their political passivity.[27]

Appearing at a time when it is clear that those living in the United States are dissatisfied and struggling with dwindling options, the PEW report begins with a dramatically different image of Asian Americans, successful and more content than "the general public," while they nurture their lives with their love of family and hard work. With regard to the headline, one might add further that not only is the suggestion of a race toward national supremacy inherently problematic for what it suggests about power and hierarchy, but the very notion of a monolithic Asian American race pitted against other monolithic racial groups is unsustainable even by mainstream standards since at least 2000, when the Census Bureau started including mixed race as a category of identification.[28]

However problematic the PEW research report might be, it offers us an opportunity to notice the growing mainstream interest in pitching Asian Americans, including Indian Americans, as the "rising" immigrant group of present times. This trend, while in the making for a couple of decades now, has been foregrounded particularly since the findings of the census report of 2000.[29] In particular, the report highlighted that Asian Americans are the fastest-growing consumer market in the United States, upstaging Hispanic groups. More notably, the PEW report concluded Asian Americans had the highest income among all U.S. groups and that they were not only likely to buy more than other groups but, very importantly, they were more likely to buy high-end products. This revelation, so to speak, was quickly absorbed by the consumer industry, and it was very common in the early 2000s to see numerous references to Asian Americans as "premium" consumers.[30] The PEW report of 2012 does little to destabilize that image; rather, it reinforces the idea that Asian Americans are the wealthiest, most educated, and most successful of all U.S. groups. Within that framework, it highlights the unique ways in which Indian Americans represent the "rise" of the Asian American. Building on the census reports of 2000 and 2010, the PEW Research team notes that the median annual income for Indian American households ($88,000) is considered to be the highest in all the U.S. households ($49,800), including all other Asian American households ($66,000).[31]

If the growing economic clout of Indian Americans is one yardstick by which their model minority success is being framed in these mainstream accounts, another key factor is their numerical strength, which is discussed in absolute and relative terms. According to the 2010 census report, there are approximately 3.2 million Indian Americans, who account for around 18.4 percent of the total Asian population in the United States, which is estimated to be over 17 million.[32] The census report of 2010 also indicates that Asian Americans account for 5.6 percent of the total U.S. population, recording a growth of approximately 4.6 percent since 1965. The year 1965 holds particular significance for Asian and Indian immigration to the United States. When the Immigration and Nationality Act was passed that year, it created a steady stream of migrants from Asia, including India. Like their Asian counterparts, Indians had been arriving on U.S. shores since the 1800s, most of them to build the U.S. nation by working on its mines, farms, and railroads. In addition to doing low-wage jobs, Asian migrants faced racism, violence, and exclusion sanctioned by the state (through its immigration policies) and dominant white society (through its social attitudes and practices toward Asians) in nineteenth- and twentieth-century America.[33] In many respects, 1965 is seen as a key moment in Asian American history. The post-1965 generation, those Indians who migrated to the United States in the 1960s and 1970s, are considered as the first generation of Indian immigrants, with their children viewed as the second generation, as U.S.-born citizens of Indian origin or ethnicity. Indian Americans are considered to be one of the six largest Asian American groups by country of origin, along with Chinese, Korean, Japanese, Filipino, and Vietnamese Americans.[34]

While almost half of the foreign-born Indian immigrants in the United States have become U.S. citizens, the category of Indian American is shifting in terms of its contours, usage, and cultural implications. One crucial example is that both in the U.S. census and the PEW research report, the term *Indian American* (like *Asian American*) is used broadly to include U.S.-born citizens, Indian-born naturalized citizens, and Indian citizens who live in the United States as permanent residents (with a green card) or who temporarily reside (a period that can stretch to more than a decade) on visas including student visas, work visas, and the like.[35] While reports that rely on quantifying the immigrant group employ the category Indian American loosely, popular accounts—whether they are in the mainstream U.S. press or the Indian or Indian American press—often use terms like *Indian Americans* and *Indian immigrants* as well as nonresident Indians (NRIs) living in the United States interchangeably.

Unquestionably, there is an argument to be made here that the generalized framework might function both to signal the fluidity of community affiliations and to create an inerasable, naturalized continuity between Indian, immigrant, and Indian American, thereby cementing their status in Lisa Lowe's memorable phrase, "as perpetual foreigners within" the U.S. nation-state.[36] In fact, one of the most important early interventions of Asian American critique within media and communication studies was to foreground the imperial and racist cinematic framework that lumped Asians in Asia and Asian immigrants in the United States in the same category of nonwhite alterity; America's white, normative logic has employed various strategies, such as Orientalizing, trivializing, or criminalizing, to produce the "Asian" immigrant as an un-assimilable outsider.[37]

The shifts in the numerical and social configuration of this immigrant group as well as transformations in the broader cultural and political contexts, in the United States and India in particular, engender new spaces for critically reevaluating the terminologies of migrant locations exemplified through the ethnically marked Indian American, the nationally marked nonresident Indian, and the transnationally inflected Indian immigrant. Such a reevaluation must also keep in mind the possibilities (some hegemonic, others not so) attached to the loose and interchangeable mobilizations of Indian Americans, Indian immigrants, and NRIs in popular understandings. Relevant here is the current demographic trend indicating not only that Asians are the fastest-growing immigrant group, but also that almost three-fourths of the Asian

American population (roughly 74 percent) including adults and children are foreign-born, not U.S.-born; in other words, the community's configuration currently overwhelmingly emphasizes the Asian American as immigrant.[38] The 1990s, which recorded the highest ever levels of overall immigration to the United States, also witnessed the most prolific levels of migration from India to the United States.[39] The migration patterns also contributed to the demographic reconfiguration of the Indian immigrant community as Indians from far more diverse backgrounds—in terms of class, caste, language, education, region, and religious background alike—than ever before came to call America their home.[40]

Several factors came together to facilitate that trend: among them, the synergy between U.S. software and computing sectors and India's science- and technology-related labor force; economic liberalization and changing attitudes toward travel, migration, and transnational lifestyles in India; developments in U.S. immigration policies impacting diverse forms of migration for study, work, temporary labor, and family needs; and more broadly, the dynamics of globalization that impacted India and the United States in the areas of labor, education, technology, capital, state, and industry.

A key immigration rule, enabling specialized labor entry, plays a pivotal role in the story about Indian immigration to the United States, and for that reason it also plays a critical role in this book. The H-1B visa was created in 1990 to accommodate U.S. demands for specialized foreign labor in several booming sectors, especially technology, science, and medicine.[41] Although a temporary, non-immigrant visa that could be availed for a maximum of six years, the H-1B was also a dual-intent visa, which means that persons who are allotted the H-1B visa can enter the United States with another intention, namely to become immigrants, provided their U.S. employers can sponsor the transition from temporary H-1B visa holder to permanent resident (green card holder) and legal immigrant.[42]

Indians have long dominated this category, receiving approximately half of all the visas annually allotted; in 2011, for example, of the 129,134 H-1B visas issued, Indian citizens received 72,438, or 56 percent of the total visas allotted; China, the second-leading nation, received 10,849, or 8 percent.[43] Along with the workforce needs created by the information economy, Indian immigration to the United States has also been shaped by factors such as research and academic study and working-class labor. While more than half of all the international students at U.S. universities are from Asian countries, India and China send far more students than any other nations.[44] According to the Institute of International Education, during 2012–13, for instance, there were 96,754 students from

India, accounting for 11.8 percent of the total number of international students in the United States.⁴⁵

Furthermore, the changes in migration patterns intersect with other shifts in the Indian American community: growing political desires, increasing clout in the field of information technology and software, greater grass-roots social activism, and increased attention to issues of race, class, gender, religion, and transnational identifications across India and the United States.⁴⁶ The first generation of immigrants, who arrived between 1965 and the late 1970s, were mostly middle-class professionals in the fields of science, technology, and medicine, thereby engendering what Vijay Prashad terms the stereotype of the Indian as "techno-migrant."⁴⁷ Since the 1990s, that stereotype continues to persist, particularly in mainstream American and Indian media; and yet it is not as dominant, at least within some segments of the Indian community, because of an increased awareness of the working-class, impoverished, and vulnerable lives of many in the community.⁴⁸ Relevant here is the example of *desi*—a term referring broadly to someone with South Asian origins—which has become an important category of racialized identification as brown subjects, especially in post–9/11 America. These shifting identifications and realignments of Indian Americans are becoming more visible through youth and popular cultures, political investments, rights-based activism, transnational networking, and media cultures.⁴⁹

The reconfiguration of the Indian immigrant constituency is also influenced by the Indian government's relationship with this expatriate group, one that has been historically characterized by indifference, and some would say even disdain. The indifference, it is commonly suggested, stems from a perception that those who leave India to seek greener pastures abroad are not patriotic citizens of the country. What is interesting in this perception is the Indian government's focus on the economically successful émigrés rather than those who have struggled in their new locations as indentured labor or poor immigrants among others. The country's official rhetoric has focused on the idea of brain drain, implying that the Indians who leave the country are draining the nation of its most valuable resources since they represent the best of India.⁵⁰

At the epicenter of the brain drain debate have been the graduates of India's prestigious technical institutions, notably, the various centers of the Indian Institute of Technology (IIT), as well as the country's premier medical and, more recently, business schools. Although graduates of IITs have been emigrating to the United States since the late 1960s, the debate became heated especially in the 1980s and 1990s when the numbers of Indians migrating to the United States swelled considerably. It was widely reported that during the late 1980s and early 1990s almost 90 percent of the graduating class from one of the IITs,

IIT Chennai, made their way to the United States.⁵¹ The graduates of these elite public institutes were not only considered the best brains in the country but were also seen as responsible for the brain drain, since they were using their talents nurtured by the state's resources for the benefit of a foreign country.

Since the late 1990s, however, there has been a shift in the official relations between India and its expatriate community, a shift that seems to be inextricably connected to the perceived economic power of that expatriate community. The economic potential of these expatriates has been on the radar screen of the Indian government since the mid-1970s, when the category nonresident Indian was first created to allow immigrants to open foreign-currency bank accounts in India.⁵² However, it wasn't until India took steps to liberalize its economy in 1991 that there were steady and successful attempts by the Indian state to attract NRI remittances and investment.

Among the key reasons for such a spurt in NRI investments has been a more aggressive drive on the part of Indian financial institutions to attract NRI money by offering attractive interest rates and investment opportunities in the real estate and equity markets of India. According to the World Bank, in 2010 India was the nation with the highest amount of remittances from its overseas subjects, an estimated 27 million people living in over 190 countries. These expats sent back home an astounding $55 billion (China, a close second, gathered $51 billion from its expats), which was a 162 percent increase from the $21 billion in remittances for the year 2003.⁵³ A large part of these remittances come from the United States and the countries of the Persian Gulf and Middle East.

In 2003, around the time when the Indian state's plan for "dual citizenship" was unveiled, it was common to hear political leaders and government officials refer to nonresident Indians and American citizens of Indian origin as India's extended family.⁵⁴ There was a great deal of excitement over the prospect of being a citizen of both the United States and India.⁵⁵ Yet since the inauguration of the first Pravasi Bhartiya Divas (Nonresident Indian Day) in August 2003, the Indian state has been mulling over the terms of engagement with its diasporic citizens. While there are still no plans to offer dual citizenship, whereby one could legally retain two passports, the Indian state created a new category—Overseas Indian Citizenship (OCI)—in 2005 to enable non-U.S. citizens to avail themselves of benefits in the financial, educational, and economic fields that were being extended to NRIs. The OCI category was an upgrade over the Persons of Indian Origin (PIO) card that the Indian state instituted in 1999 to offer some benefits to foreign citizens of Indian origin, especially visa-free travel to India. In December 2011, the state operationalized its plans to merge the categories of PIO and OCI and, as of 2013, offers one identity card—the Overseas Citizen of India card.⁵⁶

The technologized iteration of the Indian immigrant condition is also a site of cultural production of ideologies of gender, class, and cultural nationalism. It is hence significant that the two key figures—the Indian American venture capitalist and the Indian software professional on the H-1B visa (a visa enabling highly skilled foreign labor to be temporarily employed in the United States)—to emerge over the course of the 1990s and 2000s are also produced as Hindu, middle-class men who are tied to their national homeland.[57] While such a vision is mobilized by the Indian and American cultural mainstreams, it serves different agendas and purposes. The transnational aspirations of hegemonic Indian nationalism rely on the incorporation of the successful Indian in the U.S. software sectors as evidence of "India Shining" in the twenty-first-century digital age.[58] The Indian American venture capitalist—male, Hindu, and middle class—along with the technologically abled bodies of Indian migrants become appropriate figures of the (Asian) Indian "homesteading on the electronic frontier," to recall Howard Rheingold's colonialist metaphor from his much-cited book *The Virtual Community*.[59] At the same time, the representation of the successful Indian immigrant, wherein success is measured through the yardstick of academic degrees, salaries, professional status, capital, and consumer goods accumulation, aligns very well with the image of "model minority" that has been applied since the 1960s to Asian Americans within the U.S. political and cultural mainstream.[60]

Recasting Home: Site Map and Chapter Links

In using the word *recasting* rather than *remaking* in this chapter, I want to suggest that there is no new, and no stable, location to be arrived at; rather, there are only ways to "cast" the net differently. The language of webs, spiders, and nets has been central to the descriptive and connotative meanings of online media. To these existing meanings, I want to introduce a few new dimensions: in the pages to come we meet new cast members (new industry players as well as new communities that have never been central to our narratives about Indian immigrants or online users), and we learn new ways of aligning our theoretical lens to read online media through categories such as race, class, and immigration (thereby casting new light, illuminating new contours of the online world that is already so central to our lives).

My method is informed by an integrated approach that studies media texts, usage, and institutions in specific historical and cultural contexts.[61] I use a combination of textual analyses, institutional analyses, and discursive analyses to examine online media and the contexts in which they participate.[62] Websites are not discrete objects, and therefore in my analysis, I foreground the intertextual and hypertextual nature of the Web's political and cultural economy.[63] I problematize the homepage as "text" by doing a discursive analysis of its hyperlinks that lead to other sites; in addition, I include institutional analyses of the cultures of ownership, sponsorship, funding, revenue, affiliations, and tie-ins of the sites within my framework, thus noting the ideological nodes or connections across texts, institutions, target users, and cultural contexts. Some of the homepages and images analyzed in this study no longer exist online. In such instances, I draw on my personal archive of stored images and web pages and historically contextualize their meanings through popular and journalistic discussions of these sites. In other instances, I have used the Internet Archive to gain access to earlier versions of websites that are active but do not keep an archive on their own site (for example, the now defunct discussion forum on the website indolink.com can be accessed partially through the Internet Archive); in other cases, I have used the Internet Archive to examine websites (such as namaste.com) that are no longer active.[64]

I draw on mainstream Indian and American newspapers and magazines such as *Times of India, Time,* and *Newsweek,* technology magazines such as *Wired* and *SiliconIndia,* and Indian American newspapers such as *India Abroad.* Other sources include U.S. immigration policy documents, special reports on Asian Americans conducted by the U.S. Census Bureau, Indian official press releases on its emigrants, and several online magazines that routinely cover the business and advertising aspects of online media industries and cultures.

This book is organized into four main chapters plus this introduction and a conclusion. Chapter 1 interrogates what I call the "problematic of homepage nationalisms" in analyses of online media. I argue that the problematic is produced through normative ideas about online media as "global" (which all too often is synonymous with "American") technologies and cultural nationalism as a quintessentially immigrant or diasporic concern. The chapter examines the politics underwriting the categorization of the global Web and digital diasporas and links it to the continued undertheorization of "home" in home pages. Using the example of curry as a metaphor for the presence of Indian immigrants in the American software industry, I demonstrate how reading race in narratives that are ostensibly about transnational migration can illuminate the nuances of belonging or being an outsider in the immigrant experience. An interdisciplinary approach that engages the question of "home" at the intersections of race, class, and gender, I suggest, can therefore help redefine the equation between nation and diaspora in examinations of digital diasporas and help pose the question of nation more purposefully in discussion of the global Web.

Chapter 2 examines the textual, discursive, and networking politics of Indian immigrant women residing in the United States on the H-4 temporary visa, through a close reading of the discussion forum by and about these women on indusladies.com, a community website. The chapter argues that the politics of household and networking evidenced through the discussion cultures and online practices of the forum participants exemplifies the repurposing of the virtual network to foreground a particular immigrant formation articulated along relations of gender and visa-defined immigrant class. H-4 women make visible their diverse and embodied experiences of feeling like outsiders in the immigrant space. They narrativize their histories of migration from India and relocation in the United States culminating in their becoming out of place in the NRI household; in turn their testimonials unsettle idealized discourses of gendered NRI belonging, which mostly by absence of representation assume that the H-4 wives of H-1B professionals are happily ensconced in domestic bliss as NRI householders.

Chapter 3 examines the idealized construction of the Indian immigrant home and household in online grocery stores, shopping sites, and banking sites. Through close readings of these sites, the chapter reveals how the textual, cultural, and institutional politics of a diverse set of Indian and Indian immigrant players has shaped the production of an idealized version of the immigrant home as a household organized around elite imaginations of mobility, the reproduction of the filial thorough the financial, and the agency and labor of male technology professionals. It situates the idealization of the immigrant home in the context of the ideologies of e-commerce and online financial transactions that first emerged in the late 1990s and continue to be mobilized around the domestic and transnational needs and desires of Indian immigrants in the United States.

Chapter 4 explores how desi activism reimagines the Indian immigrant location and seeks to mobilize the politics of citizenship around issues of race and class. Using drumnyc.org, the homepage of New York–based organization Desis Rising Up and Moving (DRUM), as a case study, the chapter foregrounds a particular mode of citizenship among South Asian immigrants wherein belonging and rights are negotiated through technologies of race and immigration and through network cultures. The site represents its immigrant members as active political subjects in the U.S. homeland who craft a cultural location for themselves by engaging, resisting, and responding to the disciplinary strategies of the technologized racial state. In doing so, the activists of DRUM reveal how belonging is produced and enacted through the transnational online media and through immigrant, labor, and racial coalitions. Desi is here articulated to labor struggles, racial alliances, and immigrant collectives to produce desi networks as brown, working-class spaces of political leadership.

The conclusion revisits the key arguments developed in each of the four chapters and points to key implications of undertaking a study of home in the age of networks. It locates the politics of revisiting a core concept "the homepage" within the need to counter the trend toward presentism in discussions about online media. It reiterates the significance and urgency of including media institutions and their practices into our frames of analysis to better understand the complexity of home and belonging in online contexts.

CHAPTER ONE

Homepage Nationalisms

Silicon Indians and Curry Codes

Home, as Mary Douglas has insightfully noted, while not necessarily fixed in space, starts by bringing space under control; creating home spaces then involves creating regular patterns of activity and structures, both in place and in time.[1] The physical structure of the house, traditionally inscribed by notions of privacy, security, family, intimacy, comfort, and control, has long represented home at a micro-level. At a macro-level, the idea of home is usually manifested as our origin story, as the place that each of us come from.[2]

While the homeland metaphorically operates as a collective home for the family of national citizens (who in turn are invoked within the nation's origin story), for immigrants the story of home is more complex. A traditional sense of belonging—structured around origin myths, validated by legal citizenship, and residing within the national homeland—does not match up with the complex realities of the immigrant's history of migration, the necessity of relocating to a new home and nation, and the engagement with transnational cultures that shape their everyday life and practices.[3] As Ien Ang recounts in the introduction to her book *On Not Speaking Chinese: Living between Asia and the West*, when she answered "Netherlands," to the question "Where are you from?," it almost always resulted in a subsequent query, "No, I mean where are you really from?"[4] As a Chinese Indonesian immigrant to the Netherlands, her racialized embodiment of difference could not satisfactorily placate the nationalist anxiety at the heart of the question.

For the immigrant, then, belonging is a vexing preoccupation, but it is also open to negotiation. The homepage, in this context, is particularly interesting. The homepage already has the capacity to disrupt the "real" material, physical, and territorial logic of the nation-state. But in addition, it is also a potent site for the possibilities of making and unmaking traditional ideologies of home and homeland. The operative word here is *possibilities*, since homepages are imbricated within larger political and social contexts of digital capitalism, neoliberal citizenship culture, and transnational strategic alliances. As has been pointed out by many scholars, nation-states have reworked their agendas to align better with neoliberalism and flexible citizenship in an effort to remain relevant in a new world driven by global media, migration, and mobility.[5] When we consider that the Web, in the words of Tim Berners-Lee, is "not a physical thing" that exists "in a certain place" but rather is "a space in which information could exist," we might also use the homepage, drawing on Douglas's insight above, as a trope for bringing spaces—virtual, transnational, and immigrant—into our understanding of the micro-household and the macro-homeland.[6]

As we study transnational communities, such as Indian immigrants, we see the limits of epistemological frames organized around the concept of diaspora and its associated meaning as an "imagined community" without territory.[7] Derived from the Greek *speiro* (which means to sow) and *dia* (which means over), the concept of diaspora—notwithstanding critical retheorizations of the term over the past two decades—has long been articulated within narratives of dispersal, movement, dislocation, and relocation.[8] We have seen that the identities of Indian immigrants (like South Asians more generally) can't be understood without examining everything from class, gender, race, sexuality, profession, and place.[9] Similarly, belonging cannot be understood within a mono-nationalist framework and, more importantly, should move beyond, beneath, across, and around the hegemony of the "nation." Only then can we understand the politics of struggle around cultural citizenship in the contemporary United States.

I believe that we need to reexamine migration through the codes of online media. The conditions of transnational migration and network communication seem to offer up similar questions about the ontology of reality, materiality, and emplacement. Online media and diaspora are viewed as particularly compatible given their homologous relationship to deterritorialization, dispersal, virtuality, time-space compression, and transnational mobility.[10] Decentralized circuits of production, distribution, and consumption as well as the "world wide" reach of the Web have factored into the conceptualization of the online as a globally accessible network space that transcends the limitations of place, geography, and synchronous time-space.[11]

The emergence of studies of "digital diasporas" in recent years speaks simultaneously to the increasing investment within academia to understand the intersections between online cultures and diasporic spaces as well as the growing awareness to complicate the association by unpacking both "digital" and "diaspora."[12] As online media have transformed the modes as well as the meaning around travel, mobility, and place, the narrative of searching for a national home, "in both its liberatory and repressive senses," as Ella Shohat put it, is still very much present in the midst of transnational and dispersed identities.[13] However, even as we track the continued significance of the national for digital diasporas, we must also recognize the presence and play of multiple other factors that shape how online media matter to transnational communities. With regard to South Asians online, as Radhika Gajjala and Venkataramana Gajjala note, language, caste, and religion, for instance, complicate the debates over access and computer literary.[14] Further, as Rachel Lee and Sau-ling Cynthia Wong remind us, while it is very seductive to buy into the possibilities of virtual, especially the possibility of transcending the limitation of the "real" world, we must remain very "skeptical of the erasure of a category such as race via the technologies and conceptualizations of the virtual."[15]

The varied and overlapping concerns of online remediation of "home" through the concept of the homepage, the reframing by immigrant communities of the nationalist logics organizing "original" and "current" homelands, and the multi-sited nature of belonging in the household, on the street, in the workplace, in a community, locally, nationally, or transnationally call for an interdisciplinary approach that engages with the multiple contingent pathways of belonging. Therefore, instead of fitting my study of Indian immigrants and their online cultures into the category of "digital diaspora," I purposely press my research against the contours drawn by the notion of a virtualized diaspora and seek to mark the sites of tension, rupture, and reconfiguration. As Stuart Hall and Paul Gilroy have noted, identities and cultures are constantly changing and shifting; they are mobile and open to negotiation within emergent frameworks.[16] Addressing the gaps between our current theorization around immigrant cultures online and the shifting practices governing and shaping the relations between transnational communities and online networks can help us expand our understanding of some of the key issues with which this book is centrally concerned: the transnational logics of web entrepreneurism and the politics of race, class, gender, and nationalism in mediating online belonging and exclusion for immigrants.

CHAPTER ONE

A Critical Take on the Silicon Indian

While the term *Silicon Indian* locates the immigrant within California's Silicon Valley, I use the term more fluidly to indicate the confluence of a particular conceptualization of Indian-ness with that of science and technology. This figure was fashioned most intensely during the 1990s, when shifts in the technological, political, and capital investments of the Indian and American nation-states brought about more dynamic exchanges between a variety of actors in the domains of computing, software, and information technology. Popular and industry narratives about the information nation-states of America and India have repeatedly hailed the Indian—as software worker or expert, technologically inclined, math and science proficient.[17]

Historically, Indians who migrated after the U.S. reforms of 1965 were often middle-class professionals in the fields of engineering and medicine. In the 1970s and 1980s, Indian presence in the technology domain, especially computing, increased sizably. In the 1990s the figure of the Indian immigrant was sutured to information networks and Silicon Valley in unprecedented ways.[18] While the figure of the Indian American venture capitalist, exemplified through people such as Vinod Dham, Vinod Khosla, and Kanwal Rekhi, began to occupy a key space in the reconfiguring of immigrant identity, the emergence of the H-1B Indian "techie," following the creation of the H-1B visa category in 1990, furthered the vision of this community as a middle-class, web-savvy, networked group. As the following example reveals, the emergent narratives about Indian immigrants and digital technologies hinged on exemplary success stories to spread a mythology of male technological prowess.[19]

In February 1998, *Little India*, a popular Indian American monthly magazine published on the East Coast of the United States, released an Internet directory with more than two thousand listings for the Indian American community, noting "not only is this the first such directory for the Indian community, we dare say it is among the first specialized community directories of its kind, period."[20] Published at a time when, by most accounts, e-commerce was booming in the United States, *Little India's* Internet directory was reproducing an annual tradition of the magazine, which was to offer a directory of Indian American businesses, but this time with a crucial difference. For its 1998 issue, *Little India* shifted the focus from the brick and mortar model of community businesses and organizations to the e-commerce model. Prior to publication, the magazine featured the following call for directory listings on several India-related online bulletin boards and chat groups: "If your business has an internet presence, either through homepages, email access, or because it is a computer/internet related business, this is your opportunity to stand out and truly benefit from your cutting edge advantage among the most computer and internet literate ethnic group in the United States."[21]

When the directory was published in its February 1998 issue, the editorial—fittingly titled, "Grasping the Future"—laid out its vision of the unique location of Indian Americans in the emergent network economy and its implications for the community's sense of identity and power in the unfolding age of online media. As the world is "on the cusp of a momentous economic paradigm shift," the editorial notes, Indian Americans are "especially well positioned to reap the rewards of the emerging information revolution."[22] Among the reasons listed include, most notably, the fact that Indian Americans have "the highest proportion of computer professionals of all U.S. ethnic groups" (the editors suggested that the representation of Indians in the computer sector was ten times the U.S. national average). However, beyond computer literacy, it was the community's "exceptionally high educational attainment," according to the editorial, that made Indian Americans uniquely advantaged among all immigrant groups in the United States. To substantiate the point, the editorial deployed statistical data: "nearly 66 percent of Indian men and 50 percent of Indian women have bachelor's degrees, compared to a national average of 23 and 18 percent respectively," and "almost 4 in 10 Indians hold a master's or higher degree and 7 percent have a doctorate, both several times the national average." Hence, the editors remark, given the twin factors of high levels of education and numerical and technological strength in the sectors of computing and networking, it is hardly surprising that "India and Indian Americans are exceedingly well represented on the web." By way of "grasping the future," the editors opine that while the Internet will in all likelihood be a "high stakes poker game with a handful of winners and many losers," it is the "the technologically savvy [who] will hold all the cards." In a community where even the "computer illiterate ... hold a vital key to the door of the information society" (by virtue of being highly educated), the editors hoped that the directory "will serve to accelerate the adoption of the Internet," thereby giving Indian Americans "an enviable winning hand."[23]

The editorial employs the figure of Sabeer Bhatia as a "remarkable story of Indian immigrants," who along with Bill Gates and other "high tech moguls," are taking "center stage" in a U.S. economy where "already the Fords and General Motors of American [sic] have been relegated to the sidelines."[24] Bhatia, who moved from Bangalore to California in 1988 as a nineteen-year-old graduate student, created Hotmail, the email service company, in 1996. He reportedly built its user base at a record rate of 125,000 new members a day for the next two years.²⁵ This phenomenal growth led the media pundits at celebrated technology magazine *Wired* to note that Hotmail was growing "faster than any media company in history—faster than CNN, faster than America Online, faster even than the audience grew for *Seinfeld*."²⁶ Hotmail was subsequently acquired by Microsoft in 1997 for $400 million.²⁷ *Little India's* editorial referring to the very same development describes it as "the stuff on which egalitarian legends are based [where] in truth, Bhatia, and Gates before him, second only the first notes in a symphony that is transforming the global economic order."²⁸

Appearing two years before the dot-com crash of 2000, *Little India's* editorial offers an insight into a dominant narrative about Indian immigrants in the United States, coming of age via their technological expertise. It is a narrative that imagines Indian Americans as a model minority in the information age, where through individual enterprise, education, and skill Indian Americans refashion themselves as web entrepreneurs, venture capitalists, and, to quote *Little India*, "egalitarian legends." It is worthwhile to note that Sabeer Bhatia, in many ways a rare and outstanding example of entrepreneurial success in Silicon Valley, is the figure who frames the presentation of the Internet directory, which essentially is a list of websites catering to the Indian American community that were included by virtue of an application form and payment of a fee. The *Little India* editorial, which connects the unprecedented success in the entrepreneurial domain of online technologies to Indian male immigrant skills, is a very significant text. It points to a cultural transformation in the late 1990s and early 2000s, one that is in many crucial respects still ongoing.

Following the dot-com crash of 2000, the Silicon Indian migrated within the United States, finding a home in resurgent software industry nodes such as Silicon Alley in New York and emergent ones such as Silicon Hills in Austin, Texas.²⁹ At the same time, India adopted an IT vision for reimaging the nation and its location on the global stage, and regional states began recasting their capital cities as IT hubs. While the city of Bangalore in Southern India had been called India's Silicon Valley in the late 1980s, its position was increasingly consolidated beginning in the 1990s.³⁰ India's Silicon Valley, however, also had to share its limelight with emergent IT hubs such as Chennai and Hyderabad (also sometimes called Cyberabad).³¹ The changes in the Indian national and regional scene were often reliant on networking with as well as the investment of Silicon Indians in the United States, who are a key target of India's efforts to involve its diasporic population in the national economy.³² A related and interesting development during the 2000s is that the image of the Silicon Indian slowly transformed into a state of mind, an attitude that believes in the enduring power of technology to bring about development and progress. This transformation is exemplified by Chidanand Rajghatta's book *The Horse That Flew: How India's Silicon Gurus Spread Their Wings*, which references some provocative interpretations, such as the idea that India's tradition of philosophic inquiry steeped in Vedic Hindu religion makes Indians intellectually predisposed to be good at computer science and info-technologies.[33]

There are two major implications for the figure of the Silicon Indian in narratives such as Rajghatta's. First, the Silicon Indian is imagined as a Hindu male, technological expert, and the Indian nation is writ large on the body of the Silicon Indian and his Indian American networks. Second, in the figure of the Silicon Indian, ideologies of race are critical (along with class, masculinity, and religion) to the efforts to manage and consolidate the hegemonic boundaries of the nation-state—both Indian and American. As discussed in the "links" of the following section, race is implicated within the overlapping relations of class and gender in the production of technology-related stories about Silicon Indians. Race is a key factor that often gets elided in discussions of Indian immigrants and the Indian diaspora online. In the next section, using the concept of curry—the group of spices at the heart of Indian cuisine—I demonstrate how Indian immigrants in the IT field experience both a sense of belonging and a reminder of their outsider status through the raced and sensorial metaphor of curry. I suggest that curry is a code: for the American mainstream to hint at how Indian immigrants are different (as in "curry people" and "curry-smelling IT workers"), and for techno-elites within the immigrant community to appropriate cultural difference as cultural pride by (as in "curry brigade" and "curry rock music").

Speaking of Code: Silicon Indians in the Racialized U.S. Landscape

Although curry is popularly considered a cornerstone of "authentic" Indian food, it is actually a colonial invention.[34] While Indian cuisine uses a variety of spices or masalas, and the proportion of the different spices varies based on the dish, the British version of curry relied on offering a standard, fixed mixture of spices—and authenticating it as quintessentially Indian. That the fabricated version assumed greater currency as "authentic Indian food" in the West is an expression of food imperialism, whereby the British who colonized India were able to shape the production and dissemination of an English invention and offer it as an "ethnic" food. In the contemporary United States, curry often features in celebratory food-centric narratives of America's ethnic diversity and multiculturalism. Such celebration of Indian American food, however, often ignores the more problematic social meanings in historical and more recent uses of curry, including curry heads, curry munchers, curry town, and—in the wake of the Indian immigrant influx into Silicon Valley in the 1990s—the curry menace. While scholars have only recently begun to engage seriously with food and its many meanings, many of us—especially immigrant groups—have felt how food is often a reminder of difference, whether via race, class, or gender, and a marker of social inequities.[35]

In this context, the production and circulation of the "curry" metaphor online—to refer to Indian immigrants in the information technology and networking sectors—is especially significant. Two reasons are key. The first relates to the enduring power of the myth of technological neutrality. It is the idea that the codes, applications, platforms, and principles of technology have no built-in cultural bias; similarly, we too often assume that the work cultures of the information technology sectors are similarly free of bias.[36] The second reason, recalling Wendy Chun's argument, relates to the concept of software as symbolic code, immaterial, and virtual, qualities that are in turn extended to online cultures, network spaces, and new media industries.[37] Chun has argued that decoding race through software and, inversely, seeing software as racialized are particularly difficult because of two overlapping concepts: that if it is not seen or made visible, race does not exist; and that software is a symbolic code, which cannot be made visible unless it is connected to hardware.[38] In the 1990s, for example, it was often assumed that race did not matter on the Internet because of the anonymity afforded by virtual interactions.[39] That notion has been dented quite substantially through research and online media presence foregrounding race in the 2000s and since.[40] Yet, there is still a lot of work that needs to be done to uncover the complex and subtle interactions of race and information technologies. Some of that work requires reading against the grain of the preferred meanings of a given representation. Race, as we know, is often coded and not apparent. And curry, I argue, is one especially prevalent code for the racialized Indian immigrant. Below are five examples of this code in action, spanning the period from 2000 to the present. I suggest that these five instances of curry as code should be seen as links; just as the links of a web page move us across virtual space, so do these links between codes illuminate a larger picture about belonging and place for Indian immigrants vis-à-vis the U.S. mainstream.

LINK ONE: BEING BROWN, SMELLING LIKE CURRY

On the website of the popular slang dictionary Urban Dictionary, the word *stindian* is defined as "a stinky Indian, typically an IT professional on H1B visa status."[41] The stindian, we are further informed, "commonly eats the stinkiest of the stinky foods, such as chicken vindaloo (extra curry) and curry fried okra."[42] Listed among the top fifty websites of 2008 by *Time* magazine, Urban Dictionary goes by the slogan "Define your world," referring to the fact that the more than seven million entries on the site are user submissions, albeit ones regulated by the site's editors and shaped by visitor rankings. Not surprisingly, *curry* is among the words defined by users, along with more than a hundred variations of curry with a suffix added to it, such as *curryhead* or *curry muncher*. Curry is defined as both an Indian food and an Indian person, while curry muncher is defined as a person who eats a lot of curry (read: Indians) but also as an insult to a person of Indian origin. Other variations reveal sexually explicit, elitist, and patriarchal meanings attached to curry in addition to racist ones. When one considers the production and dissemination of the term through blogs, tweets, posts, and online forums, it appears that alongside the many racist usages of the term, there are others with a different agenda. Indian Americans, it is clear, have appropriated the term as a way of joking about and critiquing South Asian culture; in other cases, users call attention to the racist attitudes behind the use of curry online.

Dice is a leading job board for technology professionals in the United States, and on its discussion forum, "techtalk," conversations about immigrant labor, American jobs, outsourcing, and company management issues are fairly routine. Not surprisingly, the H-1B Indian is frequently referred to in the "techtalk" conversations. It is, however, the pejorative linking of Indian professionals on the H-1B to their curry-eating habits, in threads that are ostensibly about technology or IT jobs, that is particularly significant. For example, when Groupon announced its plans to recruit a hundred engineers from Silicon Valley in 2012, there was considerable criticism of the move by forum members. While one member dubbed it a "world-wide Indian conspiracy," suggesting that most of the jobs would be given to H-1B Indians, another member building on the motif of an H-1B army (introduced by a third member) vents frustration in the following words, "Lord knows they have a cache of chemical weapons. Anyone who's ever smelled that god awfull curry . . . they indiscriminately throw in a microwave knows what I'm talking about."[43] Previously, in 2010, in response to a report that suggested that H-1B workers are "virtually enslaved," the conversation in the forum once again quickly reduced into a discussion about the filthy habits of Indian coworkers. While for one member the presence of Indians is no less than an "infestation," for another the feeling of being trapped with Indian coworkers is expressed through having to witness their long lunch breaks "with 20 [other] Indians" and the lingering "smell of curry [that] stays with the building... as the windows are sealed."⁴⁴ On a site like Dice, as well as related job boards such as cafepharma (a job and discussion board for the medical and pharmaceutical industries), the association of Indians with H-1B armies and the smell of curry is reiterated so often that the use of *curry* seems like a lingua franca—a word whose meaning, the posters assume, is common knowledge.

The swarming armies of technology workers is nothing less than a "curry menace," as a 2003 article about the new wave of racism in Silicon Valley puts it.⁴⁵ While the article focuses on racism against Indian engineers in the IT world, it concludes: "technology workers who heap scorn on their Indian counterparts aren't necessarily doing it because they think Indians are racially inferior. More to the point, they're pissed off because strangers are taking their jobs away—strangers who didn't go to the same schools as they did and grew up in places they can't locate on a map."⁴⁶ In other words, people who are not from "here." While the question of racial inferiority cannot be solved by the simple assertion that it doesn't exist (as the article's author does), more to point here is the link between curry and place and its deployment as a sign of the Other whose presence cannot be tolerated.

In a 2011 weblog about San Diego's technology industry, which suggested that the city was a financially rewarding place for technology workers, an anti-immigrant response cynically suggests that the returns are going to an Indian outsourcing firm and "its curry eating buddies."⁴⁷ When another poster challenges the comment's underlying racism, the respondent asserts, "The comment about the curry smell can be verified as fact by anyone who has had to work around a shop where there are a clan of H-1B Indians employed. It indeed DOES smell like curry and it's pretty annoying to the nose of people not acclimated to it."⁴⁸ Additionally, the poster urges forum members to scroll the results that are generated with the search term "indian smell like curry," and to follow a "Yahoo Answers" thread on the question, "why do Indian people always smell like curry, without fail?"⁴⁹ The casual racism toward H-1B Indian immigrants, couched in descriptions of their food, is one iteration of a broader culture of racism toward Indians, Pakistanis, and South Asian Americans more broadly.

That racism, however, does not go unnoticed. The hashtag "Racist People on Twitter"—which describes itself as a "social initiative to confront some of the most racist remarks on Twitter," re-tweets descriptions of Indians and Pakistanis as "stinking people," along with other expletives that are directed toward black and brown populations.⁵⁰ Similarly, on the Tumblr blog "You are not desi," the blogger links these common online assertions—such as "All Indians smell like curry, all Mexicans are illegal immigrants, all black people are criminals, the list goes on!"—to a strategy of racial stereotyping that is advanced to secure the power of dominant white culture.[51] That such ideologies are racially charged and constructed is made bluntly clear in the following post titled, "Shit White Girls says to South Asian Girls," on the Tumblr thread "fuckyeahethnicwomen": "Ugh, that guy smells soooo bad, like curry. Oh, sorry! I forgot you're Indian. Oh sorry, you're not Indian, right. Well, you're like, white anyways and you never smell like curry! You know what I mean!"

LINK TWO: CURRY ROCK AS ANTI-IMMIGRATION ESTABLISHMENT

Standing in line with papers in my hand
All my answers practiced and planned
He asked, "Would'cha ever come back home?"
    (*pause followed by laughter in background*)
"Yes, sir, I will. Give me that H1B
"First give me that damn H1B; first give me that damn H1B"
I've gotta get me an H1B, can't wait to go see New York City.
    Lyrics of the song "H1Bees" in the album *H1Bees*

The music album *H1Bees* was released by Srikanth Devarajan, an Indian immigrant, in 2005.[52] A software engineer who entered the United States as part of the Indian workforce on the H-1B, Devarajan retells his story of leaving his family in India and adjusting to life as a new immigrant. In an interview with National Public Radio (NPR) at the time of the album's release, Devarajan reveals that his intention was to give voice to the affective journey made in the transit from India to the United States.[53] That journey, as the lyrics communicate, includes the anxiety of applying for an H-1B, the pleasures associated with tricking the U.S. state's border policing enquiries (by answering "Yes, sir, I will" when the immigration officer enquires about plans for returning to the homeland), the frustration when U.S. credit card companies deny credit card applications for lack of credit history, and the joy of taking visiting parents from India on the great American tour. During the album's release, Devarajan frequently referred to his brand of music as "curry rock" and suggested that *H1Bees* was the first album in this genre.

His assertion aside, what is interesting about the coinage is its effort to be translatable to a Western audience. While curry triggers the stereotypical Indian association, rock emphasizes the political nature of the theme. In this context, when asked why the spelling H1Bees, Devarajan referred to worker bees who labor for the queen bee, just as the H-1B workforce labors for the system with little freedom or rights. Worker bees are commonly understood as female bees who are either infertile or with little reproductive capacity; the adult queen bee, on the other hand, heads the colony and has the maximum reproductive capacity.[54] The gendered articulation of loss of freedom—feminized bees with no reproductive rights—and a reassertion of identity through the frame of curry and rock here offer a different take on the racialization of Indian immigrants wherein the issue of masculinity and its crisis emerge as key. Devarajan's song, while reinforcing the hegemonic link between H-1B visa holder and Indian men, levels its critique of systemic oppression at both the Indian and the American workplace. In the first portion of the song "H1Bees," he refers to his experience of working for an Indian company as one "worse than working for the mob." While the worker bee alludes to the American workplace's labor-intensive and restrictive treatment of H-1B immigrants (since H-1B visas are sponsored by the American company that hires the immigrants, the latter are not free to change their employer), the album's framing of its critique as "curry rock" suggests an attempt to recover lost ground (a crisis of masculinity?) by articulating it as part of a genre defined by male, anti-establishment rebels. Curry rock tries to negotiate along the hierarchies of both race and national culture.

LINK THREE: THE CURRY BRIGADE AS TECHNO-MILITARISM

The magazine *SiliconIndia* is published by the transnational SiliconIndia network, a membership organization aimed at Indians in the United States and India who work in the field of computing. The magazine was launched from New York in 1997; it was subsequently published from the Fremont, California, headquarters of the SiliconIndia network. In 2008, the magazine's online version siliconindia.com was launched, and the publication's headquarters moved to Bangalore, India, with satellite offices in Delhi and Mumbai in India and Fremont in the United States.[55] While the magazine in its early years was predominantly aimed at U.S.-based Indian professionals, since the late 2000s its interest in catering to Indian IT professionals in India has become very pronounced. The SiliconIndia network thus has organization chapters in India and the United States; its website as well as the print magazine have India and U.S. editions; and perhaps most significantly, the IT professionals who are featured on the covers and in the stories of the magazine cannot be fixed to any one national territory—as they include Americans of Indian origin as well as Indian entrepreneurs, U.S.-based H-1B professionals, and nonresident Indians. These "Silicon Indians" cannot be fixed in place, in the sense that their politi-

FIGURE 1. Photo montage using guns, explosions, and combat gear to depict Indian immigrant men on the warpath to India's IT development. Credit: *SiliconIndia*, Cover Image, March 2001

cal, financial, and technological investments traverse the geopolitical borders of India and the United States in multiple ways.

In its March 2001 issue, *SiliconIndia* ran a cover story on information technology and development in India. The cover image (Figure 1), a photo montage featuring several Indian American venture capitalists and software experts—all men, and all holding or surrounded by weapons—conveys the issue's key theme.

The image is captioned "Rules of the Game: 11 Working Principles That Will Drive the IT Industry in India." While the inside cover story argues that India is on a "warpath" to IT development, the cover image takes this idea literally: the corporate, suited capitalists are digitally altered to appear as gun-toting agents of this war. A huge military gun, appearing from the interstitial spaces between the bodies of the men, points toward the viewer, while the background is lit up with a fiery explosion. One expert dons a military helmet, while another bears the signature sideways pose of an action hero with revolver in hand. As the military signs assembled here convey the militant nature of the "drive" to the electronic "frontier," the drive is both literally and symbolically gestured through an image of a man driving a car. While much smaller in scale and occupying a marginal location within the visual economy of the cover page, the man with car motif reinforces the heteromasculine frame being erected in the narrative. The meaning is clear: Indian American men are calling the shots in India's technological reforms.

To make the connection a little clearer is the billboard-styled image of Chandrababu Naidu (the chief minister of the South Indian state Andhra Pradesh at the time), on the left lower edge of the cover, appearing above the statement, "We'll Connect You to the Internet." Reminiscent of the welcome banners that line Indian roads during official visits of political leaders or foreign dignitaries, the Naidu reference suggests two meanings. First, that Naidu, a regional political leader who had already tapped into the diasporic presence of men from his state in Silicon Valley, was an ally in this "game"; and second, that it is the Silicon Indians in the United States that are going to bring Naidu's technological fantasies and desires to fruition. By 2001, when the *SiliconIndia* cover story was published, Naidu had already established a reputation for being tech-savvy and creating the infrastructural resources to transform Hyderabad, the state's capital city, into "Cyberabad," especially by creating a technological township, known popularly as HITEC (Hyderabad Information Technology Engineering Consultancy) City in the suburbs.[56]

The visual of this increasingly important association between Indian Americans and Indian interests (which coincided with a period of slow global recovery from the dot-com bust) is significant for what it does not say about Indian Americans and the rules of the (racial) game in the United States. The technological upgrading of India, the image makes clear, requires a hypermasculine Indian American prowess; if technology is a game, it is a blatantly phallic one. The photo altering is relevant here because it inserts a sense of the absurd, of the cover image being more of a joke, not to be taken seriously. War and weaponry have long serviced dominant discourses about masculinity and nation building; in the magazine's reworking of this mythology, Indian Americans, bullish on the network nation, wield their technological supremacy as evidence of their masculinity as well as nationalism. Yet the fact that they represent themselves as Silicon Indians and not Silicon Indian Americans or Silicon Americans tells us that race is the invisible trigger here.

Drawing on the notion of race, like software code, as invisible, I suggest that this image of militant Indian Americans is not so much about the warpath India is on or the techno-warriors it needs to win that battle, but about a virtual reality closer to home. As Patricia Wise discusses in her interrogation of the polysemic term *virtual*, one interpretation is that which is "not quite there but only in effect."[57] In turn, I believe that race in the software technology sectors is always present, but because it is often invisible (in the image of Indian American masculinity, for instance) we can understand it only through its effects.

This image, ultimately, is an expression of the anxieties and desires around the racialized locations of Indian immigrant men in the American information technology sector. Silicon Valley and more broadly the technology sector are commonly constructed as places that are devoid of racial discrimination and primarily driven by talent, innovation, and creativity. Barring a few miscellaneous pieces in the Indian American press, online, and in print, discussions about the racial representations of Indian immigrants are not common.[58] At the same time, images abound in U.S. popular culture of Indian and South Asian American men as geeks, smart but socially inept, emasculated, or feminized and most often rendered in opposition to the white hetero-masculine ideal. (The character Raj on the CBS show *The Big Bang Theory* (2007–) is a popular and current embodiment of this image).[59] In the Silicon India representation, hetero-masculinity and technology operate as a code for race, revealing simultaneously the effects of dominant discourses about Indian American masculinity as well as the virtual ways in which Silicon Indians displace concerns around race into a virtual dimension of play, games, and warpaths.

LINK FOUR: BROWN BODIES OR RACIAL AMBIVALENCE?

Another image of Indian American masculinity appears in a June 2000 story published in *SiliconIndia* (see Figure 2). Titled "Austin's Power," the lead for the feature goes, "Not long ago, Austin, the Texan capital, was known mainly for its music and salubrious climate. Now it's playing a new tune, calling itself the Silicon Hills and fashioning a new high-tech image."[60] The framing half-page image, which precedes the text, is a drawing representing the physical contours of Texas that is being built by a handful of construction workers. Brown-skinned bodies, men with rippling muscles wearing construction attire—overalls, tool belts, helmets—scale the physical map of the region.

The bodies of the workers are measuring, wiring, and tightening bolts in different units of the Texas machine. This imagination of sexuality, masculinity, and industrial capitalism is yet another code for Indian American displacement of their racialized location. The narrative, which focuses on the growth of the new economy in Austin, is also a story about Indian Americans venturing into the state and changing, one might say, the rules of the game.

At the same time, there is something else going on in this image that hints at the racial attitudes—maybe ambivalence, possibly racism—that are part of Indian American life. The illustrator uses the contours of geographical territory and emblems of industrial labor to make visible the Indian American

FIGURE 2. Brown muscular bodies of Indian American men reconstructing Texas into a high-tech state. Credit: *SiliconIndia* June 2000, p. 58

presence in the age of digital capitalism (a contrast to the notion that race, like code, is invisible). Nevertheless, the class and racial marking of Texas as brown, working-class space hints at a possible association of the state of Texas with the Latino community, which is often stereotypically associated with working-class jobs. I am invested in reading against the grain of the preferred meanings here, and so while the obvious binary to decode the race factor is across white and Indian American brown (using the unwieldy language advisedly), I suggest that it is intertwined with Texas's long history of Latino stereotypes. The complexity of this iteration is that while visibly marking themselves as raced bodies, the iteration of brown masculinity is overlaid (or read as such) on a preexisting code—a stereotype about Latino class positions. In the interplay of potential alliance and possible stereotyping are the glimmerings of racially charged desires around belonging and Othering. How one is seen or not seen cannot be considered apart from how one would like to be seen.

LINK FIVE: CURRY EVERYWHERE: OF PLACE AND DISLOCATION

The final link I consider here is the widespread metaphorical association of Indian immigrants with curry, especially in journalistic pieces about the information economy and the changing landscape of America at the beginning of the new millennium. In 2000, in the midst of the anxieties about a weak network economy, *Time* magazine ran a feature about the growing trends in homeownership among Indian immigrants in the New Jersey area. In that piece, it is stated that area realtors, happy at the brisk business of their Indian immigrant clientele, often joked that these days, the suburban neighborhoods were increasingly smelling like curry.⁶¹

In another *Time* magazine article on Indian Americans and their search for cultural roots, published the same year, writer Nisid Hajari begins his column with the following words: "The great question of the immigrant experience in America is figuring out when one has arrived. Has a community made it after producing its first Member of Congress? Its first sitcom star? Its first big-bucks ceo? South Asians in the U.S. seem to have stumbled upon a simpler litmus test: the Net dominates America, and Indians dominate the Net.... Therefore, Indians must now rule the U.S. The definitive smell of the American melting pot must be of curry, no? Not exactly."⁶² Hajari's reference to the smell of curry is a direct echo of the statement made by Michael Lewis a year earlier in his celebrated best seller, *The New New Thing: A Silicon Valley Story*.⁶³ A narrative focused on Jim Clark, founder of Netscape, the book nevertheless pays attention to the growing number of start-ups in the area funded by Indian American venture capitalists. To summarize his understanding of this phenomenon, Lewis notes that "the definitive smell inside a Silicon Valley start-up was of curry."⁶⁴

While Hajari is more critical of Lewis's assertions about Indian American dominance, despite the racist overtones of using "curry" to indicate their presence in the high-tech corridors of Silicon Valley, Chidanand Rajghatta, in his book *The Horse That Flew: How India's Silicon Gurus Spread Their Wings*, addresses the racist terminology but offers a no less problematic reasoning for why the Indian Americans of Silicon Valley were not offended by it. He opines that while "in politically correct America, such a statement would have usually raised a stink ... Indians ... were way beyond noticing or complaining."⁶⁵ Why? Because, in his words, "at the turn of the century, some half a million Indian professionals, nearly half of them concentrated in California, were conquering a new, new frontier of Digital America amid a general frenzy reminiscent of area's gold rush of the 1840s."⁶⁶ Rajghatta's book, an ode to technophilia, is also a utopian story, replete with a rosy-eyed depiction of the electronic frontier, the Wild West, and conquest. Most notably, however, it employs a narrative of the "great Indian men of technology," essentially trying to prove what Hajari's *Time* magazine article was trying to counter, namely that if (a) the Internet dominates America and (b) Indians dominate the Internet, then the conclusion can only be (c) that "therefore, Indians must now rule the U.S."⁶⁷ Rajghatta's account of the late 1990s rush to create e-commerce sites, such as ethnicgrocer.com and namaste.com (discussed in chapter 3), is not coincidentally entitled "Curry Fever." It becomes clear in the book that Rajghatta revels in appropriating the term and wielding it to cook up a new mythology about the "natural" propensity of Indian American men to be good at code.

Curry finds other uses in his mythology. Covering Indian American affairs for an Indian news organization, Rajghatta in 1999 refers to Indian immigrants in the U.S. software industries as the "curry brigade" and the definitive architects of "Digital America."[68] The underlying message of aggressively leading or charging ahead in a technological war is also what makes link three, the cover image of gun-toting Indian American venture capitalists, another representation of the "curry brigade."

CONNECTING THE LINKS

The curry image that emerges in these diverse links extends the discussion about race and technology to include the domain of the sensorial, specifically that of smell. The olfactory system mediates both a racialized anxiety of the Other, as well as the desire of that Other to access a more inclusive space of cultural belonging. When neighborhoods or start-ups begin to smell like curry, we see a reproduction of a master narrative of colonialism where white culture is overwhelmed, nauseated, and appalled at the smell of its racial Other. Curry then is a virtual signifier of the real, transcending the body, soaking the environment, and, most importantly, transgressing the boundaries laid out by mainstream America for its "tech-coolies."[69] Those boundaries become visible only at the site of their disruption; curry, associated with cooking and the latter predominantly with women's space and labor, is also used here to domesticate and gender-ize the racial Other. When realtors joke about their curry neighborhoods, one can discern the unease that structures the joke—that there is something unsettling about having Indian immigrants in our neighborhood. Could their racial and cultural difference affect our ways of being in this white suburbia?

While curry start-ups and curry neighborhoods speak to the constant othering of Indian Americans in the United States, the Indian immigrant's mobilization or appropriation of curry—with masculinity, rock music, and gun imagery—is equally significant. While the curry brigade is a clear expression of a techno-masculinity coming to the aid of two homelands (the Indian American venture capitalists are rewiring both Andhra Pradesh in India and Austin, Texas, in America), the "H1Bees" song is bit more complex around issues of gender and nation.

Race—specifically, the processes of racism, racial marking, and racialization—functions invisibly at the site of techno-masculinized encounters between Indian American and white American subjects. Class and cultural privilege do not make the immigrants immune to the regimes of racism in the United States; social media and online discussions offer a glimpse into the attempts, albeit marginal, to counter the effects of curry racism. Yet, it seems that instead of confronting the issues of racial hierarchies and racism, the immigrant digerati often rely on covert and displaced references to their "not white, not quite" status. In their hesitance, ambivalence, or refusal to engage around the question of race, one can read a desire to ascend to the very top of the hierarchy of model minorities as the "rising" Asian Americans and the Indian diaspora par excellence—categories that in turn are hinged on the axes of class, patriarchy, and nationalism.

The Problematic of "Homepage Nationalisms"

The most prolific discussions of the relevance of nation and ideologies of nationalism in studies of online media occur within studies of immigrant, migrant, and diasporic cultures. These studies, increasingly collated under the category of *digital diasporas,* also focus heavily on non-Western contexts beyond the United States. On the other hand, the unit of nation rarely factors into the analytical and critical frames shaping discussions of the institutional, technological, textual, and cultural contexts of the "global" Web in the United States. As a result, the fields of *digital diasporas* and the *global Web* are being shaped by uneven responses to the dialectic between the national and the global. This unevenness leads to what I describe as the problematic of *homepage nationalisms.*

In recent years, the term *digital diasporas* has increasingly been used to mark the prolific and dynamic online cultures of diasporic communities around the globe. Andoni Alonso and Pedro J. Oiarzabal define digital diasporas as "the distinct online networks that diasporic people use to re-create identities, share opportunities, spread their culture, influence homeland and host-land policy, or create debate about common-interest issues by means of electronic devices."[70] By calling attention to the role of online media in mediating belonging, the idea of digital diasporas is fruitfully expanding and complicating our understanding of the current processes of transnational identity formation.[71]

Academic studies of online communication within diasporic groups began to emerge sporadically in the mid-1990s, concurrent with the rise of web-based media. Much of the early work focused on community formation online, calling attention to the ways that cultural nationalisms began to manifest online. For example, interrogation of the politics of gender and religion in diasporic "community" websites revealed the cultural tensions in collective efforts to imagine a virtual diaspora.[72] Similarly, close textual and discursive analysis of diasporic websites showed how issues such as age, generational ties, language and technological savvy are crucial for immigrants to negotiate the everyday practices of crossing between nationally marked zones online.[73]

Appearing intermittently in journals and edited volumes, these important early examinations of diasporic cultures online put the thematic of new media and migration on the table (of contents), even if they did not emerge as crucial to the dominant theorizations and conceptualizations of the field of new media studies, particularly as it was being imagined in the U.S. academy. In this context it is important to note that while the label *digital diasporas* is gaining greater visibility in new media studies, it is rarely seen as a co-constitutive feature of online media. Instead, U.S.-centric conceptual frameworks such as the *global Web* are more readily granted an originary status for understanding the emergence and the constitution of online media.

There is now a small but growing number of sophisticated analyses of new media in migrant, immigrant, and diasporic cultures.[74] However, in most of this work, the definition of diasporic communities continues to be framed in terms of a homeland/host land binary. Moreover, the basic unit of analysis for interrogating digital diasporas remains the nation-state.[75] Another crucial gap in the existing scholarship on digital diasporas relates to the institutions that produce the online media that target, speak to, and participate in diasporic communities. Ignoring the institutions of diasporic media and their production processes reinforces two troubling stereotypes and myths. The first, as Lisa Nakamura outlines in her analysis of race and cyberspace, is that the online cultures of minorities are best understood through consumption practices (which clearly mark their cultural difference) and not their cultures of production (which are seen as derivative of mainstream culture).[76] The second myth is that the institutional histories and ongoing practices of online media emerge in a "neutral" global context.

It is imperative to ask how the diverse communities that are included within digital diasporas are articulating a different set of politics of location, identity, and belonging than what is conventionally ascribed to them. How are the politics of race, class, and gender within immigrant constituencies reframing the debates over cultural identities and locations? How, in turn, do newer understandings of immigrant cultural politics—mediated through online media—shift the terms of engagement with nation, homeland, and migrant subjectivities? Further, how might the rearticulations reveal the contours, limits, and power of the idea of nation in existing and emergent configurations of individual and collective identity? We must engage these and related questions to arrive at a more nuanced understanding of the cultural politics of digital diasporas, as well as online cultures at large.

While the notion of digital diasporas is a useful way to think about the Web, one of the most problematic ways of thinking about it remains the notion of the *global Web*. One prevalent myth about online media is that its virtual networks transcend the physical and symbolic boundaries of the nation. Such an idea is expressed through the following description of the Web by its "inventor," Tim Berners-Lee: "[The Web is] about anything being potentially connected with anything. It is a vision that provides us with new freedom, and allows us to grow faster than we ever could when we were fettered by the hierarchical classification systems into which we bound ourselves. It leaves the entirety of our previous ways of working as just one tool among many. It leaves our previous fears for the future as one set among many. And it brings the workings of society closer to the workings of our minds."[77] The notion of the connectivity transcending the limitations of geography and culture has taken a deep hold in the cultural imagination and has shaped our thinking about online communications, communities, commerce, and culture. The announcement by Google of its Project Loon—an experiment begun in 2013 to wire the remote corners of the world using high-altitude balloons that would create a wireless network—can be understood as one of the latest expressions of this cultural imaginary.

As scholars and critics have sought to understand this new technology over the last two decades, it is difficult to resist the narrative of new media as a paradigmatic break with "old" media. Although critical issues of history, cultural context, and the many continuities and overlaps with "older" media are being brought into the discussion, they nevertheless operate as marginal to more general, and typically more celebratory, discussions of the shimmering possibilities of new media. Such generalizing narratives, often underwritten by Anglophone, American-centric biases, imagine new media as a *global Web*.[78]

One of the most insightful critiques of this tendency emerged in 1998, when Guillermo Gomez-Peña introduced the idea of a virtual barrio to counter the dominance of Western, Anglophone metaphors of "electronic frontiers" and global expansionism in new media studies. Peña's virtual barrio calls attention to the marginality, if not invisibility, of racial and class differences online, while also symbolizing the need to "brownify" its Euro-American white spaces.[79] In a similar vein, Vinay Lal has noted that the "perennial American language of frontier is incurably a part of the language of cyberspace enthusiasts."[80] Relatedly, Wendy Chun has argued that the techno-Orientalism that underlies much of cyberpunk's fascination with cyberspace and the "Orient" can help us better understand the erasure of race and nationality in "dis-orienting" constructions of cyberspace and virtual travel.[81]

In the generalized concept of the global Web, factors such as capital, technology, architectural protocols, and institutional politics are assumed to be neutral, immune to nationalist ideologies.[82] Yet we know that it is not the case. For example, in a study of search engines and their information algorithms, Vernadette V. Gonzalez and Robyn Magalit Rodriguez revealed that the dominant associative linking of gendered search terms like *Filipina* was to sites associated with maids and prostitutes, thereby indicating a cultural and racial bias built into the technological system.[83] The Domain Name System, a fundamental protocol of the Web, also offers a striking example of the recurring tensions around national boundary markings in the global symbolic order of online media. Irina Shklovski and David Struthers have documented how country code Top Level Domains (ccTLDs) become important sites for negotiating ideas of national identity, state control, and boundary crossings for the people of Kazakhstan given the ongoing reorganization of ideas of statehood and nationalism in the country.[84] Country codes (such as .kz for Kazakhstan) are typically added after the top-level domain (such as .com or .edu), and while their need from a governance point of view is justified in terms of better targeting and streamlining of net traffic, the implementation of the protocol has caused confusion, and its politics of marking nationality have been critiqued.

What these trends and scholarly analyses reveal is that new media are revising our understanding of national boundaries. The universalizing notion of an ideologically neutral Internet or a global Web might be a tempting ideal, but it does not capture the complex and varied ways in which the technological, institutional, and financial domains of the Web and online media are shaped by national and transnational factors. In turn, we must seek out the nationalist impulse in the technical and institutional contexts of online media, in order to destabilize the presumed neutrality of the global Web. It is also crucial to highlight the ways in which ideologies of homeland and diasporic belonging are not reproduced neutrally or singularly in online discourses. Relatedly, we must foreground instances where the institutional and financial networks associated with immigrants online cannot be entirely contained within dominant ideologies of nation-states and the business practices of transnational corporations.

The notion of the global Web is problematic because it fails to turn the focus on the ways in which national imperatives shape the so-called borderless world of online systems, technologies, and capital. The frame of digital diaspora, on the other hand, predominantly foregrounds the national and the original homeland and insufficiently highlights how the digital diasporic experience is mediated by other markers of difference besides the national. This lopsidedness in the frames of engagement with online cultures, technologies, and media evidenced in the categories of global Web and digital diasporas can be understood as a problematic—the problematic of homepage nationalisms. A critical step in addressing this problematic is to revisit the key trope that is embedded within the unit of the homepage—the trope of home.

Revisiting the "Home" in Homepage

Home—like borders, portals, gateways, frontiers, highways—is a spatial trope. Wendy Chun and Jerry Kang have argued that spatialized tropes assembled around online technologies are a way to map but also to manage, contain, and sustain the power struggles that underwrite digital cultures.[85] Yet, despite or perhaps precisely because of its rather obvious placement in online taxonomy, the idea of "home" in the homepage has not received the sustained analysis that is necessary given the complex and shifting nature of belonging, mobility, identity, and social relations.

It is almost as if the homepage is assumed to be predefined, preconstituted, and always already understood. Instead, we might go against such a tendency and assume that there is no given "home" in homepage cultures, and that there are only ways of knowing, accessing, and producing online spaces as homes.

Building on understandings of the Web as an information space represented through the vocabulary of hypertext, scholarship on the personal homepage has paid some attention to the literal and metaphorical associations between physical homes and virtual homepages. For example, Daniel Chandler in his extensive studies of personal homepages employs the imagery of construction and remodeling a brick and mortar building to describe the creation of homepages. Referring to the use of the sign "under construction" for websites, Chandler writes, "although the Web is a virtual environment, the use of roadsigns alludes to the writing of web pages as a physical act of building, and clearly writing a web page is authentic labour involving the expenditure of effort and energy. However, the construction involved is more than the construction of the sites themselves: 'homepages' on the web are one of the most dramatically visible signs of the construction of reality."[86] Sherry Turkle stretches the home metaphor one level further when she draws a connection between the hypertextual page and the widely dispersed organization of digital information on the Web at large: "If we take the home page as real estate metaphor of the self, décor is postmodern. Its different rooms with different styles are located on computers all over the world. But through one's efforts, they are brought together to be of a piece."[87] Nina Wakeford in her study of feminist appropriations of Web technologies has noted that the usage of a term such as *homegrrls, netchicks,* and *geekgrrrls* in URL site names illustrates a new kind of "semantic alliance" between women and computing cultures.[88] However, alongside the new usages exist more traditional associations of the "home" as a physically demarcated expression of private space and activity; Wakeford's examples here include page maintenance being referred to as house cleaning and the graphic use of icons such as doorways and living rooms in personal homepages.[89]

More broadly, a feminist take on online technologies has treated the analogy between physical and virtual homes through a discussion of the gendered work cultures in the computing industry as well as through a more complex understanding of the social relations that shape the feeling of being at home online. Melissa Gregg and Susan Leigh Star have problematized the idea of being "homed in cyberspace" albeit in different contexts. While Gregg's work reveals the perils of telecommuting for the familial dynamics in a household, Star posits the notion of homing as the opposite of the category of *home*.[90] Homing signals a process toward belonging or not—within homepages—unlike home, which reproduces familiar, taken-for-granted assumptions about one's access or even desire to be at home online.

An important point here is that while online technologies are changing the household or one's sense of belonging (to be at home), how exactly that dynamic is getting played out in different scenarios needs to be continually examined. In addition, one cannot assume that the dynamic is necessarily positive for the subjects involved. Like Star, I contend that the moments when one feels out of home or "homeless in some sense" online can be very revealing of the assumptions made about who can belong online and how. Furthermore, in the case of immigrants, as Kyra Landzelius argues, "to make oneself 'a(t) home'" in cyberspace is to problematize the nature of home [and] to do so in the name of culture and/or ethnicity... is to complicate further the relationship between identity and place."[91] Even as ethnic immigrant enclaves proclaim themselves online, it is the contestation, contradictions, and debates embedded within them, as Emily Noelle Ignacio's work tells us, that might be the most devastating evidence for the lack of stable national discourse in digital diasporas.[92]

Home Travels

Drawing on interdisciplinary theorizations of the home—from diaspora studies, Asian American studies, transnational feminist studies—and bringing them to bear on the idea of the homepage is an acknowledgment of the processes by which we construct home and homeland. As David Morley writes in *Home Territories*, "only a truly interdisciplinary . . . approach, which can synthesise the various potential insights generated in . . . conventionally separated analyses, can supply us with an effective understanding of the issues at stake in what I take to be one of the most central political questions confronting us, as we attempt to construct a viable cartography of the world in which we now live."[93]

That "world in which we now live" must include a recognition of the ways in which transnational media and migration continue to destabilize the very notion of the home or the house. Myria Georgiou's provocative and stirring question is worth recalling here. After noting that the diasporic home often involves dual or multiple houses (in former and current homelands, most likely), she wonders, "Which house would that [home] be anyway? Which *one* home is home?"[94] Feminist cultural geographer Doreen Massey, among others, has argued that home is not a static place but a dynamic space informed by social relations.[95] Building on that observation, we might ask how the homepage, as an articulation of situated belonging, poses new contestations as well as opportunities for conventional associations of home with a household and a homeland.

The notion of being at home without being taken back home, while seemingly straightforward, is a complex idea that is constructed, negotiated, and in some instances resisted through the political, economic, technological, and cultural domains of online media in the Indian immigrant community in the United States.[96] By bringing the everyday, banal realities of *homeland* into proximity with the immigrant home through the particular form and content of homepages, online media rupture the dichotomies of "here" and "there" or "then" and "now."

The homepage as a transnational space of belonging also becomes relevant when we consider the role of media in the multicultural United States. Given the marginality of racial minorities and immigrants in mainstream media, the homepage provides a crucial link for minorities in the experience and management of their lives as transnational cultural subjects. And in that regard, the homepage can challenge us to see how online media catering to immigrants is not limited to the reenactment of ways to reconnect to the homeland. Rather, a vital detail that such homepages bring to the fore is that there are many other desires, problems, concerns, and agendas that are just as important, if not more so, in the immigrants' experiences around belonging. While the trope of home often stabilizes its meanings around security, familiarity, privacy, and self, the reality of the immigrant home, seen through the lens of online media, is undoubtedly more complex. One must therefore ask if "rooting not travel" has been central to hegemonic notions of culture, are homepages reinvigorating the concept of "home" as something that travels?[97]

CHAPTER TWO

Out of Place in the Domestic Space

H4 Indian Ladies Negotiating Belonging

H4 Indian Ladies is an active and prolific discussion forum on Indusladies.com, one of the most popular community websites for Indian immigrants. The H4 Indian Ladies forum was created in 2005 and appears under the geographically marked section titled "USA and Canada" on the website's discussion page under the category of "neighborhoods."[1] That page has five geographical categories, aiming to appeal to Indians living all over the world; the USA and Canada section is second to the India section in the number of active threads and follow-up posts. As of January 2014, there are over seven hundred threads on the forum, covering the gamut of experiences specific to Indian immigrant women who live in the United States on the H-4 visa.[2] As noted earlier, the United States Citizenship and Immigration Services (USCIS) issues H-1B visas to foreign workers who are affiliated with a "specialty occupation" and perform duties that are "specialized and complex."[3] The spouse accompanying the H-1B visa holder, as well as any dependents under twenty-one, receive the H-4 visa from USCIS. Since its creation in 1990, the H-1B visa has been allotted to Indian nationals more than any other national group; that proportion is increasing, and as of 2013 it is estimated that more than half of all the H-1B visas issued annually since 2006 have been to Indian citizens.[4]

While there is no gendered clause in the visa category per se, the male-female ratio of H-1B allotment over the years has been found to be roughly 75 percent to 25 percent, respectively; as for the H-4 visa, it is overwhelmingly allotted to women applicants.⁵ This statistic holds true even in the case of Indians and in turn shapes the dominant perception of H-1B Indian contingent as almost exclusively male. Relatedly, within popular representations of Indian immigrants, the figure of the male H-1B professional occupies a central role while H-4 women are for the most part absent.

The H4 Indian Ladies forum represents one of the handful of online spaces where the immigrant condition, as shaped by the gendered H-4 visa, is visible. Equally important is the nature of that representation. As a public discussion, open to anyone with Internet access who is willing to create an account with the site, H4 Indian Ladies allows participants to use online media to engage with women in a similar situation across the country and in the process to produce a collective social identity (there is no need for an account to access and read the forum discussions). Prior to the creation of the forum in the mid-2000s, there wasn't any clearly defined online space for H-4 visa holders. Throughout the 1990s, a random thread or two on community websites would fleetingly remind users of the predicament of women on the H-4 before returning back to more pressing matters: namely, the questions and concerns of H-1B immigrants. It was routine for some of the leading community websites of the 1990s such as Samachar, nriworld.com, and INDOlink to address the needs of the H-1B immigrant through classified ads, news, immigration help, and forums while completely ignoring the predicament of the H-4 spouse. In the early 2000s, leading portals such as Sulekha.com brought intermittent attention to the H-4 immigrant through the site's personal essay feature, and Rediff.com carried a couple of stories about domestic abuse in H-4 households.⁶ Thus while the H-4 immigrants were discussed in a few instances, they were at most a reminder of the presence of H-4 women in the community and not much else. The uneven attention resurfaces in social media, with the H-1B issue getting greater and more diverse coverage than H-4 matters.⁷

In 2014, nine years after its creation, the H4 Indian Ladies forum continues to be the leading online discussion for this particular group of Indian immigrants. In the age of Web 2.0 and social media, "the H-4 condition," as it is often phrased, has emerged in other outlets as well. For example, individual entries about the dilemmas of H-4 spouses were published on a few feminist blogs—Poonam Bhatke's blog and Apu's World, in 2010 and 2009, respectively—and in a handful of single entries on wordpress blogs since then.⁸ More recently, in 2011, a Facebook group—"H4 visa, a curse"—was created with the aim of creating support and advocacy for H-4 issues.⁹ The group also maintains a Twitter account and has found an ally in an immigration lawyer who champions the cause of H-4 visa reform. The group and the lawyer have collaborated to create a couple of online radio shows that focus on the H-4 visa.[10] While the Facebook group for H-4 women is gaining new members steadily, it appears to be more focused on immigration reform and as a result seems to be less of a fluid space for a range of conversations. Interestingly, some of the key elements of recent social media and blog sites—sharing personal histories, debating immigration policy reform, encouraging advocacy—have long been central to the activities of the H4 Indian Ladies forum. We can view these more recent expressions of H-4 visibility online as a proliferation or dispersion of the elements embedded within the forum since its creation in 2005.

Against this backdrop, I want to explore the discussions on the H4 Indian Ladies forum and how the hopes and frustrations of these women reconfigure our ideas about the Indian immigrant household.[11] Specifically, this chapter asks: How does the Indian immigrant home, typically relegated to the domain of the ethnic, the domestic, the private, look different within the public domain of online media? And how do the voices that emerge online redefine the notion of being at home?[12]

I argue that the women of the H-4 forum mobilize online media to render the "private" cultures of their immigrant home and household "public." They make visible their diverse experiences of being outsiders in the Indian immigrant world; in turn, their narratives of feeling out of place in the home—the very place where, traditionally, they are supposed to most belong—unsettle idealized notions, seen both in Indian and American culture of the gendered spaces of immigrant belonging. The participants on H4 Indian Ladies, many of them well-educated professionals, find themselves in a new country, unable to work because of restrictive immigration laws and confined to their homes. These H-4 women link the gendered nature of their experience of home and household to patriarchal structures that govern both the process of immigration and the principles of the Indian family. As we track the ways these women repurpose online media to articulate the burdens of gender hierarchies and a visa-centric class system, we witness a tactical subversion of the idealized representation of the Indian immigrant as a Hindu male software professional on the H-1B visa. In these discussions we see Indian immigrants exploring everything from the logistics of work and leisure in a new country to their sense of agency and self-definition.

Two key topics that recur on the forum are home and work. Though some of the forum conversations address the theme of labor in terms of domestic chores, childbearing, and child rearing, a majority of the discussions frame work as labor away from home-centered life. While all the posts and threads are accessible under the forum's main page, at the very top of the listings are two "sticky threads," discussions that the moderators deem most important and relevant to the participants: "H4 Wife: Things to do?" and "Looking for job in H4 status: Expert opinions needed."[13] The titles of the two threads go back to the original wording of an initial post dating back to 2005. Beneath that initial post are hundreds of responses, some a direct response to the first query, and some the work of the forum moderators, who it appears decided to collate similar posts and generate a larger metathread organized around the two main queries about home and work issues for H-4 wives. Beyond these two threads, members post similarly themed queries in the section of the forum that is outside the "sticky" domain. The sticky threads are a spatial foregrounding of what seem to be two key recurring concerns around the H-4 condition for many of the women on the forum; while one revolves around the limits of the pleasures of home life, the other revolves around denying the pleasures of work life.

What American Dream?
Critiquing State and Patriarchy

While the following quote is taken from the "H4 Wife: Things to do?" thread, the sentiment it bears is also evidenced quite frequently in the second sticky forum, "Looking for job in H4 status," as well as other threads in the H-4 forum that comment on the unfair laws regulating H-4 women's movement and agency: "Coming to the US was a dream as everyone says, but thatz only for our hubbies who go to work as they were doing in India . . . We take this dream and happily come to the US and then after a year start feeling the effects of turning into a homemaker 24/7/365 days."[14]

In this section, I draw out some of the views expressed by the H-4 forum members around life as an NRI living the "American dream." While the latter conjures up images of wealth, commodities, and abundant civic and public service resources, being an NRI in the United States has often been viewed as a great escape from the highly competitive and scarce resource world of India while enjoying the perks such as yearly vacations in the Indian homeland, the high exchange rate between the dollar and the rupee currencies (which translates into greater economic freedom in the Indian setting), and the cultural capital associated in middle-class India with living "abroad."

However, as the following perspectives shared by the H-4 women reveal, while making oneself at home in the United States is a crucial desire for H-4 immigrants, how they understand and define it is always political. Recalling Chandra Talpade Mohanty's rhetorical question, "Is home a geographical space, an historical space, an emotional, sensory space?," the critiques of the un-dream-like reality of the NRI life by H-4 women reveal that there cannot be stable definitions of the NRI home but only historically contingent ones that are shaped by specific contexts of transnational relocation.[15]

New entrants to the United States often post about being ill-prepared for the H-4 lifestyle and lament that combined with the pressure to marry a U.S.-based groom is a lack of information about what living on the H-4 visa actually entails. While most of the forum members are either on the H-4 or have previously been on it (before acquiring a green card or U.S. citizenship), Indian women contemplating a move to the United States on the H-4 visa appear to visit the site to post questions and gather information. Speaking to such a contingent in a thread titled "Daily Routine of H4 Ladies," a fellow member offers this cautionary note: "Know what you are getting into before considering marriage to an H1B person . . . don't jump, get married to an NRI just for the desperation of landing in this country (some of my friends were) and then complain about not [being] able to work . . . get mentally prepared that you might sit at home the whole day . . . if you can't then rethink about getting married to a H1B."[16] Given the high desirability of an NRI groom in the Indian middle class, and especially the H-1B software engineer "type" over the course of the 1990s, the 2000s, and continuing to the present, the above post counters the glamorized vision of NRI homes with a sobering appraisal of it as a potentially undesirable space when viewed from close quarters.

In the "H4 Wife: Things to do" thread, a member residing in India and awaiting her H-4 visa to enable her to "follow" her H-1B husband to the United States writes: "My worst dream is going to the US and remain jobless for one year as I have been working for the past five years . . . What type of job opportunities are there for ladies like us? Please help me in preparing myself well before I land in the US. I am very anxious about moving to the US. Your feedback would help in shaping my future."[17] While the above post suggests that prospective H-4 women are trying to understand the reality of their life as NRIs prior to arriving in the United States, another post speaks to the inadequacy of information in understanding the lived nature of the experience: "When I came to the US as a new bride in 2007, I was shocked to find the ways in which my freedom was curtailed. Though I was warned about it, I didn't expect this."[18]

While the H-1B visa has become a signifier for skilled, foreign, science, and technology labor in the United States, the H-4 has become a code for dependency. There are important legal and cultural dimensions to such a description. In U.S. immigration law, since the H-4 visa is linked to the category of the H-1B, an H-4 visa can be initiated only if an H-1B application is approved for a family member. When the H-1B expires, the corresponding H-4 automatically ceases as well. While individuals on the H-4 visa can stay in the United States as long as their H-1B in-status spouses, they do not share the same immigrant rights as their more privileged "skilled worker" partners. To maintain legal status, H-4 subjects have to strictly follow the rules and restrictions to which the U.S. immigration law subjects them. These regulations include being barred from employment, not having a social security number, and being unable to independently pursue activities such as dealing with financial institutions (banks, for example) without the consent/authorization of the spouse.[19]

Underpinning this legal framework of H-4 dependency is the cultural ideology of U.S. immigration where some rights and privileges are guaranteed to the migrant whose labor is deemed useful by the state while accompanying migrants, such as family members, are excluded or restricted since they represent, perhaps in the official perspective, the unintended consequences of foreign labor inflows. What makes this position on desired migrants and their dependents further problematic is the imbrication of gendered visa politics with hegemonic family and national cultures. A member posting in the thread "H4 Wife: Things to do" succinctly invokes the tradition that puts pressure on young women to be married sooner than later, when she states, "I was one of the most brilliant student in my school and my college days and was planning to come to USA for further studies and got married instead."[20] While members frequently allude to the Indian middle-class family values whereby they are "brought up to do well in studies," they also point to the disjuncture brought about by NRI marriages.

In the thread "Looking for job in H4 status," one of the most active threads on the forum at large, a member resorting to model minority imagery attempts to connect the H-4 women's dependency to the American state's inadequacies in channeling the potential of its minorities. She argues: "Most people on the H4 visas are well educated and would easily be able to contribute [to] the American economy. We are law abiding and give so much to the American economy. All our talents are wasted and skills are rotting sitting around for backlog center to clear the LC's [labor certification for H-1B work permits] and for retrogression to end. Meanwhile we practically have no life and are completely dependent."[21] In the same thread, another member's critique of the American state's restrictive H-4 laws reveals how race can inform the class identifications among NRIs. After noting that the H-4 visa "sucks," she turns her attention to the state and wonders: "but why are they worried about prospective citizens for 1 million Indians who are in the highest tax paying bracket contributing so much work and are law abiding citizens $$$$ in USA (contributing to their wealth) when they are allowing 10 million Latinos to jump across the border EVERY Year? Really idiotic . . . just goes to show how 'smart' they really are. 😠"[22] To which another member responds: "They are worried for political reasons. All these Immigration matters are monitored by the govt. and they have to make sure things are under control when it comes to the population—it is a different story about illegal immigrants and it is sad what is happening in that area. Again everything leads to politics . . . sadly."[23] Laced in this exchange is the idealization about Indian immigration being always legal, elite, and desirable.

Some of the posts also indicate that many of the participants struggle between their critique of the "unfair visa" of the United States and appreciating the country as the "land of opportunities." Hence ambivalence often marks their conversations about the process of immigration. A critical point in that process occurs when the H-1B applicant (with his dependents) appears for an interview at an American embassy in India, and U.S. officials determine whether or not the applicant secures the H-1B visa. To appear eligible, as one member recounts, a prospective H-1B applicant can "suppress [my] qualifications because they did not want the Embassy to think that the immigrants could be prospective citizens."[24] Similarly, while discussing their interviews, often with the intention of helping others awaiting their H-4 interviews in India, the women list the questions they were asked by immigration officials. The questions all revolve around knowledge of their H-1B husband's prospective or ongoing job and employer details in the United States and their ability to confirm a marital relationship with the H-1B visa holder by showing pictures from the wedding album and accurately identifying date of marriage. For many of the women, who even at the time of the visa interview are possibly continuing in their professional lives as doctors, chartered accountants, teachers, and engineers, the visa interview, as they share on the forum, evokes ambivalence toward an imminent journey that is possible only if their identity is suitably silenced.

Others try to negotiate it by adopting a liberal perspective on transnational labor flows and national prerogatives. For example, one member reconciles with her inability to work by stating that although "America[,] the world of opportunities[,] is very cruel to H4 like us," she can see how "from the American's point of view they need to have such restrictions to have opportunities for themselves too!"[25] Another member reiterates the same point in her statement that the "rules seem terribly unfair, but the rules are there for a good reason and I feel that since I am a visitor here in this country, it is especially important for me to follow the rules."[26] Others reveal a more informed reasoning of the restrictions placed by the H-4 visa, calling into attention the fact that another temporary dependent visa, the L-2 (given when married to an L-1 visa holder), does not carry the same restriction on work eligibility. One member states that following her professional career in India working for an MNC (multinational corporation), she moved to the United States on the L-2 visa status (since she married someone on the L-1 visa status), which allowed her to continue working. Then "came the news that my husband had to move to the H1B visa for the Green card process (God knows how when it will get over), and I was put on the H4."[27] For another member, a chartered accountant who gave up her job in India and followed her H-1B husband to the United States, the problem is a more practical one—the Obama administration's measure that increased the fees for H-1B applications, which in turn reduced her prospects for getting a company to sponsor her own H-1B visa application.

The emotional response to the H-4 predicament, especially the sense of being confined within the home, also varies greatly. For example, while one member stoically states that she has decided to move on (mentally), since "nothing can be done about this visa for the next 100 years unless USCIS does something," for some others, going back to India or at least imagining the possibility is a temporary relief, as exemplified in the following post: "I regret my decision everyday now . . . I just wish I had never come here. I am fed up now and I want to really go back and get a real job and make a career for myself. Even if I earn Rs. 100 in India I will be happy than just sitting here and staring at the walls and thinking of ways to keep myself busy."[28]

The disjuncture between the idealized NRI life (comfortable, pleasant, and exciting) one is supposed to have and the reality of everyday existence is another key site of frustration. As one post puts it, "people back in India think I should be happy because I am in such a cool place but life without any friends and work becomes as much useless as if you are in some rural area."[29] The problematic assumptions about rural and urban life notwithstanding, of particular importance here is the fact that while H-4 life can be isolating, what might intensify that desolation is the fear and inability to openly discuss it with others in the social or familial circle. That fear might arise from one's own desire to sustain an image about the NRI life or from knowing that there will be family backlash to such revelations. This issue—the gap between how women experience their lives as middle-class housewives on the H-4 and how they are perceived by their extended families in India—has been previously addressed by feminist social justice organizations, particularly in the context of domestic abuse within the home.

Immigration reform advocates and feminist activists have first drawn attention to the fact that the H-1B is most often granted to men and the H-4 to women. Subsequently, they have problematized the gendered politics of the visa typologies H-1B and H-4 by pointing to the underlying assumption that men are the economic and social heads of their families wherein their wives are dependent on them. Critics of the H-4 have argued that such a systemic privileging of patriarchal notions of family and gendered relations engenders a vulnerable space for immigrant women on the H-4. In this regard, the work of South Asian community activist organizations such as Sakhi and Manavi has been critical. Working with domestic abuse cases in South Asian immigrant communities, these women's social justice groups have illuminated the links between the vulnerable legal position of women on H-4 visas and the incidence of their victimization within the household.[30] Until 2000, the legality of an H-4 spouse's stay in the United States was tied inextricably to the maintenance of marriage with the H-1B visa holder. It has been noted that such a suturing of marital status with the legality of the migrant's status has contributed to cultures of fear, silence, and suffering for some women on the H-4. Many women in contentious home situations could not afford the material and symbolic costs of disrupting or challenging the status quo. Community organizations have argued that in such instances, the lack of access to economic freedom (to secure a lawyer, buy a ticket), fear of deportation, and the cultural embarrassment it would bring to the family "back home" operate as key deterrents. Many women are caught between a rock and a hard place, between a tough domestic situation strengthened by legal favoring of the H-1B holder and a patriarchal culture where women are expected to uphold marriage, tradition, and family values, no matter what. Following advocacy efforts urging a reauthorization of the 1994 Violence Against Women Act, a new class of visa, a T visa, was created in 2000 to help H-4 spouses in domestic abuse situations to continue to live and work in this country provided they cooperate with the law.[31] Under this new immigration pathway, persons on the T visa could legally work their way to a green card and permanent residency in the United States.

While the example of immigration reform through the inclusion of the T visa offers an instance of successful advocacy for H-4 women and immigrants' rights, there is another important policy change that is being advocated for by H-4 right activists since 2012 and, as of January 2014, is under regulatory review of the federal government.[32] It involves allowing a select group of H-4 visa holders to pursue employment—those whose H-1B spouses have successfully advanced their green card applications to the final stage of processing and acceptance. In other words, this imminent policy would offer the spouses of "almost" U.S. permanent residents the "right" to work as part of the greater spectrum of rights accorded to those legally recognized as immigrants. That such changes are perhaps being brought about by action not only on the part of social justice organizations but also the very women who are intimately aware of the situation is indicated through the online campaign on the H-4 forum initiated in 2007–2008 to support a petition to "improve conditions for H4 individuals."[33] Such campaigns have more recently emerged in other online efforts such as the "H4 Visa: A curse" page on Facebook.

One could argue that these efforts toward immigration reform, though small, are significant because they allow H-4 subjects, mostly women, the freedom to be employed sooner rather than later in the transition from temporary migrant to U.S. permanent resident. But on the other hand, the gains suggested through this measure do little to disrupt the fundamental framework of the immigrant state that recognizes H-4 rights solely through the lens of H-1B desire and potential and frames the issues of rights, as Monisha Das Gupta has argued, through a narrow conceptualization of nation-bound citizenship.[34]

Not Feeling at Home: Not Belonging and Domestic Discontent

The H-4 forum presents an interesting case study of divergent views on the politics of the time-space of the NRI household from the perspective of Indian women who are, as the following post states, "traveling in the same boat," of the H-4: "We are sailing in the same boat which is taking us nowhere. I am also here on the dead H4. I used to be a pretty busy person in India managing my work 'n' home. But here it's just home."[35] This metaphor indicating companionship built around similar modes of navigating the immigrant life is frequently brought up in forum discussions. However, what the discussions ultimately reveal is a lack of consensus over what being at home in the H-4 status means for its subjects. They also illuminate the extent that the lived experiences of space, time, and subjectivity for immigrant women on the H-4 are being altered by online technologies. Further, the H-4 forum exemplifies a space for critique, subversion, and negotiation of their expected roles vis-à-vis home and labor.

The discussion forum foregrounds how this group of women feels about their officially and culturally sanctioned role as "dependent spouses" of the H-1B immigrant, and how they respond to the notion that they ought to be at home in the private NRI household. It also exemplifies a first-person representation of Indian immigration, a form of narrative that, as Sandhya Shukla has noted, has been accorded very little space in the community imaginary.[36] For a minority of women on the forum, the fact of being on the H-4 is quite inconsequential to their reflections on being in the United States as an Indian immigrant. But for the vast majority the mobility—and most often, immobility—induced by their visa status is a key source of contest and frustration. That said, the diverse perspectives of the forum members are nearly always defined by the borders of the household and the constraints—both in time and space—of being in the United States on the H-4.

To return to the metaphor of the boat, there is no singular description of the H-4 experience that emerges as definitive. This is particularly relevant in light of the fact that the little media attention that has been paid to the H-4 women's context (preceding discussion practices) has tended to lump them as a group with certain pressing concerns such as their vulnerability to abusive situations. By exploring a forum like H4 Indian Ladies, we can get a better understanding of this context of immigrant life in the United States from the standpoint and views of the subjects who have for the most part been spoken for.

Home life—particularly routine activities in the household, the pleasures and limits of the domestic, and the contours of necessary possible and desired forms of labor in and out of the home—informs many of the topic threads on the H-4 forum. Here I foreground a few examples and explain how and why these conversations offer significant insights into some of the ideologies and practices shaping the contemporary NRI household.

One of the primary ways in which the private space of the home emerges on the forum is through its associations with boredom, lack of extended familial or neighborly relations, and restricted choices for work and labor. The following post from 2005 initiated the longest running thread of the forum, titled "H4 Wife: Things to do?"

> I got a bachelors degree in India—I was working for a good company in India making decent earnings—I got married to a H1B visa holder, which put me in H4 visa status (yes, that dreaded H4) 😩—Being H4, I can't work or earn a single dollar.—All I can do is stay at home and stare at the four walls (Not ready for kids yet) Does the above profile sound similar to you? Are you a fellow H4 visa holder as well? Please share how you use your time without getting bored to death. I meet lots of H4's who are in the same boat and this thread could be useful not only to me, but to fellow H4 travellers as well.[37]

In the post, the member hails her "fellow H4 travellers," inviting their input on how to use "time without getting bored to death." Also, in a style reminiscent of a professional résumé, the member describes her profile in bullet points. The order in which she presents the facets of her profile is very revealing and, more broadly, is illustrative of a dominant mode of self-presentation on the forum. Many members first begin with their professional history before offering their reflections on their current lives on the H-4. The breakdown of the narrative along the lines of pre- and postmarriage scenarios not only juxtaposes life in India with life in the United States but also indicates that for many members their memories of India are associated with activity, pursuit of interests, and economic independence while their realities in the United States are implicated within inertia, restrictions, and loss of economic independence. It is not the American dream, but rather the end of their dreams for many of the members on the forum.

Household time-space in many cases is expressed through metaphors of physical confinement and immobility; phrases and terms such as "boxed in," "four walls of boredom," "staring at four walls," "stuck in the same boat," "dead bored," and "torture" are very commonly used in the post accompanied by emoticons and gifs (such as bonk, 😊) to indicate frustration, anger, sadness, and exasperation.[38] For some, the feeling of being stuck in their present scenario is exacerbated by the realization of how little or no preparation they had for what home life as the H-4 wife of a H-1B immigrant entailed. The disclosure by some members that they did not realize the full consequences of their decision to marry and migrate to the United States supports the claims of existing research that women among skilled immigrant groups routinely give up their professional and personal networks for the sake of marriage with a partner whose career will take them abroad, and that very often they make these decisions without full knowledge of what such a life entails for them.[39]

Many of the women who allude to their busy life in India prior to marriage and immigration discuss it within the context of their academic life or, more commonly, their professional lives. As one former medical professional puts it: "I am a doctor and have had my own practice in India. Imagine from treating 20–30 patients every day, all you get to do now is cook and mop the house!!! Grrr."[40] On occasion, some of the participants offer a brief professional biography, indicating their occupation or what professional degree they hold (with MBA, computer engineer, and chartered accountant being mentioned most commonly in this group) and how many years of work experience they have. This is usually followed by a timeline of their marriage, migration, and homebound status in the United States.

There are a significant number of women on the H-4 forum who advance the view that their sense of confinement is a result of a loss of the productive work life that they were accustomed to in India; for example, one member stated she "never thought sitting idle would be more challenging than those stringent deadlines and deliverables 😊."[41] That said, however, there are many others (some of whom were professionally active in India) who view the boredom primarily through the lens of transnational migration and the loss of familiar networks of family, friends, and community that it engenders.

It might be noted here that it was a similar experience of loss of the familiar network that inspired Malathy Jey, the creator of Indusladies.com, to imagine a virtual gathering space for women like her. Here it is not the restrictions of labor outside the home that are seen as having a bearing on the isolation of the immigrant housewife. Rather, it is the fact of being Indian in America, being in a neighborhood with very few or no Indians, and going through the rhythms of domestic life with little or no interaction with the outside world; as one member describes it, "no long chats with the *bai*, no conversations with neighborhood aunties/uncles, no friends relatives coming home."[42] Another member admits that although for a while it seemed that "the only sound thinking I did everyday was about what to cook," it was not for long since cooking while being essentially alone without any company became a time of displeasure rather than pleasure.[43] The lack of activity in the household and the restrictions around mobility and work for many H-4 women make them evaluate India and America within a sense of national time, where "life is slow here indeed . . . unlike in India." The temporalities of household and homeland are intermeshed through a subjectivity that is deeply political.

Along with such nostalgia-tinged references to a familiar time-space, forum members frequently include emoticons and phrases such as "sad," "depressed," "lonely," "losing my mind," and "going crazy" to indicate the isolation and displacement they feel; alluding to the fact that they are "losing interest in daily chores," they also invite suggestions from fellow members on appropriate activities "to achieve a sense of fulfillment."[44] Their expressions of nostalgia, physical and emotional ill-health, and suggestions of disorientation as a consequence of the displacement they encounter in the immigrant locale illustrate a case of what Jigna Desai has insightfully theorized as "homesickness." Exploring the various ways in which the British Asian women characters in Gurinder Chaddha's film *Bhaji on the Beach* embody social and physical illness—experiencing vertigo, domestic abuse, dizziness, unplanned pregnancy—Desai posits that these modes signify "diverse embodiments of gendered migratory subjectivities" that she urges must be (re)located within diasporic contexts of racism and heteropatriarchy.[45] Following Desai, I read H-4 forum members' modes of "homesickness" not as a way to pathologize them but rather to see how by bonding over talk about feeling sick staying at home all day, their narratives point to the intermeshing of female agency and restrictions; homemaking in turn becomes the very source of their homesickness.

When the H4 Indian Ladies forum members discuss their feelings of depression and isolation as a result of feeling confined to the home, the responses they generate, particularly from other senior members of the forum, insightfully point to the fluid meanings associated with home that are shaped in great part by one's ability to traverse beyond the physical confines of the individual home and the metaphorical boundaries of the immigrant space. The seniors in question either indicate their seniority within the H-4 context (they have been on the H-4 longer or previously) or the website (senior ILites who have long been Indusladies.com members) or both (long-standing IL members who are now green card holders or U.S. citizens). They intervene in the conversations to reassure and support the unhappy members as well as offer strategies to cope.

Such interventions from senior members of the H-4 club find resonance with those in the forum who feel that there is an overwhelming focus on the negative aspects of the H-4 status and not enough on the positive energy needed to overcome the hardship associated with the visa status. It is in that vein that a member's call for "H4 success stories" invites "H4 ladies who have overcome the H4 panic syndrome and have found some positive engagement and satisfaction while on the H4 boat" to post their stories about "small, small achievements," which in turn can illuminate the fact that "being on the H4 is not that depressing at all."[46] Here the act of online navigation away from the heteronormative patriarchal space of immigrant home and nation leading to collective bonding and sharing can be understood as a negotiation of the "homesickness" where reorienting their sense of displacement (disorientation) includes expressing agency through virtual mobility.

These interventions also bring up fairly conservative and reductive categories of "Indian" and "American" in the process of articulating a transnational experience of moving from a familiar culture to a new one. The ability and legal permit to drive is often the first strategy shared by fellow members by way of becoming agents of their time and space. For many women, getting the information that they were legally permitted to get a driver's license was a revelation of sorts; in such instances, the H-4 forum serves an important role of a community information desk drawing on the shared knowledge of its diverse members. In addition to driving, other activities commonly cited include shopping, baby sitting, and volunteering at or and visiting libraries, with the underlying notion that these leisure or interest-based activities would interrupt the isolation and boredom faced by immigrant women in the home.

The activities suggested often serve as codes for "Indian" and "American" time-space and are employed to further either a culturally nationalist ideology of the immigrant life or a liberal perspective on becoming Indian American. For example, while babysitting implies taking care of Indian kids, volunteering at the local library is presented as a way to be a part of an "American" community by embodying some of their values (volunteering) while partaking of the resources meant for the public good. In this context, the forum also offers continuing evidence of the hegemonic politics of religion and culture in shaping conservative narratives of Hindu Indian women's responsibilities and activities in the immigrant household while also serving religion as a site for the reproduction of their ideals about authenticity.[47] While the forum is not restricted by religious affiliation, Hindu identity serves as the dominant code for the community. It is expressed through the absence of references to other religions besides Hinduism and correspondingly through the dispersed visibility of Hindu referents such as information sharing about Hindu websites, rituals, and activities in the local area temples and references to *sloka* chanting (chanting verses from Hindu sacred texts) as an activity to avoid feelings of depression.

The hegemonic construction of Indian immigrant women as "authentic" symbols of national culture in diasporic settings has been addressed and critiqued by feminist scholarship on migration and transnational identities.[48] Such scholarship has also pointed to the imbrication of religious activities with the immigrant women's domain. While the H-4 forum indicates a continuation of older practices such as visiting physical temples, it also bears witness to newer iterations that are digitally mediated; examples include practices such as reading Hindu scriptures online, visiting virtual shrines, and performing online rituals. While not a commonly discussed topic on the forum, the use of the virtual, interactive, digital environment for religious activities within the domestic household by NRI women destabilizes some of the fixed meanings of the private associated with the individual home and those of the public associated with transnational online spaces. Elsewhere I have noted that the virtualization of Hindu temple cultures, shaped in large part by a targeted appeal to the Indian diaspora in the United States, is mobilized around a discourse of the virtual home, whereby the private space of ritual (the immigrant's domestic home) intersects with the public cultures of Hindu temples (the priest, sermons, ritual services) through the strategic mediations of the interactive, digital, hypertextual homepage of the physical temple.[49]

In considering the sphere of reproduction, it is significant that the discussions about children and the reproduction of the family occupy a more or less marginal location within the conversations on the forum.[50] On the H4 Indian Ladies forum, however, two specific contexts in which the theme of having children emerge are worth mention here. In the first, starting a family is presented as a non-option in queries about things to do while on the H-4 (e.g., I don't want to have children in the next x years). While indicating their current lack of interest in having a child is a way to ward off any responses to their post that present childbearing as a meaningful activity, it also points to their investment and desires around self that are not tied to the ideal of motherhood. In the second context where the theme of motherhood emerges, having children is presented as an end to the ordeal of boredom, as it would introduce normative household activities organized around childbearing and rearing. In the latter case, it is worth noting the instrumentalist approach to the act of reproduction as a "thing to do," which would in turn engender meaning as it recasts empty home time-space into a series of household activities associated with raising a family. Brief though they might be, these expressions must be read as significant moments of disruption to the conservative ideologies that naturalize the relation between women—their bodies, identities—and reproduction of the family and in that way produce "Woman" as teleological sign of nurture and Nature.

The forum at large also reveals a contestation over the meanings associated with the H-4 household. There is significant tension over imagining certain forms of labor as productive and others as merely time-passing activities. This is most clearly evidenced when members who present a positive take on life on the H-4 are applauded by a few others for being refreshingly different from the dominant "sad" stories about feeling stuck and depressed. Some use such opportunities to remark that home life sans working outside the home can be a very productive use of time and constitutes meaningful work as well. An example of negotiating that notion is expressed in the following "survival" tactic shared by one member, which is to "run your home like a business."[51] The post elaborates on the virtues of streamlining and organizing all household activities including cooking, grocery shopping, and doing laundry before concluding that running a home is a job just as demanding as any outside job. The implicit target here are the posts made by fellow members who indicate being unable to legally hold a job outside the home is linked to their sense of frustration of wasting time and feeling unproductive. This is also revealed in other posts such as the one where a member suggests having a pet as a way to generate emotional companionship at home, but she notes, not once but twice, that this advice was not meant for those who want to "earn or productively utilize their time as an H4 . . . not for someone who is looking to do something serious."[52] The forum also offers evidence of the identity struggles for many women that are engendered, in some part at least, by the visa hierarchy of the H-1B and H-4.

A particularly insightful thread in this regard is one that pits "H1B ladies vs. H4 homemakers."[53] In the first post, a member shares her unpleasant experiences with H-1B Indian women, who, she contends, have always shown "attitude" in their interactions with her. She then implies that the attitude stems from a sense of superiority based on their visa status, namely the H-1B, and polls the community on their experiences. Of the twenty-four responses to the first post, almost all reinforced the notion that there is indeed a class system within the Indian community that is hinged on their immigrant status; other members broaden the spectrum of snobbery to include those with green cards.

The diverse comments that emerge in this context highlight the struggle between desire and distance for some of the H-4 women. On the one hand, they distance themselves from the H-1B women by configuring the H-1B women's lives where they work all day in the office and come home to cook and clean as "a life of slogging," which they would rather not have; on the other, they reveal resentment over the lack of sisterhood among Indian women, particularly because, as one post states: "Very few Indian ladies come here on an H1 by themselves. Generally, they come on H4 or some other dependent *visa*. So for some years everyone has been on the same boat. Whats the point of looking down on something you yourself went through some years back?" A second post by the thread starter offers this timeline of progress: "Every single H4/gc/new citizen started at the same *point*—and everyone knows that its a matter of time, then people will get where they are—like X years=h4 to h1, x+y years = house, etc. (after filing for GC of course)—so its a timeline, deal with it, you're not doing something above your peers!"[54]

The contradictory, vexed nature of H-4 women's discussions over the superiority of the H-1B women and green card holders simultaneously points to their critique of the hierarchy in the community of visa holders but also to their own investments in such a social ranking, which in turn are embedded within ideologies of immigrant mobility, citizenship culture, and nonresident Indian lifestyles. A critical component of that lifestyle is hinged upon home ownership in the United States, a trend that reports in 2012 indicate is only getting higher among Indian immigrants. On the H-4 forum, a member critiquing the "keeping up with joneses" syndrome afflicting the NRI community at large elaborates: "Another big thing is buying a house. Those with homes tend to look down at those who rent (especially if you have been here a while) . . . There may be reasons for us not buying a home." Reflecting on her own position she adds, "frankly . . . it is a headache to maintain a home here—doing all the cleaning, maintenance, lawn mowing by yourself."[55]

In a study of gender relations in the context of the migration of Indian software professionals to the United States, S. Uma Devi lists gender stereotyping and a mythification of high-tech masculinity as key to understanding some of the thought processes shaping the work ethos in the information sector. In particular, the author focuses on the H-1B and H-4 visa category and examines how women entering and working in the United States on these two visas offer important narratives about the contradictions between the discourse of economic restructuring and the liberatory potential it offers women. While her H-4 subjects with professional qualifications felt restricted by the expectations of domestic and reproductive labor inside the home, the H-1B professionals working in the male-centric software sector had to reconcile their professional ambitions with caregiving, oftentimes choosing to self-regulate their aspirations regarding their careers.

Devi concludes by arguing that her subjects' experiences "highlight the deepening contradiction between the economic and social restructuring between the spheres of production and reproduction."[56] By juxtaposing her insights with the visa-centric gendered class divide that is suggested in the above-mentioned posts, the online media becomes witness to the internationalization of the discriminating practices of the state and its problematic implications for hierarchical power narratives within the immigrant community. The H-4 forum demonstrates that participating in the online networks of Indian women in the "dependent" visa category is not predicated on any essential notions of the Indian immigrant condition or Indian womanhood. Rather, it is shaped by and speaks to a politics of shared location within the regimes of U.S. immigration policy, as well as Indian migrant cultures underpinned by conservative ideologies of gendered familial structures.

Building Home Networks: Negotiating Space, Rethinking Rights

The gendered logics of immigration and migration have provided privileges to the Indian male H-1B professional in the form of economic citizenship in the United States while producing a "crisis of rights" for immigrants such as the H-4 subjects.[57] However, the combination of being stuck at home, having online access, and being invested in making virtual connections with others in the same situation has given H-4 women new and profound means to engage with the concept of belonging and the right to work. As the private home for many of the women in the H-4 forum becomes a space of struggle for identity and equality, the forum and the creation of an H-4 network are new temporal and spatial expressions of an imagined, political space of belonging. The creation of the H-4 forum, with members sharing information about immigration law, creating petitions, writing about their experiences, and producing their exchanges, is also an expression of what Tiziana Terranova discusses in terms of the productive elements of "immaterial labor" in online contexts.[58] The mediation of the H-4 household through the homepage is a reminder that while the image of home is built upon a mythology of comfort, stability, inheritance, and familiarity, the realities of home, as evidenced through these women's voices, stress contingency and struggle. With the example of the H-4 forum, we are also witnessing one of the many uses and meanings of online media as a domestic technology. It is an example of the technology being "domesticated" and being used to represent the domestic.[59]

In particular, the inclusion of online activities within the domestic routine, the tactics of working online from home despite legal restrictions placed on their employment by U.S. immigration law, and the use of the online to create personal and professional networks based on shared physical locations, social interests, and work-related expertise point to the key ways in which the participants of the H-4 Indian Ladies forum mobilize the Web around their time-space relations with and in the household.[60] Their use of the online adds new insights to the call made by B. Ruby Rich to "imagine a truly interactive computer/telephone system that seeks to break women's isolation, replace the extended family with virtual communities, and enhance women's empowerment through strategic linkages."[61]

Surfing the Web, gathering information from the Internet, online media usage (watching Indian television shows is often mentioned), and creating blogs are some of the web-centric activities that are very commonly included in the list of things one can do to negotiate the confining nature of the H-4 life. Lynn Spigel has suggested that "terms like 'surfing' or 'information superhighway' serve as the contemporary version of a much older fantasy about travel to distant locales that telecommunications has historically offered its publics."[62] While some members add going online or Web surfing alongside other activities such as shopping or watching television, a few include blogging as an unique opportunity to reimagine oneself in a public space through an expression of one's tastes, interests, and experiences. In a few instances, members disclose that they have cooking blogs but don't reveal the URL for their blog. While this might be related to the need to keep their identity private on the forum, the women do address the fact that blogging about cooking was a way for them to feel useful, for in addition to the pleasures associated with writing on a topic of interest to them, they imagined their blogs as a community resource for anyone interested in recipes or cooking methods. The focus on cooking as a way to help fellow Indians in the immigrant landscape resonates with the observation by Sharmila Rudrappa that "the family and home [in the immigrant space] lose their naturalness and reveal themselves not to be a priori sites; instead they are produced actively in the everyday practices of speaking the mother tongue, cooking and eating familiar foods, and raising children according to norms and values central to an 'ethnic' imaginary."[63]

Another way in which online media emerge as an active resource is through the sharing of hyperlinks by members on their posts; these links pertain to news about H-4 women (immigration policy issues, media coverage), H-1B processing (online list of companies that are likely to hire H-1B labor; official press releases on quota and processing dates), links for online courses (software skills–related courses being quite commonly mentioned), as well as Indian community sites that are potential resources (for example, Sulekha.com, another popular Austin-based website, which is discussed in the next chapter, is mentioned many times as a great site to place or find jobs such as catering or babysitting for local Indian immigrants).

An active and recurring theme on the discussion forum relates to employment in H-4 status, such as in the thread titled "Looking for job in H4 status: Expert opinions needed." Discussions about the possibility of employment are in a majority of cases initiated by participants who are recent entrants into the world of the H-4 and are trying to figure out the ropes of navigating the restricted work world of the dependent status. This figuring out includes both knowledge gathering about the networks and strategies employed by the women who have been through the status or those who have been in the H-4 status for a longer time. While all forum participants post messages using their user names/IDs, some indicate their location in the membership hierarchy of the site community at large by stating "New ILite," "Junior ILite," or "Senior ILite" alongside their user names.

Very often it is the senior ILites who respond with the "expert" view. Expert advice includes not merely reproducing facts but sharing information that the H-4 member might not necessarily be aware of—such as this member's post: "The H1B quota for the year 2005–2006 starts in October 1st. However the government will start receiving applications by April 1st itself."[64] Here the notion of H-4 women as experts offers a stark contrast to the often male immigration experts on Indian American websites, blogs, newspapers, and community spaces. In the participatory cultures that we see here, H-4 women become active producers and distributors of shared knowledge.[65]

The H-4 network also serves as an informal knowledge-sharing resource where strategies to gain entry through the system of checks and controls initiated by U.S. immigration are gathered. Providing updates on the H-1B visa quota and application process is one of the top agendas in this context. While many provide date lists and reminders relating to the application process, others share links on companies that are likely to be hiring H-1Bs in a given year; others share lesser-known details, such as how getting a master's degree in the United States and then applying for an H-1B visa would allow them to circumvent quota-based restrictions (and the possibility that one would not get a visa because the regular cap of 65,000 visas has been reached).

The techno-feminist positions advanced by the women repurpose the status of the H-4 visa holder, conventionally relegated to being an invisible and silenced migrant, and rearticulate it to a cultural citizenship that is primarily enacted through participation, debate, resource building, and a work subculture mediated through the Web. While the idea of women using the computer at home to nurture an interest is now becoming part of the lore about H-4 readjustment to U.S. life, the H-4 online forums uncover another dimension of the negotiation between home, visa-induced location, and Internet technologies, in the form of discussion about "working from home."

Working—that is, working to earn income—when on an H-4 visa constitutes illegal activity. Some posts share strategies such as working for Indian companies online and getting direct payment to Indian bank accounts; others talk of collectively doing something since "we are anyway unwanted citizens"; still others talk about scams, failed ventures, and working successes. In sharing these strategies, some members remind interested parties to keep a "low profile." Sometimes members mention their success with these illegal activities but refrain from saying more, while leaving an email address for private messaging. The linking of employment with the tiered structure of cultural citizenship is important here. By referring to their status as unwanted citizens, the women reveal the gendered divides created within the NRI home due to the state's regulatory practices. While H-4 women are middle-class transnational subjects and inhabit the same U.S.-based household as their H-1B husbands, their ability to belong in the immigrant home setting is severely restricted.

However, in their attempts to find a reentry into the home as a space of belonging, rethinking the possibilities for work by tinkering with the technology of the information network appears as an appealing option. While at one level the appeal lies in the fact that they can generate some income and feel productive, for some members it also seems to lie in the pleasure of transgressing an oppressive rule. This is somewhat reminiscent of what Vivek Bald terms "tweaking of the circuitry."[66] Bald is discussing South Asian taxi drivers' use of CB radios and specifically their appropriation of the technology to access private subfrequencies meant for South Asian immigrant drivers, thereby creating a common space of support. However, it is possible to read, at least partially, the H-4 women's real and aspirational appropriation of the transnational network for pleasures relating to work, income, and identity as examples of tweaking the network circuitry to forge new pathways of belonging.

The mode of virtual working generates two types of dominant critiques. In one, members reject this move as clearly illegal and likely to end in disaster and deportation. These members also angrily point out that H-4 women willingly walked into their current situation and so need to just stop grumbling. Others reflect a more ambiguous sentiment, pointing to the illegality but also reminding interested virtual workers to exercise caution. As one member writes:

> I just want to remind all you H4 wives out there that it is illegal to work (i.e. *make money from* providing a service) as long as you're on an H4 visa. This doesn't mean you can't work, or that some H4 wives don't work in some way. But whatever work you're doing would be illegal. I'm not sure how you might be caught, or what the repercussions would be, but I think it's something to keep in mind. You should be fully aware that if you do manage to find a money-making opportunity, should you be found out by the authorities, they would not accept ignorance of the law as an excuse. It may seem like an unfair law, but it is the law here. Please be careful, whatever you decide to do.[67]

While earning income, moving away from boredom, and recovering a semblance of their active, professional working lives prior to coming to the United States are some of the key motivations, the responses to solving the problem of not being able to work and get paid in the United States propose some interesting solutions. A common suggestion is to work for an Indian immigrant company and ask to be paid in cash. The assumption here is that those in the Indian community will be more interested in helping out the H-4 visa holder since they might have some understanding of the predicament. It is also indicative of how cash is a way to leave no trace for illegal work activities in the United States. A fellow respondent suggests freelancing for companies in Europe and asking for payment by wire to an account in India.

In one instance, when forum members ponder the legality of working for a company in the "home country" and receiving payment in Indian currency, an "expert" chimes in with a broader perspective that reinforces the legal intertwining of H-4 women's actions with the family's immigrant status: "I can certainly understand the frustrations of wives on H4—I too was one. It is hard to come here and sit around at home while the most productive years (career wise) are wasted waiting for a green card. However the legal implications of working on H4 are pretty serious and can impair your/your husband's green card app. Even if you work without pay, if it is a job that normally would pay a salary, it is illegal." She goes on to advocate looking for jobs outside the IT sector as a way to improve one's chances of getting an H-1B visa approved.[68]

Another member identifying herself as a practicing immigration attorney strategically offers a cautionary note while inviting the participants to get in touch with her privately if they wanted her legal advice. " I know you ladies are talking about the H4, not having the opportunity for working. But few of them are telling they are working in other ways, but you have to [be] really careful with that . . . you have to be really careful about the status, it is also going to affect yours and your husband and family status if something goes wrong."[69]

While clearly the discussion above is about legal status, the conversations of the H-4 women point to the complicated interconnections between their own dependent status and their gendered performance of the family's status in the immigrant context. Middle-class prejudices, cultural tradition, and husbands' status come into play in this telling post, where a member referencing the job of a friend's wife as a worker at Subway recoils rhetorically at the horror of being outed in the Indian community for doing such work. "But come to think of the outcomes, if any person who knows u comes to the store u r working & they spread to others in a cheap way 'hey such and such's wife is working at the Indian groceries billing man!!', it will look cheap for ur husband."

Here, while the anxiety is not around the labor per se, it is triggered by a reflection of what that labor means for the NRI family's class standing in the Indian immigrant community. This is established when the member adds a little later in the same post that where she lives there are no Indians, and that she is willing to work at Dunkin' Donuts but is unable to get a job because she does not have a work permit.[70] The irony here is that the Indian woman who worked at a Subway shop potentially risking her husband's status got the job because the owner of the shop was a Gujarati Indian; in other words, while for many H-4 women working "illegally" for cash can materialize more easily within the immigrant community–owned businesses, it comes with the fear of losing status not within the boundaries of the regulating state but those operating in the transnational middle-class community formations of Indian America.

Technologies of Home, Gender, and Information

If, as Nina Wakeford has noted, metaphors of home abound in online media, then pursuing the textual expressions of home, its symbolic associations, and its material, discursive, and affective consequences can help us understand both the contemporary meanings of home as well as the ways that technology shapes belonging.[71] Unlike the technological determinist perspective where technology has a life of its own and is an inevitable force of progress or is an autonomous domain of tools, machines, and gadgets shaped by neutral qualities, the critical cultural studies approach to digital technologies implicates its emergence and proliferation within power relations and the production of knowledge. The symbiotic and symptomatic relationship between technology and society that Raymond Williams wrote about in the 1970s can be explored in the new context of homepage cultures where new media technologies and households become open to renegotiation in their social meanings.[72] And by considering it within immigrant spaces, a context that has been very marginal to theorizations about new media as well as the way that media shapes the household, I hope to contribute to debates over gender, technology, and immigration in ways that shift the analyses from seeing them as disparate to being mutually constitutive.

Immigrant Indian women on the H-4 visa are through U.S. immigration policy relegated to the domestic sphere, the space of the private, immigrant family, and to that extent are imagined as invisible within the public domains of law, labor, and citizenship. Nevertheless, the online forum initiated by H-4 Indian immigrant women on the Indusladies.com site resists such clear divisions and moreover complicates ideas such as "mobile privatization" and its inflection, "privatized mobility." Raymond Williams's concept of mobile privatization, first developed in the mid-1970s, describes the twin modes of mobility and privatization that increasingly characterized social life in the age of industrialization, as technologies of communication, transportation, housing architecture, and planning generated a culture of mobility and an ideological emphasis on the idea of privacy.[73] Television, Williams notes, particularly through the mode of broadcasting managed this contradiction of outward/inward by bringing the world to the private home, thereby retaining the idea of travel and public spaces but within the confines of the private home.

Lynn Spigel, more recently, has argued for an inversion of the term into "privatized mobility" during the 1960 U.S. television culture as the home was experienced "as a vehicular form, a mode of transport in and of itself that allowed people to take private life outdoors."[74] Television and broadcasting have been recognized as domestic technologies of communication in that both the television set and the cultural practices of viewing as well as discourses within its texts are enmeshed within the social and spatial organization of the household along gendered division of labor, leisure, and public/private sphere.

The entry of digital communication technologies into the home is "marked by their differential positioning of men and women and their differential incorporation into the masculine and feminine spheres of activity within the home."[75] In thinking about the home and its reshaping through the advent of new media technologies, there has been an interest in considering how the home becomes more efficient, networked, and intelligent through the synchronization of its space and activities through digital machines. Notions such as the "smart home" and so forth exemplify a conceptualization of the reimagined home space at the level of everyday existence as its rhythms are transformed by new technologies.[76]

Considering such historical analysis of social spaces and their mediation of the domestic through home technologies such as the television, we must contend with the white, middle-class normative subject that is positioned as the media user and mobile subject in such theorizations as well as the fantasy about travel and mobility that underwrites much of these debates. Simply stated, immigrant women on the H4 engage the home technology of the computer and the online network within the embedded contexts of transnational migration and travel as well as the regulation of their mobility and relocation into the private immigrant home by the state.

Paying attention to the usages and meanings generated around online imaginations of H-4 location and home spaces, I want to consider the strategies of negotiation and exploration advanced by the women participants of the H4 Indian Ladies forum within a broader framework of feminist repurposing of computing technologies. Granted, there are some very conservative positions that are expounded on the forum, but my point is not to frame the forum as a radical, counter-hegemonic space that articulates a virtual belonging apart from deep-rooted cultural histories of gendered belonging in the domestic space or middle-class Indian cultural nationalisms in diasporic settings. Rather it is to reveal the contradictions and complexities that shape H-4 women's inhabiting of socially sanctioned and personally imagined spaces of belonging. The interactive nature of the network frames the responses the women have to their home life and its contours but also reveals the range of responses others in the community have to their ideological and affective positions.

The specific practices that emerge in such interactions, such as information sharing, hypertextual linking, historicizing, and blogging, exemplify what several scholars writing at the intersections of digital technology and feminist critique have identified as feminist repurposing of what in the mid-1990s Margaret Wiley termed as the "male territory" of digital technology.[77] Careful to avoid essentializing the networking woman as a digital extension of the nurturing female, feminist writings, especially those acknowledging the problematics of difference, including but going beyond gender relations, have worked hard to contest the masculinized contexts within which ideologies of female technophobia, feminine cultures of media, and technology consumption emerged and gained currency.[78] Further technology as a sign has also functioned to denote cultural progress and civilization and as a paradigm created a homology between culture/nature, production/consumption, masculine/feminine, high-end/low-end, and hardware/software; in the context of computing technologies, Aihwa Ong, for example, taking the instance of South East Asian women producing the microchip that underwrites online media technologies, has noted that digital capitalist formations reproduce these older homologies while masking the intimate connections between transnationalism, race, gender, and labor.[79]

Yet, even as online media participate in familiar ideological constructions of the idealized masculine and feminine vis-à-vis technology, we are also witnessing a realignment of these ideas of gender, space, and technology through the virtual homepage. To consider the private home in the context of the public homepage is advancing the kind of feminist legal positions that have urged for an examination of the "public" world of law that governs immigration policies and migration with the "private" world of the family to nuance our understanding of immigrant experiences.[80]

Considering the private-public interrelationship in these instances is also to build on existing debates over changing roles of women in the scholarship on Indian immigrant communities in the United States. For example, in her ethnography of Indian professional women who migrated to the United States in the 1980s, Padma Rangaswamy notes that for several of her respondents, the home was a key site though not exclusively the only site for women to feel a sense of identity and self. Pointing out that many of her respondents had an active career outside the home, Rangaswamy however, notes that for many of her subjects, work was defined not in contradiction to but in affiliation with home. In other words, working was also framed as a way of consolidating the home and desires around home life.[81]

Madhulika Khandelwal in her study of Indian immigrants in New York City lists several factors including re-creation of extended family networks in the United States since the 1960s, increased numbers of women in the workforce in pink- and white-collar jobs, and the reorganization of women's labor around cooking and childcare in the home as contributing to anxieties over family and gender in the community.[82] Other scholars have noted that even as patriarchal tendencies exist and erupt in particular forms such as domestic abuse, there is no denying that narratives of family, gender roles, and home life are being rewritten as immigrant contexts get more complex. For example, the revelation about domestic abuse of immigrant women in South Asian homes that became public in the 1980s is one instance of the shifting lines between public/private and home/outside concerns in the community at large. While airing the so-called shameful details of patriarchal family life in immigrant homes revealed a new articulation of a private concern in the public sphere, the emergence of South Asian women's organizations providing shelter and rehabilitation for abused women in the mid-1980s signaled community activism around the gendered violence of the South Asian home.[83] That middle-class, professional women in the software and computing sector were not excluded from such patriarchal violence further contributed to demystifying the glorified successful lives of IT Indian Americans.

Cyberspace as Women's Space: The H-4 Forum within the Gendered Economy

The Austin, Texas–based Indusladies.com was started by Malathy Jey a year after she relocated from India to the United States in 2004. A software engineer by training, Jey decided to start a website aimed at Indian women like herself who, as a result of transnational migration, experienced a loss of familiar female networks of support, advice, friendship, and conversation that had been a part of their everyday life in India. In an interview, Jey notes that the intent behind starting the website was to create an "online home" for Indian women.[84] In the years since its inception, Indusladies.com has grown exponentially; currently the heavily advertiser-driven site claims over 217,000 registered members, over 1.6 million visitors a month, 150,000 discussions, and over 2.85 million comments. The site, which runs entirely on user-generated content, is one of the most prominent and visible online spaces mobilized by and for "Indian women from around the world who ... ask questions, get help, read and write blogs, engage in a dialogue and along the way build authentic and enduring friendships"; that said, the most active nodes of this global community are located in India and the United States.[85]

Given the user-generated content on Indusladies.com, it is not surprising that discussion forums along with blogs occupy a high visibility within the site. While some of the topics informing the forums include parenting and kids, marriage, spouses and in-laws, fashion and beauty (with threads in the 6,000 range and, in the case of the marriage forum, posts upwards of 113,000), a significant and active section of the forum universe, titled "neighborhoods," is defined by region, where five geographically labeled forums hail users located within particular areas of the world: India; the United States and Canada; Asia-Pacific; Africa and the Middle East; and Europe. Each region-forum in turn has several subforums organized under it. As of January 2014, in terms of the number of threads and posts, the USA and Canada forum (13,118 threads and 82,313 posts) is the second most active region forum, with the India forum (14,052 threads and 100,175 posts) being the most active.[86]

Although the site is predominantly imagined as a global, virtual community of culturally nationalist subjects who are Indian women, the specificity of place is marked within sections of its online content. A forum like H4 Indian Ladies then pushes the encounter with place even further as the posts call attention to the temporal, spatial, and affective dimensions of being in place, be it at the level of the nation, the state or city, the neighborhood, or the individual home. The idea of belonging to an online community such as H4 Indian Ladies is, of course, an imagined construction, a process that may be intellectual and emotional, but its only physical element is for participants to sit at a computer. And yet that sense of belonging is produced through active negotiation of place-bound notions of identity, agency, power struggles, and community. If the U.S. state and Indian nation together produce a temporality that renders home for many H-4 women into a space of absence, the presence of forums like H4 Indian Ladies must be viewed as an intervention, a means to remake home by producing it within a historically and culturally specific community, even if that community only exists online.

The H4 Indian Ladies forum invokes the idea of place while simultaneously exemplifying how place is remediated through virtual, hypertextual, transnational modes of communication and engagement; in this regard, it illustrates within a specific context (life in the United States on the H-4 visa) what Indusladies.com exemplifies at a general level. Interesting to note here is the play on the term *Indus*—a reference to Indian-U.S. culture and its emerging pathways in the form of the website as well as an allusion to the Indus civilization (roughly 2000 B.C.E.) at the site upon which the modern Indian subcontinent exists. In its present form, the site is a virtual community of "Indian women from around the world"; it is also the case that India and the United States are most active nodes or, we might say, hegemonic links within the site's hypertextual network.

While the H-4 designation speaks to the women's visa-centric identity in the United States, the phrase *Indian Ladies* invokes a historical discourse embedded within colonial and postcolonial patriarchal narratives about the Indian nation, where ideal Indian femininity (ladies and their lady-like behavior, pursuits, and investments) was tied to middle-class Hindu women and their spiritual and cultural pursuits within the home. Steeped in notions of authenticity and respectability, the imagination around Indian femininity and womanhood was also underpinned by a spatial logic of hemming in the feminine (a symbol of the nation's honor) within the private and domestic space of the home.

One could say that by the linking of a phrase historically suggestive of the private to the public space of the discussion forum, the H4 Indian Ladies forum (and Indusladies.com) points to realignment between ideologies of gender, class, and spatialized social roles. The juxtaposition of the "H-4" category with "Indian Ladies" speaks to the unique location and lived contexts of the forum participants; it is also revealed in an ongoing power struggle over ideologies and identities among the forum participants. While for the most part the women avoid any direct and aggressive confrontation with each other over conflicting ideologies around home and gender roles, there are moments of intense debate or difference where the group seemingly united by the H-4 status is repositioned into different constituencies with very different cultural and political investments in questions of gendered home, work, and national spaces.[87]

Another aspect about Indusladies.com that is relevant to the present discussion is that the site offers one of the few examples, if not the only one, of a highly successful, commercially supported community site, explicitly framed as women's space that is also the entrepreneurial creation of an Indian immigrant woman. It bears relevance that Indusladies.com emerged in 2005, a period marked by the emergence of social media networks and participatory cultures. One must acknowledge that Indusladies.com with its heavily commercial-driven content nevertheless also functions as one of most visible and current spaces online where a women-centric or feminist alliance among Indian immigrants is being forged.

In the 1990s, there were websites, including Sawnet.org (South Asian Women's NETwork), which imagined the online as a feminist South Asian transnational space but did so in a noncommercial, activist website context. In the late 1990s, for example, community website INDOlink.com had a discussion forum specially marked as a "Women's Corner."[88] While within the larger context of the Women's Corner Forum H-4 topics remained marginal at best, there are early traces of online interventions into a culture (H-4 and women's experience of immigration) and a space (of work and home life) that are most substantially presented through a forum like H4 Indian Ladies. One post from 1999 simply titled "H4 visa" (February 11, 1999) on INDOlink's Women's Corner is quite illuminating. The author of the post offers a critique of the illusionary nature of life in the United States for immigrant women like her, who enter the country on what she terms a "quickie visa" (in that an H-4 is granted fairly quickly as opposed to an H-1B visa) but end up with "heartache, frustration and [losing] self confidence"; fellow participants responded with a mix of practical advice, empathetic support, and matter-of-fact disapproval of the pessimistic sentiments in the original post.[89]

INDOlink.com promotes very conservative heteronormative ideals of family, parenting, and immigrant sensibilities. In the context of the site's larger discursive agenda, the separation of a forum for "Women" while labeling other forums along subjects of interest such as "Politics" and "Bollywood" functions to mark difference without necessarily engaging it. Further, and this is particularly relevant given the themes explored in this chapter, INDOlink.com had a separate discussion forum titled "Immigration." The textual politics of such an arrangement reproduces the narrative offered by the U.S. state and the Indian nation that women and their "questions" ("Why can't I work?" "Can I get a driver's license?" "Am I unwanted here in the US?") are the unintended consequence of a global order imagined around gendered migrant labor regimes and patriarchal transnationalisms.

Indusladies.com, in this context, interlinks the themes of women, commerce, and community within the same framework on its website. As a result, it offers a new image of the confluence of the political and cultural economies of the Web, and of how the Web is shaped by gendered, Indian, transnational spaces. In *Cyber Selves: Feminist Ethnographies of South Asian Women*, a book published in 2004, the year before Indusladies.com was created, Radhika Gajjala reflects on the concept of cyberfeminist e-commerce: "What might cyberfeminist e-commerce from below look like? Is such a contradictory 'e-commerce' at all possible? What are the collaborations, connections and issues that might emerge?"[90] The immediate context for Gajjala's reflections are grounded in her collaborative work with Annapurna Mamidipudi around the production of handloom fabrics in India (creating knowledge through print) and the construction and engagement with digital spaces (producing knowledge through the digital). Yet I think Gajjala's rhetorical questions point to an underlying issue: we have seen that digital capitalism can contradict the ideals of feminism, but can digital capitalism also contribute to feminist praxis?

With Gajjala in mind, I suggest that Indusladies.com is better understood as a contradictory space: the site's dominant representation—of privileged cosmopolitan women upholding the transnational, middle-class Indian family—must be read alongside the expressions of disenfranchisement within the home and critiques of patriarchal institutions that are embedded within the discussion forums of that same site. And in the specific context of the discussions about home and work on the H-4 forum, Indusladies.com plays a critical function in creating a space—in the digital capitalist realm, in the transnational Indian women's family, and within the abundant discussions about Indian immigrant life in the United States.

Given my earlier critique of the website INDOlink.com for relegating women to a "corner" in the discussion universe, it is important to acknowledge and address the fact that even within the discussion universe of Indusladies.com, the H4 Indian Ladies forum exists as a separate forum within the USA and Canada forum. In other words, is the gendered marking of the H-4 forum any different from the Women's Corner on INDOlink.com? I contend that there is a difference and distinction between these two iterations of women's space online and in the immigrant context of NRI life in the United States. Here the linking of visa-nation-gender politics is specific to the immigrant context being discussed; furthermore, it is the dominant assumption of H-4 women's invisibility, and the concurrent hypervisibility of the H-1B male, that makes a forum like H4 Indian Ladies a dynamic site of intervention.

The H-1B Immigrant: Coded as Primary

Although the U.S. Congress has issued an annual cap of 65,000 H-1B visas, the numbers actually allotted have fluctuated quite a bit. For the fiscal year 2012, the USCIS issued a total of 262,569 H-1B visas; for 2011, the number was 269,653; and for 2010, a total of 192,990 H-1B visas were issued.[91] In the mid-2000s, we notice that while the year 2004 saw 287,418 visas being issued, in 2002 the number was 197,537, and in 2006 it was 270,981.[92] The larger trend to which these fluctuating numbers point is the steady increase in the number of H-1B visas being issued over the past decade; relatedly, the numbers increase in the midst of tensions in the U.S. Congress over the influx of foreign labor.[93]

In many of the debates over the H-1B, Indian software professionals have been cited as evidence both for the need to continue the current policy and for the need to police or curtail it. Thus, when Bill Gates, the head of Microsoft and long-time advocate of loosening regulations concerning the H-1B visa, testified in 2008 in front of the Science and Technology Committee of Congress, he noted that the current cap "is arbitrarily set and bears no relation to the U.S. economy's demand for skilled professionals." That demand, Gates argued there and elsewhere, is to obtain the most qualified technology professionals, such as those being trained in Indian science and technology institutes (like the Indian Institute of Technology, the IITs) for the United States so that the nation can continue its claim to be the world's number one innovator in the fields of science and technology. It is pertinent to note here that in his 2008 testimony Gates references his company's inability during the year 2007 to hire a third of the qualified foreign-born professionals they needed, simply because of the low cap on the H-1B visas that were being allotted that year.[94]

While Gates was employing these facts to argue in favor of immigration reform that would lead to loosening of control over the H-1B visa, critics of Gates's stance and, more broadly, the labor flows engendered by the H-1B have pointed to the fact that top companies receiving H-1B visas invariably tend to be Indian software and IT companies in the offshore business. For example, in 2007, eight of the top ten beneficiaries of H-1B petitions were Indian companies; Microsoft at number five and Intel at number ten were the only U.S. firms in this elite list that year. In both 2007 and 2008, the top three beneficiaries were

Indian companies Infosys Technologies, Wipro, and Satyam Computer Services, ranked at numbers one, two, and three, respectively. The implication here goes beyond the Indian professional as H-1B employee to the Indian company as the H-1B employer, a development that turns on its head the very idea of the United States as the national beneficiary of the foreign-labor program that is the H-1B. I employ this data here to indicate the diverse ways in which the connection between India, H-1B visas, and Indian software expertise unfolds in the U.S. context.[95]

It is fair to say that an earlier mythology of India residing in the minds and hearts of its diaspora is being reworked in dynamic ways as the virtual networks through which India meets its Indian diaspora dramatically alter the temporal and spatial contexts within which transnational belonging is engendered. As the meanings and implications of being an NRI in the United States are shifting, a great part of the ideological recasting is being mobilized around the technological, financial, and cultural capital associated with the Web. By this I mean that contemporary understandings of being an NRI are not only built around conventional ideas of transnational migration and being away from the homeland of India, but also are increasingly being woven around NRI desire, need, and ability to harness the potential of new technologies, new communication modes, and new economies.

What occurs as a result, then, is that the modes and politics of transnational belonging are up for remaking. As a virtualized India emerges through new technological pathways, it offers a new site to produce, circulate, and engender the ideology of the NRI. In this intersection between new media and the national, a key development is the online participatory cultures that have emerged around NRI subjects. They reveal, among others, the critical need to expand the analytical and cultural frame beyond India and emigration to include the United States and immigration. Alongside neoliberal state and corporate practices that produce a consumerist version of NRI citizenship, mobility, and technological agency are alternative discourses that highlight the gendered ideologies underpinning techno-centric immigrant labor migration and U.S. regulatory practices. In turn, they help us understand how the Web is a dynamic space where national belonging, citizenship, migrant rights, technological networks, and community formation are being actively fostered, contested, and negotiated. While conservative narratives hoisting the NRI on the platform of authenticity and national culture abound, there are several other narratives that disrupt such alliances between nation and NRI, authenticity and cultural practice; such narratives often do so by focusing on the micropolitics of belonging in temporal and spatial contexts of everyday life and activities.

The privileging of the H-1B Indian and its overlap with the figure of the NRI is most clearly evidenced in commercially supported community websites that strategically target key groups within the loosely defined Indian American constituency. For example, in the mid- to late 1990s, Samachar.com, one of the first community websites to be hugely popular among Indian immigrants in the United States, regularly featured jobs and services explicitly targeted to the H-1B Indian; a recurring and prominently placed advertisement was for the site H1Bjobs.com.[96]

The advertisement for H1Bjobs.com was widely circulated through similar websites targeting Indian immigrants but was also featured regularly in the leading Indian American newspaper *India Abroad* and the popular technology print magazine *SiliconIndia*. In a flash and click advertisement typical of the period, the main page of H1Bjobs.com displayed the image of a suit-clad man covering his face in anguish as he remains chained to a chair by a heavy weight, while posing the question, "Does your consulting company leave you feeling like a hostage?" This thematic of feeling like a hostage in the work environment becomes more charged when considered in the context of H-4 women's sense of confinement to the domestic sphere.

The suggestion that H-1B Indians feel restricted by their work environment, which in turn is interconnected with their immigration status, is one that resonates in other websites where NRI issues are addressed. For example, in the same year that the H1Bjobs.com site and the advertisement mentioned above were created, 1999, another community website, NRIOL.com, featured an essay titled "The Problems and Hardships of H1B Holding Visa Employees" on its user-generated content section of the site. Essentially a letter of protest addressed to the U.S. immigration office, the article gives vent to the frustration of the author, an Indian male on the H-1B visa, at the lack of sensitivity of regulatory bodies in considering the life of the immigrant on the work visa. "Nobody thought of the feelings, emotions, career and life of an H1B employee, who comes from thousands of miles away, leaving his job, society, family and relations, with great dreams."[97] Created and maintained by U.S.-based immigrants, NRIOL.com privileges a conservative and India-centric understanding of the transnational spaces inhabited by NRIs. Its tagline, "Home for Non Resident Indians Worldwide!," reflects its address to the global NRI. However, the site is U.S.-centric in most respects and articulates by and large a culturally nationalist vision of the NRI subject.

For instance, exploring how the affluent, successful, technologically advanced NRI community can help the home country of India has been a steady thematic of the site. Within such a cultural narrative, the male H-1B Indian occupies a pivotal role along with the Indian with the U.S. green card. The site has a section titled Welcome2America, meant to help newly arrived NRIs with all essential information and resources. While the subsection in this link that relates to visas covers all the official categories whereby Indians can migrate to the United States, such as the H-1B and J-1, it nowhere addresses the category of the H-4. As the next chapter further elaborates, privileging the H-1B Indian within representations of NRIs and, furthermore, producing the domain of the H-1B as a space of techno-masculinity and capital are common features of commercially developed culturally nationalist "Indian" community sites.

While this strategy emerges most clearly in the news-, immigration-, and employment-related sections of a given site, matrimonial services inform another key context where H-1B desirability and its masculinized coding resurface. Popular early sites such as Samachar.com and INDOlink.com exemplify two different trends that emerged with regard to online matrimonials. Indolink.com, a California-based web company started by Indian Americans with the goal of "Linking Indians Worldwide!," replicated the print model of the marriage bureau where users would send in short descriptions of themselves and their desired partners. An in-site search engine represented by an Electronic Matchmaker and a flashing heart would cull the relevant entries based on keywords entered. While this represents an early model of matchmaking online and included, among others, H-1B Indians, there was nothing in the textual address of the service that privileged them. In the second model at this time, exemplified by Chennai-based Samachar.com, the matrimonial section outsourced in that the site featured hyperlinks that in turn led to commercial matrimonial service sites such as Shaadi.com.

Shaadi.com (*shaadi* is Hindi for "marriage") is arguably the leading online matrimonial service in the world and one of the most highly successful and visible players in the transnational Indian American domain. Over the years, Shaadi.com has added several new features to its search functions; in what can perhaps be viewed as evidence of the site's appeal among NRIs, Shaadi.com allows its clients to list or search for permanent residency status within its "smart search" option. While Shaadi.com's inclusion of immigrant status helps us understand the role of visa and green card classifications in contemporary constructions of marriage eligibility among Indian immigrants, the venture H1Bmarriages.com focuses on the community who are either on an H-1B or intend to marry someone in that status. The site claims to be "the first ever matrimonial portal exclusively for NRI's and technical professionals, designed by technical professionals."[98] The site's services include wedding planning, travel packages for honeymoon destinations in India, and an online selection for e-brides and e-grooms. H1Bmarriages.com not only exclusively caters to the H-1B professional, but it also blurs the lines between NRI, H-1B, and technical professionals by using them interchangeably on the site.

The site's visual and textual strategies on the main page extend the meaning of H-1B as a male-defined occupation. Framing the upper left and right corners of the main page are small, pixelated images of women that appear in a loop with the accompanying phrase, "Looking for a perfect match?" The size of the image and its focus on the face is reminiscent of a passport photograph, but with a seductive twist. The politics of this mode of seduction become more clearly visible through the central image of an "Indian" bride, with downcast eyes, as she presumably recites romantic verses about undying love. What we see here is the reenactment of an ongoing function of women as seductive objects. Reading these images intertextually with previously mentioned representations of the H-1B Indian as a male, techie professional, one can see how the virtual in this instance serves the function of privileging a masculinist perspective on transnational migration, labor, and digital capitalist property relations. H1Bmarriages.com relies on textual and visual practices that invite identification with the heteronormative male gaze and render the female body, and potential immigrant, as an object. Following Patricia Wise's invocation of one of the meanings of "virtual" as "not quite there, not quite real," and her argument that women in patriarchal cultures are, in this sense, produced as virtual objects, one can see in online consumerist spaces like H1Bmarriages.com an extension of an older mode of domination into newer online media.[99]

Technologies of the virtual, assembled around such practices as online matrimonial services, digital photographs of brides and grooms, drop-down menus indicating match preferences, and honeymoon packages following success in "looking for the perfect match," operate within a textual, aesthetic, and sexual economy of the Web that is underwritten by a logic that normativizes the channeling of the Web's potential to the pursuit and management of the transnational H-1B male Indian immigrant's sense of feeling at home, happy, and in place. It includes orchestrating a community space like NRIOL.com and its "welcome2America" sections to make the transition from India to the United States comfortable for the H-1B NRI, creating employment sites like H1Bjobs.com, where the hostage metaphor is used to create an emancipatory ideology of the Web for the new immigrant digerati, and finally sites like H1B-marriages.com, which suture ideologies of information, technology, new media networks, H-1B labor, and U.S. immigration within a gendered imagination of H-1B identities and NRI marriages.

The H4 Indian Ladies forum is a very significant case study to consider how new media, and their particular networking practices, produce new narratives about the NRI home and household. Ideologies of home and household on the forum point to the contestation over traditional articulations of the Indian immigrant home and to the ways that home is being reconfigured in transnational online media. The forum is a dynamic and ongoing illustration of how H-4 Indian women use online interactions to reconstitute their sense of self and their frustrations as home-bound immigrants. As they compare notes about daily grievances and share information about what the future might hold, H-4 women are utilizing the transnational digital network to also do something far bigger: to articulate a critique of the hegemonic and patriarchal regimes of the immigration system in the United States and of the Indian family. Utopian conceptions of new media celebrate the breakdown of boundaries. And yet the H4 Indian Ladies forum reminds us yet again of the contradictions of modern migration, where the mobility of information, capital, and labor is underwritten by the immobility of raced, gendered, classed bodies.[100]

The narratives of the H4 Indian Ladies forum challenge the dominant ideological sign of the H-1B as "the" Indian immigrant in the age of new media culture and the NRI home as that of the H-1B holder. By offering alternative readings of what the NRI household is and how its material, affective, and temporal realities differ from its ideal construction, the forum posts deconstruct, to an extent, the NRI household and reveal the gendered power hierarchies of masculine cultures of immigration and work in shaping the dominant meanings of home space in Indian immigrant contexts. The H4 Indian Ladies forum allows us to get a closer look at the ways in which migration and relocation is experienced in the contemporary moment. Embedded in the desires and anxieties of these women, and their fraught relationship to the H-1B household, is a new layer in our understanding of that household. This layer is often subsumed by the weight of the status quo and by the burdens of Indian ideas of the family and American ideas of the immigrant; but if we listen carefully, we uncover a flurry of voices eager to be heard. These voices dispute any totalizing narratives of the Indian immigrant household.

We must consider the revelations the forum members offer against the backdrop of their absence within dominant community imaginations, online and elsewhere. There is one notable exception to this overarching absence: media attention to the problem of domestic abuse and violence against immigrant women on the H-4. However, in the absence of any other narratives about H-4 women and their diverse experiences, this attention to abuse, while important and absolutely necessary, can serve the troubling notion that immigrant women—especially immigrant women of color—lack agency.[101] The presence of the H4 Indian Ladies forum thus makes visible a range of experiences that have been ignored or rendered in limited ways.

CHAPTER THREE

The Wired Home

*Commodified Belonging
for the Transnational Family*

On July 2, 2012, India's largest private sector bank ICICI launched a Facebook page for the banking services it targets to nonresident Indians (NRIs).[1] The launch was one in a series of measures by the corporation to use social media platforms to strengthen its decade-long investment in the global NRI community, especially those in the United States. Starting in the late 1990s and intensifying through the first decade of the twenty-first century, ICICI built a strategic relationship with Indian immigrants in the United States through its online banking services. The effect was remarkable: ICICI catapulted itself into a dominant position in the transnational banking and remittance business. In 2013, ICICI was named the best remittance business bank in Asia by the prestigious financial services research company The Asian Banker. In 2009, the bank's NRI services were named the best in Asia for demonstrating excellence in a business model that taps into global labor migration to generate and diversify its revenue.[2] As its NRI Services Facebook page demonstrates, the banking giant cleverly utilizes themes of culture, tradition, and bonding to promote its online banking services.

A quick scroll of the bank's posts show numerous references to Bollywood, cricket, India's multireligious festivals and customs, and iconic historical figures, alongside tips for online banking; the company is making a clear effort to build a public image for itself on the social media stage. As its June 16, 2013, status update states, quoting Warren Buffet, "Price is what you pay; value is what you get."[3] That value comes from participating in ICICI Bank's array of services and activities besides banking. For instance, in addition to giving tips on creating strong passwords for secure financial transactions, the "services" provided here include a quiz for the potential user on Indian cinema on the occasion of its one-hundredth-year celebrations in 2013, a note of congratulations for the U.S. National Geography Bee champion, Indian American Satwik Karnik, and a wide array of tidbits on Indian indigenous arts and culture.[4] Throughout the page, a common thread is the idea of the NRI as a mobile, transnational worker who nevertheless maintains strong ties to his former homes and homeland. Hence, even as the ICICI NRI page acknowledges the America-centric everyday life and achievements of its target community, it constantly shores up ideologies of the family and the homeland that point to the "Indian" core in the transnational mix. This dynamic—celebrating the transnationalism of the NRI in order to emphasize a nationalist vision of the immigrant family and its cultural and financial investments—is not unique to ICICI. Since the early 2000s, a wide array of websites, from Rediff.com to sulekha.com and including Indian American media companies like *India Abroad*, have built this image of the NRI as proudly transnational but still rooted to tradition.

While the previous chapter focused on online narratives of home created by marginalized Indian immigrant women on the H-4 visa, this chapter explores how online businesses represent the transnational familial life of Indian immigrants via the Indian American marketplace. I am using the phrase *Indian American marketplace* to refer to the exchange of money, commodities, and services built primarily around the Indian immigrant user base in the United States. Electronic commerce and services built around Indian foodstuffs and household goods, banking, money remittance, and real estate purchases are some of the most dynamic sectors in this marketplace. This chapter is organized around three particularly revealing case studies—Namaste.com, Indiaplaza, and ICICI Bank—each of which helps us to understand a particular facet of the ideal image of the contemporary Indian immigrant family and home. Through a close reading of the sites' textual, institutional, and discursive strategies, the following analysis uncovers a gendered appeal to the virtual home consumer, a Hindu middle-class ideal of traditions, a masculine bias in representing financial networks, and an Indian nationalist vision of contemporary immigrant consumer desires and cultural anxieties.

What links these varied concerns is the recurring narrative of the Indian immigrant home as a "wired" home. The representation of the wired home triggers an array of associations—of network savvy, financial comfort, privileged residence, and desired levels of privacy and mobility—and ultimately operates as a symbol of immigrant prowess. The wired home helps the NRI and his family to overcome the physical limitations of migration, as well as structural limitations to global leadership and success in the information technology era. We have seen that it is impossible to discuss the networking cultures of H-4 Indian women without continually running into the dominant figure of the Hindu middle-class H-1B man. Here we deepen our understanding of this figure, all too often taken for granted as a stand-in for NRIs as a whole, by exploring the efforts to commodify the NRI life within discursive constructions of the wired immigrant home in the United States.

The distinctions between where an online media company is based (whether in India or the United States) and how it frames its identity (whether Indian or Indian American) are important considerations in the politics of belonging online. Several online ventures, either e-commerce sites or commercially supported community websites, have emerged in cities across India and America with the express purpose of meeting the cultural needs of the Indian immigrant community while also capitalizing on this constituency to turn a profit. Many of these companies make the idea of home central to the image their sites project. Though these sites all have the same aim—to sell something—the way they do so varies widely, as do the diverse iterations of home that emerge in their efforts to attract customers. *Home*, as a result, can refer to feeling "at home" in more than one country, to a virtual space of belonging, or to a person's primary and secondary residences. But girding these varied incarnations of home is the persistent notion that home must be wired.

In online narratives of home, what is most crucial to the politics of belonging is how the homepage is articulated to reimaginations of the familial and the transnational. As migration patterns have destabilized the Indian nuclear family in very significant ways, online media have entered the picture as key mediators of the changing equations between the immigrant family and the national homeland, between the nuclear family and the transnational one, and between the Indian family and the American social context. At the same time, as online media articulate transnational belonging along the lines of flexible citizenship, these transnational practices are also reflected in their institutional practices. In the new mediations of these familiar scripts, time and space are made virtual. Online media come to embody both the physical homeland and the temporal process of migration; as websites try to make themselves appealing, they rearrange traditional expressions of Indian cultural nationalism with new visions of a transnational lifestyle.

This chapter argues that the textual, cultural, and institutional politics of a diverse set of Indian and Indian immigrant players have shaped an image of the ideal NRI home, an image that is built on ideas of elite mobility, wired transnational familial spaces, and techno-masculine labor and agency. As a result of this image making, we often see the NRI family as a dual-sited network spread across India and the United States. While the commodification of the cultural is intertwined with the latter's ability to be mobile through virtual pathways (of immigration, websites, H-1B homes), the hegemonic narrative is predicated on the idea that physical distance and the dispersion of the household into two units present challenges that could, however, easily be navigated through an active engagement with resources and products offered by online media. Shopping sites, such as online grocery stores, and web-based services, such as money remittances and real estate brokers, are each critical innovations that further the notion of the NRI home as a wired, mobile, multi-sited space of belonging.

The sites discussed here emphasize online media as the link that can maintain—and strengthen—the bond between parents and children, in turn creating a homology between the Indian nation and its diasporic progeny. As in patriarchal narratives, the narrative about home is focalized through the NRI male, who wishes to seamlessly integrate his work life in the United States with the life of his extended family in India. The wired NRI home exemplifies what George Lipsitz has referred to as new media's promise of "romances of patriarchy and patriotism promising secure, stable, and homogenous homes and homeland."[5] Particularly important for understanding the NRI home is that e-commerce and financial services homepages have become key agents for the maintenance of this relationship between home and homeland. It is not surprising, then, that the codes of transnational citizenship, and the ways that we imagine belonging, are often written in capitalist, rather than cultural, terms—the financial is the new filial. The promise of the homepage, to invoke Madhulika Khandelwal, is to "to shrink the distance between households, thus strengthening extended family networks."[6] At the same time, in the very act of targeting the NRI, rather than the family based in India, commercially oriented online media reproduce what Bandana Purkayastha has described as a transnational network where the "nuclear family is the node and located in the United States, but the extended family is a field of relationships."[7] The articulation of this new, transnational, virtualized NRI home nevertheless relies on conventional ideals of gender and class norms. In other words, even in the age of new media, tradition still sells.

Home Shopping Sites:
India Inc. and Indian American Networks

The home shopping site embodies both the commodification of the home space—by giving each of us the ability to shop from home—but also, and more crucially, a reconfiguration of cultural ideologies about relationships, comfort, and "authenticity" through online media. These two e-commerce sites—Namaste.com and Indiaplaza—are particularly interesting because of the notion of home they project, by aligning the homepage of their shopping site with the home of the immigrant consumer, imagined through the flow of money and commodities. In crafting their identity as home shopping sites, Namaste.com and Indiaplaza invoke the dual contexts of India and the United States. This invocation is strategic not only because of the transnational cultural investments of their target users—Indian immigrants living in the United States—but also because of the institutional investments of the parent companies that own the sites. Thus ideologies of the domestic, the private, and the familial are strategically incorporated by e-commerce sites to establish their institutional and cultural identities.

Underpinning the transnational logic of the doubly flexible online identity are familiar scripts of gender, patriarchy, and cultural nationalism that are repackaged to sell a neoconservative image of the Indian immigrant home. While the home in its physical and virtual avatars is framed in a transnational context, the commodification of Hindu-centric family, culture, and tradition reveals that the home shopping sites' investments are essentially in the online expansion of India Inc.[8] Driving that point home literally is the institutional transformation of Indiaplaza, which has migrated from its U.S. home to a new location in India. The company is no longer a U.S.-based Indian American entity but rather an Indian company based in Bangalore and Chennai with the U.S. as secondary market.[9]

Both Namaste.com and Indiaplaza began in the late 1990s as home shopping sites based in the United States and funded by Indian American venture capital. Namaste.com closed its virtual doors in 2002, and Indiaplaza is now more invested in the online consumer market in India, rather than the Indian immigrant base in the United States. The end of Namaste.com and the transformation of Indiaplaza are not irrelevant to the discussion about home and e-commerce cultures here. If anything, these structural changes show that the ideal projected by these sites—that home can be a mobile concept, and that belonging can be found virtually—can only be fully appreciated by examining the institutional contexts and practices of online media businesses. In that context, Namaste.com and Indiaplaza are pioneers, some of the first examples of what is today a booming segment of the Internet, and as such they created the template for the many e-commerce sites that market to NRIs today, such as Cbazaar (which sells saris) and Desimart.com (which sells Indian groceries).

Namaste.com was created by ethnicgrocer.com, a company based in Evanston, Illinois, in 1998.[10] As the name suggests, there is a deliberate attempt to invoke a quintessentially "Indian" identity through its URL. The traditional greeting associated with India and underwritten by Hindu culture is here used to welcome online users, and particularly Indian immigrants, to the online "ethnic" grocery store. When ethnicgrocer.com was launched, the creators indicated that while their initial target customer base for the Namaste.com site was the Indian immigrant community in the United States, their larger vision encompassed creating a presence within multicultural America and reaching a wider consumer base interested in diverse food cuisine.

Like physical versions of the Indian grocery stores in the United States, Namaste.com was in the business of selling many other consumer items besides food, including media such as DVDs and CDs, jewelry, kitchenware, international phone calling cards, and religious ritual–related items. The website's color scheme of red, maroon, and mustard yellow invokes a visual association with Indian spices, especially yellow turmeric and red chilies, while the elaborate borders and designs spatially organizing the homepage seem to mimic the embroidered patterns one might immediately and stereotypically associate with Indian attire, especially the sari. Prominently advertised on the site were the gift items that were available for Namaste.com customers to buy and send to their "family and friends across the US," or their friends and family "back home."[11]

While Namaste.com sold everyday items used in Indian cooking such as lentils, rice, condiments, and vegetables, it was special events, mostly Hindu festivals and a few American holiday traditions such as Thanksgiving Day, that functioned as strategic moments to link the homepage with the maintenance of the domestic and the familial space. For example, in the year 2000, in the days and weeks leading up to Diwali, a Hindu festival occurring in October and marked by lighting lamps and exchanging gifts, Namaste.com employed the following text to advertise its range of products: "Share your joys with friends and family back home. This festival season, call home with our specially priced phone cards. Also *send gifts* to mom and dad or your best friend in India this season. Send mithai [Indian sweets] dry fruits, fresh cakes, silk Kanjeevaram saris, Titan watches and much more."[12] In the following promotion featured to coincide with the year-end festivities, the site shifts the focus to the immigrant household with its offer of "exciting grocery products that can grace [the] dinner table." Included among the delectable delights are "Neera's products which are a collection of delicious chutneys and relishes, Amul products like Ghee and Gulab Jamuns, fresh fruit and vegetables like lychees and okra and a host of Haldiram snacks and fresh mithais."[13]

In the multiple references to Indian food and consumer items there is a particular emphasis on the traditional, high-end, and high-quality product.

For instance, Amul, a dairy company, and Haldiram, a manufacturer of traditional North Indian snacks, bear the stamp of quality, long history, and national reputation given their popularity in the Indian food market. Similarly, Titan watches and Kanjeevaram saris link together ideas of high-quality tradition with high-end cosmopolitanism. Titan is one of the leading Indian watch brands, but more importantly it was one of the first Indian companies to sell the idea of the watch as a fashion accessory, not just a timepiece but also a piece of glamorous wrist jewelry. While the Titan brand can be viewed as a representation of the Indian cosmopolitan lifestyle, Kanjeevaram silk saris, a particular style and design of silk saris made in the South Indian state of Tamilnadu, have for multiple generations been a symbol of the enduring beauty and grandeur of the traditional. In the global marketplace of new and glitzy products, including designer saris, the Kanjeevaram sari is often used to exemplify the idea that tradition can "never go out of fashion."[14] While the array of products Namaste.com sold were marked as quintessentially "Indian," Indian-ness is represented through the quality check of tradition and middle-class cosmopolitanism.

The sale of international and long-distance phone cards online was one of the earliest uses of the commercial Web targeted at Indian immigrants in the United States. While there were a few Indian American online telecommunications businesses that regularly advertised on popular community websites of the mid- to late 1990s such as Samachar.com, Indiaworld.com, sify.com, INDOlink, and Rediff.com, U.S. giants such as AT&T and the erstwhile MCI were also frequent advertisers. One of the key strategies that smaller Indian American phone card businesses adopted to gain a foothold in the market was to offer a lower charge per minute rate than AT&T and MCI. Following this web tradition, Namaste.com pitched its phone cards, "a key mode of keeping in touch with the family," as a guarantee for "calling India for less [than] what AT&T would allow."[15] Namaste.com's offer, which was "20 cents or less," was about cost saving but was packaged within terms that imply a shared understanding of the constraints that come both in the form of the high rate of international calls set in place by U.S. conglomerates as well as having family members in a different country. Unlike food items, phone cards per se are not inscribed with national affiliations; yet by referring to American and Indian (American) differences in charge rates, Namaste.com invited a cultural affiliation that would hopefully translate into net gain.

The notion that the virtual gestures necessary for a successful online shopping transaction can be indicative of an Indian experience is best expressed in the site's use of a classic phrase commonly heard in Indian markets, whether in India or in Indian neighborhoods across the world: "the 100% guarantee." On its FAQ page, Namaste.com reassured its customers about the genuine Indian quality of its products by giving them "the 100% guarantee" that shopping on the site would ensure "an authentic shopping experience."[16] The phrase "100% guarantee" and sometimes just "100%" ("hundred percent," not "one hundred percent," is typically how it is said in India) is very commonly employed across all levels of commerce, by street vendors to high-end retail store employees, to reassure the hesitant prospective buyer regarding the quality of a given product. For instance, one is given the 100% guarantee that a color will not run or fade or a fabric is 100% cotton. While certainly the usage is not limited to the Indian landscape or cultural space, within the institutional context of Namaste.com, it was a definitive gesture toward the trademark Indian quality of Namaste.com's products.

Namaste.com needed to reassure its potential customers that shopping at its virtual warehouse would be an authentic experience because it was a virtual grocery store, not a physical one. When Amazon.com first arrived on the scene and quickly became successful, Jeff Bezos, the creator of the site, noted that books (Amazon initially dealt solely in books of the analog variety) seem like a good product to sell at a virtual store because there is almost no chance of a letdown for the customer (thinking of the product per se and not its content); furthermore, there is no desire for a potential buyer to do a quality check by touch, look, smell, or other yardstick.[17] In contrast, Namaste.com's services were acutely vulnerable to the quality "fail" given their palate and sensory-centric appeal. Hence mobilizing the authenticity of its wares by using a guarantee phrase that might resonate with their user base's memory or understanding of India is crucial to its business strategy. Besides, the pleasures associated with shopping in Indian grocery stores in the United States can include for some much more than just buying a product and paying for it. Ethnic grocery stores serve multiple functions, one of them being a meeting ground for fellow Indian immigrants and informal building of local community networks. In such a context, Namaste.com had to labor toward articulating the immateriality of the virtual within the materiality of the real, the authentic.

Namaste.com remediated the grocery store in the Indian immigrant landscape by redirecting the affective, sensorial, and embodied pleasures of shopping at home (in India) or for home products (in the Indian grocery stores in the United States) through the acts of logging onto the site, filling the online cart, and making a safe financial transaction; these virtual acts in turn held the promise of reconnecting with the extended family in India or replenishing and nourishing the household here in the United States. Remediation, as Jay David Bolter and Richard Grusin have theorized, involves a refashioning, where "what is new about new media comes from the particular ways in which they refashion older media and the ways in which older media refashion themselves to answer the challenges of new media."[18] By drawing on their conceptualization and applying it within the contexts of the technologies of the grocery store in producing authenticity and belonging in immigrant spaces, one can view Namaste.com as a site of remediation.

Indianizing their customer service was not the only reason for Namaste.com's desire to promote itself as an authentic cultural carrier. Namaste.com, as it turns out, sold Indian products that were already imported into the United States. When an order was placed, the product was shipped from a U.S. location, not an Indian one. This is clearly an important issue to address, and Namaste.com did so by once again taking to the FAQ section of the homepage to reassure the customers that the parent company ethnicgrocer.com had ties with leading U.S. importers of "authentic" Indian products, which in turn were making their way to the virtual aisles of Namaste.com.[19]

The institutional interests and investments of ethnicgrocer.com are worth considering here for a moment. Founded at a time when e-start-ups were all the rage in the United States, ethnicgrocer.com was created in late 1998 by two Indian Americans, Parry Singh and Subhash Bedi. In its initial years, the parent site ethnicgrocer.com claimed to be the largest online supplier of ethnic foods, music, health, and beauty products in the United States, having obtained distribution rights to more than fifteen thousand products from over thirty-five countries. When Singh and Bedi were named the "Year 2000 Emerging Entrepreneur of the Year" for the Illinois/Northwest Indiana region by Ernst & Young in June 2000, it was a recognition of their company's successful entry and financial performance in the online world of ethnic markets and bicultural consumers.[20] The company, while invested in the Indian immigrant business, was also interested in tapping into the ethnic market at large, a desire revealed through their two other enterprises alongside Namaste.com—QueRico.com, a grocery store targeting Hispanic users, and HuanYin.com for Chinese immigrants.

In 1998, the site was fueled by the idea of moving beyond the brick and mortar model of ethnic grocery stores and re-creating them in the virtual marketplace. It is important to locate such a market concept of an online grocery store within the late 1990s trend toward e-commerce and virtual shopping as well as the market rhetoric and desire to tap into the "ethnic" marketplace. By the late 1990s, a lot of the discussion about the ethnic marketplace was beginning to expand its focus from the Hispanic community (which was being written about and targeted since the early 1990s in some form or other) and to include Asian Americans. When ethnicgrocer.com was created, there was no dearth of optimism over dot-com startup business models, but what distinguished the company and its website was its strategic entry into the imagined "ethnic" food marketplace by pitching its wares to specific immigrant groups.

Ethnicgrocer.com exemplified an instance of Indian American web entrepreneurship that was tapping into desires regarding not only immigrant lifestyle and ethnic markers but also the potential of the Web and digital capital to generate niche ethnic markets. In 2000, Namaste.com and its parent company, ethnicgrocer.com, secured $34 million in financial investments from leading American corporate entities such as Integral Capital Partners, Kleiner Perkins Caufield & Byers, Amerindo Investment Advisors, Merrill Lynch, Benchmark Capital, and KB Partners.[21] Indian American venture capitalist Vinod Khosla, who has been dubbed by *Fortune* magazine as the "greatest venture capitalist of all time," was one of the company's early backers.[22] A general partner at Kleiner Perkins, one of the key investors in Namaste.com, Khosla once described ethnicgrocer.com as a "revolutionary business." He went on to add that Namaste.com "is a true, born-on-the-Web business model that cannot be replicated in a brick-and-mortar format. The company has built the foundation of a defendable long-term business by quickly and successfully implementing an exceptional international supply chain technology platform."[23]

It is easy to overlook the implications of such a description in the present moment when Namaste.com no longer exists as an online entity, and there is a plethora of home shopping sites online. But what Namaste.com and ethnicgrocer.com demonstrate is the harnessing and linking together of web space, immigrant cultures, and venture capital to reimagine how established (for example, U.S. importers of Indian commodities) and emergent (online phone card businesses) circuits of capital and cultural belonging can be virtually mobilized within the transnational spaces of the homepage. At the same time, by linking together new media technologies, ethnic groups, and digital capital in its business model, the company was harnessing the potential of industry rhetoric about multicultural markets and the U.S. industries' newfound drive and commitment to reach its increasingly diverse and ethnically distinct consumer-citizens. As a start-up that requires venture capital and funding, the concept of an online grocery store specializing in ethnic products taps into the software industry's desire to generate new business models appropriate to the transnational virtual networks facilitated by web-based technologies. Ethnicgrocer.com's investment in the ethnic market at large instead of just the Indian market in the United States also points to an interesting trend within the business practices of some Indian American companies online. The desire for defining themselves as transnational rather than local players in online media is perhaps reflected in the fact that ethnicgrocer.com's name was soon changed to TransEthnic, Inc.

In this discussion about the cultural politics of home and belonging within the textual and institutional contexts of Namaste.com, the site's advertising campaigns, especially a blast of advertising messages that were circulated around 2000–2001 across multimedia platforms, speak eloquently to the ideological underpinnings of the "wired transnational home" within technologies of gender, class, and hegemonic nationalism. While I briefly outline the key facets of the advertising campaign, I closely analyze an advertisement that appeared in the print version of the publication *SiliconIndia*.

To coincide with the Diwali festival in October of 2000, Namaste.com enlisted the services of AdmerAsia, the New York–based agency specializing in Asian American advertising and marketing since 1993.[24] In a television advertisement, two young children, a boy and a girl, are shown creating a *rangoli* (a design made with colored powder) on the front porch of their home, which is ostensibly located in the United States; the camera then moves away from the front porch and follows the line of lit *diyas* (earthen lamps) that dot the path leading up to the front door of the house. As the camera literally marks the spatial movement from porch to door (leading into the house), the advertisement ends with a female voiceover urging the viewers to "Bring India Home!" Diwali is a festival rooted in Hindu mythology and tradition, and rangolis are markers of traditional practices that are grounded in home and hearth while their association with festivals indicates their symbolic role in marking auspicious or celebratory events. A reductive representation of the Indian immigrant condition in America is engendered when the campaign is described, by an executive overseeing the effort, as "built around juxtaposing different cultures: the modern India with the greatness of America."[25] In addition to the Diwali-themed advertisement, two other television spots employed scenes such as the performance of traditional Indian dance and musical instruments (*tabla*) to reiterate the site's slogan, "Bring India Home!" The television spots aired on Indian satellite channels available in the United States such as Zee TV, Sony, and TV Asia (that are part of the South Asian international packages available through U.S. providers, DISH, or DIRECTV).[26] The advertisements were also featured in select U.S. cinemas where an Indian immigrant audience could be easily reached; for example, the advertisements were regularly played on one of the fourteen screens in the Regal Kaufman Astoria Cinema in Long Island, New York, where Bollywood movies are played regularly.[27]

Another advertisement, part of the print campaign that was featured in the Indian American newspapers such as *India Abroad*, depicts a man selling Bhelpuri, an Indian snack, near the Brooklyn Bridge in New York, while the text urges the reader to "Get your *Bhelpuri* Fix@Namaste.com."[28] Bhelpuri is a very popular Indian snack whose defining characteristics are its mix of sweet, spicy, and tangy flavors and its preparation style, where the ingredients are mixed only at the time of eating to keep the different textures of the snack distinct. A key image associated with the snack is the traditional way of selling it; the Bhelpuri vendor carries around the snack and stall accessories and literally sets up shop at crowded public spaces such as market squares, beaches, and the like. Completely aligned with Namaste.com's vision to be the virtual link to "experiencing India in America," to quote a company executive, the advertisement depicts the Bhelpuri seller in traditional attire, a kurta pajama and neck scarf that is a familiar sight in both urban and rural spaces in India. The authenticity of the food is articulated to the embodiment of tradition in the form of the Bhelpuri vendor, and the extraordinary role of the virtual vendor, Namaste.com, is indicated through the exaggerated real effects of bringing India home; it is literally like having a Bhelpuri vendor sell freshly made snacks in one's home space, such as Brooklyn.

Irrespective of the specific themes that were featured in the different advertisements, print and television, all of them ended with the site's slogan phrase, "Bring India Home!" In addition to advertising in the United States, Namaste.com also circulated its advertisements in Indian magazines such as *India Today* and the national daily newspaper *Indian Express*.[29] While it is not entirely clear why the site chose to reach India-based clientele, one possible reason is that magazines such as *India Today* have a lot of U.S.-based subscribers. It is interesting to note that the Namaste.com website, *SiliconIndia* and *India Abroad*, the magazines where the advertisement was featured, and AdmerAsia, the New York–based advertising agency that produced the feature, are all based in the United States. Yet, they were partaking in the reproduction of an imagination about Indian nationalism that is hegemonic in a transnational, immigrant space—that the national culture lies in its "authentic" traditions and everyday practices or symbols, which in turn can be transported intact across the national boundaries to engender home spaces in a new location. When that new location is a link between the immigrant home in the United States and the virtual space of the online Indian grocery store, Namaste.com has to tweak its message of home and belonging to articulate "authenticity" to that which is outside the boundaries of "national" and the "real." The tweaking of this message is clearly evident in a striking advertisement for Namaste.com that appeared in *SiliconIndia* in August 2000 (see figure 3).[30]

A page-length advertisement, it centered on a visual of two presumably Indian women against a blurry backdrop of New York City's Times Square

CHAPTER THREE

FIGURE 3. Advertisement for Namaste.com reproducing an ideal image of Indian women in the immigrant setting of the United States. Credit: *SiliconIndia*, 2000, 69.

at night. While yellow cabs in motion, people crossing at street intersections, neon lights, and electronic billboards advertising Canon and Coke re-create familiar images of New York City, these referents are blurred as if to capture the mobility of capital, people, and technologies underpinning the grid of the iconic "global city."[31] In contrast to this backdrop are the still and relaxed bodies of the two women as one of them applies *mehendi* on her companion's hand. Contributing to the visual effect is the strategy of photo editing whereby it appears as if the women are seated on the sidewalk of a street in Times Square. However, the divergence in the scaling of the two juxtaposed settings—street scene and women applying mehendi— makes it appear as if the women tower over the street (they appear larger than the cabs, street signs, and some buildings); in addition, the women are depicted as oblivious and impervious to their surroundings and street activities (sidewalk traffic, at the very least).

Headlining the advertisement is the caption "Beauty Secrets of India @ Namaste.com," while just below the image is the following text effectively listing the kind of wares sold by Namaste.com: "from bindis to mehndi, and kangans to jhumkas, all that you need for the classic Indian look is at your fingertips. So no matter where you live everything you love about India, movies, snacks, music, health and beauty products, is just a click away."[32] The visual then foregrounds the women against the city street as a metaphor, a symbol of its ultimate message that is succinctly rendered through Namaste.com's slogan, "Bring India Home."

At an obvious level, Namaste.com is here selling its ability to transport the cultural artifacts and products that are associated with India to the immigrant's home in the United States. The references to movies, food, music, and beauty and health products fit into a historical ideology about the production of nationalism in diasporic Indian locations wherein territory is delinked from cultural citizenship and instead practices of consumption and reproduction of cultural values hegemonically associated with the nation become salient.[33] At another, more subtle level, however, the narrative upheld by the advertisement remediates hegemonic ideals of gendered Indian transnationalism in the new media contexts of the Web, including its textual, cultural, and institutional economy. To understand that, I offer a close reading of the visual and cultural narrative implied in the advertisement described above.

The mode by which "India" is represented in the Namaste.com slogan "Bring India Home" is crucial here. The nation is imagined through the frames of authentic, traditional culture, which in turn is sutured to women's bodies inscribed with traditional Hindu, middle-class signifiers. The women's attire, which is elaborately decorated traditional clothing, their facial and bodily accessories including the *bindi* (forehead decoration) and the jewelry, the featured ritual of mehendi application, and equally importantly the use of Sanskritized Hindi words such as *kangans* for bracelets and *jhumkas* for earrings, together privilege a dominant reading of the women as Hindu and middle class.

When the advertisement employs the logic that shopping for "Beauty Secrets of India @ Namaste.com" is all one needs for the "classic Indian look," it subtly marks one of the two women as the ideal embodiment of such a look. She is depicted as having light skin and long hair and being elaborately adorned—the latter indicated in part by the clothing and bindi and in part by her continuing beautification through mehendi application.[34] Applying the mehendi is her partner, who while also coded Indian within the broader textual scheme is clearly playing a secondary role; she is depicted with short hair, darker skin tone, no bindi, and less elaborate clothing than her companion. The bearer of the classic Indian look, however, actively invites the gaze of the viewer of the advertisement and potentially the targeted user of the site. As previously noted, *SiliconIndia* targets Indian technology professionals in the United States and is heavily invested in reproducing information technology as an immigrant male domain. Thus, what we have here is a reproduction of an idealized image of

Indian femininity that circulates within Indian and Indian immigrant popular culture but is here strategically employed to simultaneously service an older and emergent hegemonic narrative about the nation.

The older hegemonic narrative, as scholars have noted, is one where immigrant Hindu middle-class women are invested with the task of maintaining ideals of authentic culture and tradition; such a narrative invested in the continuing dominance of the heteronormative, patriarchal Hindu nation simultaneously locates its immigrant men within the public sphere actively participating in the domains of the economy and politics.[35] The emergent narrative, I argue, in this chapter and throughout the book, reframes the public, masculine domain strategically to include information technology, computing, and networking as key elements and tweaks the idea of active participation of Indian immigrant men within such domains to technological leadership and capital-wielding game changers.

What we see in the Namaste.com advertisement is a fragment of that emerging narrative, where Indian immigrant masculinity is being linked, albeit through the strategy of ex-nomination—the power to name everything except itself—to dynamic, mobile spaces of production of digital technologies and capital.[36] If, as the tagline line suggests, Namaste.com will help Bring India Home, one must ask, who is already at home? I suggest that the Hindu, middle-class information technology professional, who is the target reader of *SiliconIndia* magazine and the target clientele of Namaste.com, is the implied inhabitant of the "home" in the United States. One can begin to define this group by reading the text obliquely—hence they are not just in the midst of the digital capitalist world, but they are key movers of it (hence the imagery of Times Square in motion); they are immigrant subjects who are nostalgic not just for Indian food, movies, and clothes, but perhaps most of all for traditional Indian women who could be brought into the home space. After all, in the online warehouse that is Namaste.com, it is the women who are located centrally within its narratives of culture and consumption.

Women as embodiments of authentic, unchanging tradition and culture are a familiar sign servicing the mythology of the nation; this role of women is a cultural reality that in historical and contemporary contexts has been well documented and proved across different social and cultural national settings.[37] According to Roland Barthes, myths are created by visual signs linked with already present ideological assumptions. These myths then "perpetuate and reinforce the values and preferences of the dominant ideology."[38] Scholars of diaspora and immigrant culture and politics in the Indian and South Asian American contexts have noted that while some of the conservative notions of

"Indian womanhood" are articulated with cultural ideologies around creating and maintaining immigrant homes, families, and community, the process is not a simple transnational replantation but involves negotiation with the everyday realities and practices of a given immigrant locale.[39] Thus, while the mythology of the Indian woman in immigrant settings might exist, it is constantly being reproduced in ways that realign with the conservative interests that are invested in such a mythology in the first place. In this light, it is significant that Namaste.com resorts to presenting Indian women as the most coveted or alluring of the products that are up for consumption through the virtual networks of capital, migration, and technology initiated by digital capitalism. Their allure, however, is not just in their ability to be authentic but also to be virtual and mobile. If they represent India, it is also an India that can be brought to the United States, not through family reunification laws, visiting relatives, or personal trips back home, but through the fact that India exists online. This point is reinforced by the fact that the website Namaste.com and its parent company ethnicgrocer.com were start-ups by Indian immigrants based in Illinois.

Furthermore, in the emergent narrative of home for Indian immigrants in the United States, where is the labor and role of Namaste.com? There are a couple of significant points here. One, instead of the narrative of return, conventionally associated with diasporic modes of belonging, Namaste.com is foregrounding the narrative of bringing something home, while locating the latter in the United States. The use of New York to signify the immigrant location is also interesting; in addition to being the quintessential immigrant city in the mainstream American imaginary, New York has also occupied a key location in the Indian imaginary about America.[40]

It is important to note here that Namaste.com doesn't use "India" and "home" interchangeably. While conventional and reductive discourses about diasporas create narratives about diasporic and immigrant desire to either return to the original homeland or, at the very least, to keep coming home (a continual movement between home and away), the Namaste.com advertisement makes India the mobile culture that comes to the U.S. home. In this regard, we see in the Namaste.com's narrative of home an emergent discourse that posits the immigrant location as the home and envisages a movement of particular cultural elements of India outward into the digital and the transnational domain. The strategic mobility of the culturally essentialized markers of the Indian nation and their transnational transit and relocation in the United States have been discussed previously by scholars who have sought especially to understand how the notion of little Indias and ethnic enclaves emerged and are being sustained through the social, cultural, financial, and institutional networks within the multigenerational Indian community in the United States. In many respects, a central idea embedded within such cultural reproduction is the idea of bringing India to the new home of the immigrant.

A second point about Namaste.com's role is that it positions itself as a key link in the remapping of home territories as a result of new media and migration. While the gendered expressions of cultural nationalism bound up with ideas of authenticity, pleasures of and in the body, and consumption are embodied through the women, the "home" that is already a space of inhabitation for the targeted immigrants is not physically represented but exists virtually. I use the term *virtually* in two senses here: in the sense of virtual as not a physical place but an experience of its time-space effects; and in the sense of the "not real"—exceeding the real, transforming the real, or a hyperreal.[41] In the advertisement image, we don't see any physical space other than the public square of New York City dotted by the signs of global capital, mobility, finance, and culture that in turn are blurred to produce a sense of speed and movement. In other words, the U.S. home that *is* depicted does not reveal its inhabitants, only the flows in which they participate (or alternately produce). The home, in this reading, is (virtually) accessed through its time-space effects: a fast-paced, cosmopolitan lifestyle in the global city.[42] These new centers, located within physical geography but exceeding it, as Saskia Sassen has noted, are produced through a realignment of capital, human resources, and digital networks that in turn reveal a new grid of nodes and links across physical, social, and cultural geographies that make up the global city.[43]

Unlike the Statue of Liberty, which has been often used to mark the entry of the Indian immigrant to the United States in visual cultures of photography and film (particularly the NRI cinema from Mumbai), we see in fact a digital city space that is recognizable as Times Square but also as a global space of flows.[44] In addition, the dynamically different experience of home that would transpire if one availed of Namaste.com's services is also rendered virtually—and here I imply *virtual* in the sense of that which exceeds the "real," or hyperreal. Buying and consuming Indian snacks, movies, and beauty, we are urged to feel, will reproduce the pleasures of the "Indian familiar" in the American setting of the immigrant's home, in ways that are unimaginable (cannot see them as really possible). Perfectly suited to this discourse then are the hyperreal effects of the digitally altered photo of the "new" home—the familiar, stable, grounded feeling of private comforts in constant interaction with the dizzying nature of life in the public square, represented by leisure-pursuing Indian women right in the middle of New York City's Times Square. In this latter sense of the virtual, the implication is toward the virtual as not real (we know the women are not on the sidewalk) exceeding the real (blissfully applying henna while oblivious to their surroundings) and hyperreal (they appear larger than the city buildings) yet having very real material effects, be it bodily affect of implied users, the discursive embodiment of gendered, transnational subjects, or the production of virtual bodies at home on the homepage.

In this reimagining of home spaces, women, and street, *private* and *public* are simultaneously invoked and juxtaposed to perform the task of recuperating a hegemonic vision of Indian transnationalism. While the need for recuperation is engendered by the disruptive potentialities of migration and new media (for example, by upsetting conventional expectations about gender and social roles), the mode of recuperation involves linking patriarchal desires about space, gender, and home with emergent desires about technology, masculinity, and immigrant belonging. The pleasures of eating Indian snacks in the United States, in the *private home*, are interwoven, when we consider the visual narrative, with the pleasures (past and future) of comfort—including snacks—made "real" by Indian women.

What is distinct about Namaste.com's allusion, however, is the intertwining of the virtual with the mobile, the digital with the immigrant, the homepage with the home. The role of the homepage in mediating the immigrant home by offering a commodified, mobile version of India—one that reconfigures place through sensorial pleasures associated with it (movies, food, beauty products, and women)—is where this narrative of reproducing India in the United States differs from previous expressions of cultural reproduction in the immigrant space. Here, India exists in the virtual store of the Illinois-based shopping site, and to access it one requires not a physical journey (to India or the Indian grocery stores in the U.S. neighborhood) but a virtual action (a click).

Namaste.com's investment in privileging the United States as the site of belonging for Indian immigrants must be understood within its institutional context as well. It is not just the target clientele that are located in the United States; Namaste.com itself was based in Evanston, Illinois. The virtualization of India in this example is shaped by different trajectories: the globalization of the food and culture industries, the emergence of network economies, and the transnationalization of its subjects. Highlighting the indeterminacy of a "real" India that resides within a particular geographical boundary but nevertheless retaining its power as an ideology (even as it shifts its contours), Namaste.com provides an instance of the remediation of the national through the encounter with the virtual. In this narrative of authenticity and mobility in the age of the information capitalism, Namaste.com then presents itself as an indispensable "server" facilitating the realization of imagined desires around everyday life and living in the immigrant locale. It will serve up virtual India and its constitutive elements to the immigrant client who clicks and initiates a request for service.

In February 1998 when the Indian American magazine *LittleIndia* released "the first and most comprehensive printed internet directory for Indians on the net," it enlisted the services of two "net gurus" associated with two popular India-centric search engines of the time, B. G. Mahesh of Bhaarat Ek Khoj and Amritpal Singh Notta of India Central, to pick and choose what they deemed the best of the lot.[45] In the category for shopping sites, both gurus named as one of their top picks Indiaplaza, a California-based shopping site targeting Indian immigrants with its offerings that included movies, groceries, clothing and accessories, books, flowers, and other lifestyle products.[46]

In 2013, sixteen years after its creation, Indiaplaza continues to be a visible and successful presence in the e-commerce market. However, there have been some significant and interesting transformations in the company's institutional identity and market goals that reveal a crucial facet of the reconfiguring of the ideologies of home within Indian immigrant web spaces during this period. In the context of transnational migration, it is not just immigrant subjects or commodified culture that are mobile across the India-U.S. national border; online companies also relocate from one nation to the other. As web companies shift their home locations, they also enter into a new dynamic with advertisers, sponsors, and funding agencies in their new homeland while recasting their relations with their "old" institutional family members they left behind in the homeland of their origin. In the case of Indiaplaza, while continuing to target the NRI market in the United States, the site is no longer solely in the NRI business, nor is it based in the United States anymore. Today, Indiaplaza, arguably the "world's largest India-centric online shopping company," is based in India's Silicon Valley, the city of Bangalore in the South Indian state of Karnataka.[47]

Created in 1997 by San Jose–based siblings Vijay and Sheila Shah, Indiaplaza offers a significant and ongoing example of an e-commerce site that articulates the transnationalism of the Web to specific and multiple nodes of Indian American networking and belonging. To begin, the story goes that Vijay and Sheila Shah routinely helped out in their family-run Indian grocery business, Sunshine Groceries, in Canoga Park, California. Vijay notes that over the years, his family's business grew from groceries to include videos, fast food, fashion, and home appliances, thus in many ways giving him the first inspiration for the idea of an online shopping mall. Also shaping his business ideas were his years spent living in India, which, he suggests, helped him feel more connected to India than many of his Indian American twenty-something peers (Vijay was twenty-four years old when he created the site). In 1996, when the idea for an online venture was beginning to appear attractive to him, Vijay, a former e-commerce consultant to Fortune 500 companies, also noticed that while "the mainstream was flooded [with e-commerce sites], there wasn't much going on in the ethnic markets." Instead of focusing on a single product or a range of products in one or two categories, a convention that was common for many popular sites at the time, Indiaplaza focused on "a solution and not a particular product."[48]

The solution was to offer a mix of products keeping in mind the problem of the Indian immigrant niche clientele—namely, to get access to India-related products and goods that would make everyday life in the United States easier to navigate. The Shahs' own upbringing as transnational subjects living in India and the United States, watching their parents' business in the ethnic brick-and-mortar marketplace on the U.S. West Coast, and their sensibilities about what is "necessary" for Indian immigrants to feel at home in the United States all shaped their online business venture. Those everyday life needs, as imagined and serviced by Indiaplaza in its initial years, included groceries, religious items, fashion, and art (such as bindis, jewelry, paintings, sculptures), health products (ayurvedic medicine), cultural taste and interest–related items (such as tablas, sitars, and other typically Indian musical instruments or cricket goods), investment services for nonresident Indians, and free postal service to cities in India.

Indiaplaza's banner advertisements were regularly featured on the leading portals of the time such as Chennai-based Samachar.com as well as community websites such as the Bay Area–based INDOlink. The advertisements typically featured a cultural festival or religious occasion. For example, Raksha Bandhan, a North Indian Hindu festival celebrating the relationship between a brother and sister, is featured with the text "reunite your tie with your brother, reunite the tie with your sister, reunite the tie this raksha bandhan . . . with Indiaplaza.com," while the accompanying image depicts a woman's hand tying the traditional rakhi or sacred thread on a man's wrist.[49] Raksha Bandhan is a patriarchal cultural tradition where a sister conducts rituals including a fast and prays for the long life of her brother; the ritual also invokes the idea that the sister's spiritual practice is in exchange for the physical protection her brother provides her during her lifetime. Implicit here is the notion that women are vulnerable and need male protectors for their physical and social mobility. Like Namaste.com, discussed previously, Indiaplaza mobilizes patriarchal traditions to reimagine its identity with Indian cultural citizens outside the nation's boundaries.

Also relevant here is the transnational nature of the institutional infrastructure and the Indian American alliances that underpinned this online entity. While for the first year of its existence Indiaplaza was self-funded, it thereafter began receiving funding from Indian American venture capitalists.[50] While based in the United States and receiving funding from Indian American and other U.S. angel investors, Indiaplaza also entered into strategic partnerships with Indian companies such as India Book House, the nation's largest distributor of books and magazines; Haldiram's, one of India's oldest (founded in 1937) and largest food companies specializing in sweets and snacks; and Sumeet Center, a leading Indian company in the business of food mixing and grinding appliances with offices in the United Kingdom, the United States, and Singapore, as well as India. In addition, Indiaplaza also entered into a partnership with Citibank, the international banking arm of the financial services group Citigroup and one of the first banking companies in India to advertise and invest in the web marketplace aimed at Indian immigrants.[51]

For the first decade of its existence, Indiaplaza urged its U.S.-based clientele to send gifts, phone cards, and other consumer items to friends and family in India, while it remained rooted in the U.S. landscape. The company's warehouse and place of operation shifted from San Jose, California, to Austin, Texas, in 2005, but the big move was not to occur until two years later. In 2007, Fabmall.com, India's leading e-shopping company, acquired Indiaplaza.[52] Fabmall.com, previously also known as Fabmart.com, was created in 1999 by India-based entrepreneur K. Vaitheeswaran, who recruited a few of his close friends in a partnership. While Fabmart.com initially sold only music CDs on its website, by 2001 it had expanded to include groceries, books, media products, and lifestyle items such as watches. By 2010 the company had undergone several institutional changes leading to a greater investment in the offline grocery chain marketplace in India. Chief among these changes were its 2004 merger with Trinethra, India's largest offline grocery chain, and subsequently its acquisition by the Aditya Birla Group, India's premier business house in 2006. More importantly, Fabmall.com decided to make a strategic foray into the NRI marketplace in the United States after having slowly built its reputation as the leader in the Indian e-commerce market. When Indiaplaza was acquired by Fabmall.com in 2007, the company Fabmall adopted the brand name of Indiaplaza. However, in a move that was pioneered most successfully by Mumbai-based Rediff.com in the early 2000s, the now Bangalore-based Indiaplaza created two websites, one for its U.S.-based clientele and one for its India-based customers. While the URL address www.indiaplaza.com led users to the U.S. site, the URL www.indiaplaza.com.in, with the addition of the country code *in*, heralded the new node of operation for the company.

From 2007 to 2011, Indiaplaza's institutional identity has reflected its transition from a transnationally invested U.S.-based company to a transnationally invested India-based one. The transition is also marked by contradictions such as assigning the dominant URL address to the U.S. version of the site while adding the country code to the India site. In the case of the Indiaplaza company, while the main operations were in Bangalore and Chennai in India and secondary operations in Austin, Texas, the URL addresses signified a reversal of the hierarchy by positing the U.S. site as the primary home of the site. While the dual websites and tri-city physical offices spoke to negotiations of place and online identity that Indiaplaza was undergoing through the 2000s, the company's decision to wind down its U.S. operations and focus primarily on the Indian market as of February 2011 is significant. The site offers products and services to Indian immigrants in the United States, but factors such as limited shipping and product sales only for special events make it obvious that investing in its U.S. market is secondary to its Indian interests. While Indiaplaza continues to receive funding from U.S. investors such as IndoUS Venture Partners (IUVP) as well as The Indigo Monsoon Group (IMG), it has discontinued its strategy of two websites in favor of one site that operates from India for its worldwide users. In a move that is very telling, given the previous discussion of the hegemonic power of U.S.-based URLs, the India-based site now uses the URL indiaplaza.com, without any country code identification.[53] Since April 2010, Indiaplaza has maintained a Facebook profile and uses its page as a marketing tool to promote its latest products and special deals.[54]

It is important to note that while both sites discussed in this section, Namaste.com and Indiaplaza started off as U.S.-based shopping sites invested in Indian American capital networks and Indian immigrants, Namaste.com along with its parent company, ethnicgrocer.com, has exited the online grocery market. Indiaplaza, on the other hand, continues to be very active, but like Namaste.com it has also exited, for all purposes, the U.S. web marketplace. Indeed, Namaste.com eventually could not sustain itself in the competitive field of venture capital–driven e-commerce. But the narrative it shored up for the online customer, where the virtual mediation of the household was articulated with the production of authenticity in the immigrant landscape, is one that has increasingly been mobilized by other online players invested in the transnational politics of the home cultures of Indian immigrants in the United States. On the other hand, the case of Indiaplaza highlights, particularly through its institutional shifts in the 2000s, that the idea of Indian American networks is not a fixed one, nor is it one where the relation is one of equal power.

Banking on Homeland Technologies

In its January 10, 2003, issue, *India Abroad,* a leading Indian American weekly newspaper, featured a special issue on the "The Day of the Diaspora."[55] The paper included a special four-page commemorative supplement that was sponsored by India's leading Internet bank, ICICI Bank. On the front page was a colorful image of the twenty-second India Day Parade held on Madison Avenue in New York on August 18, 2002.

The celebration, which is an annual event organized by the Federation of Indian Associations (FIA), marked the fifty-fifth anniversary of Indian independence from British rule on August 15, 1947. The image in *India Abroad* depicts the culmination of the parade at Madison Park, where the sixteen thousand participants gathered to watch a two-hour long cultural extravaganza including a performance by the grand marshal of the parade, Bollywood actress and new immigrant Madhuri Dixit.[56] The image foregrounds the Indian flag raised high above the jubilant crowds as they enjoyed the festivities of the day. Right beneath the image is the caption, "The Day of the Diaspora." And just below the caption in a horizontal bar is the sponsor's message: "It's not that lonely at that top, when we're right there with you. ICICI Bank: The Indian Face of Global banking."[57] The remainder of the four-page commemorative supplement is devoted to ICICI Bank's banking options for nonresident Indians, interspersed with sponsored messages aimed at the NRI community: "Just like you, we're making India proud"; "High Achieving NRIs, congratulations! We have a lot in common"; and "You've given India a reason to be proud. We'd like to believe we have too." On the last page, ICICI Bank (which was created in 1955; its Internet bank site was created in 1996) offers a glowing account of the recognition it received in 2002 alone, including *Global Finance Magazine*'s "Best Consumer Internet Bank in India Award," United Kingdom–based *Banker Magazine*'s "Bank of the Year in Emerging Markets Award," and a rating as "The Best Managed Bank in Asia" in *Euromoney Magazine*'s annual poll of Asia's best-managed companies.[58]

The four-page commemorative supplement described above frames *India Abroad*'s news stories for the week of January 10, 2003. Prominent on the newspaper's regular front page was the headline "Dual Citizenship Likely for People of Indian Origin."[59] The accompanying story about the first Indian diaspora convention held in New Delhi, India, on January 9, 2003, was in the news for two key reasons. First, the Indian government had declared that January 9 was henceforth to be known as Pravasi Bharatiya Divas (a Hindi phrase that means Nonresident Indian Day).[60] Second, the Indian government, for the first time in history, was planning to grant dual citizenship for persons of Indian origin (PIO) in select countries around the world. The phrase *persons of Indian origin* is widely used in discussions about the Indian diaspora (and is often used interchangeably with *people of Indian origin* as in the above-mentioned *India Abroad* news article, which refers to foreign citizens of Indian origin), and dates from 1999, when the Indian government began issuing PIO Cards to foreign citizens of Indian origin for a nominal fee.[61] *India Abroad* made its January 10 weekly edition a commemorative issue on "The Day of the Diaspora" to mark the January 9 Pravasi Bharatiya Divas (Nonresident Indian Day) and the promise of dual citizenship for PIOs.

The special supplement on "The Day of the Diaspora" is significant for several reasons within the context of this section about online banking and patriarchal nationalism. The first has to do with the ownership of *India Abroad*. In March 2001, the New York–based thirty-one-year-old and longest-standing Indian American publishing company was acquired by the Mumbai-based online media giant Rediff.com.[62] Since its acquisition, *India Abroad* has been reframed as "A Rediff Publication," and equally importantly, the India-based Rediff.com has reinvented itself as "an Indian American" company. By acquiring India Abroad Publications, Rediff.com assumed control over the oldest, largest, and most profitable Indian American newspaper in the United States. CEO and chairman Ajith Balakrishan's comments at the time of the merger offer an insight into Rediff.com's institutional plans: "The integration has provided our audiences with a superior online [and] offline product offering, thereby reaching out to new users across both mediums. It has given an opportunity to our half a million Rediff USA online user base to enjoy the same high editorial values of Rediff.com in the print medium. The new edition will allow us to consolidate our leading position as one of the preferred online and offline India destinations among the Indian-American community in the United States."[63]

By the time Rediff.com acquired *India Abroad* in 2001, it had established itself as a leading and popular India-related website in the United States. A commercially owned community website, Rediff.com initially became more popular with NRI users than the users in India; its content included multiple channels covering India and U.S.-related news, Bollywood, finance, politics, astrology, and matrimonials.[64] CEO Balakrishnan has suggested that since by the mid-1990s India did not have the necessary bandwidth and many citizens lacked access, it was not surprising that Rediff.com was more popular in the United States than in India. Taking note of the number of hits the site was getting from the United States, in 2000 the company launched two different versions of the site, Rediff USA and Rediff India. While there wasn't much of a difference in the content in the early years of this transformation, the U.S. site prominently featured advertising targeting the NRI consumer.

Prior to its acquisition of India Abroad in March 2001, Rediff.com bought two other Indian immigrant businesses catering to the NRI market in the United States.[65] Considering the time period of these acquisitions, it is possible that the two businesses in question were trying to survive the dot-com crash, while for the financially successful Rediff.com, the purchase presented an opportunity to enter aggressively into a market that it had been eyeing since the late 1990s. In February 2001, Rediff.com acquired thinkindia.com, a privately held U.S.-based portal focusing on Indians worldwide, founded with the financial backing of several Indian American angel investors; at the press release following the merger, Rediff's Balakrishnan reiterated his company's mission to "make Rediff.com the online portal of choice for Indians worldwide," adding, "We will do this by helping all Indians living outside India connect with their community, both in India and in the countries where they live."[66] As a result of the merger, Rediff.com was able to customize its content, services, and marketplace offerings for NRIs in the United States; for instance, shortly after the merger, Rediff.com launched its dedicated pages for Indians living in major U.S. metropolitan areas such as the San Francisco Bay Area, Los Angeles, Chicago, Washington, D.C., New York, New Jersey, and Houston, with the city-specific page offering local information on Indian events, news, movies, restaurants, and businesses.

In March 2001, Rediff.com bought Value Communications Corporation; an online communications company that focused on Internet-based marketing of international phone services, it was created in 1996 by Illinois-based Indian immigrants Arvind J. Singh and Sandeep Shrivastava. The company placed its phone card advertisements, most of which were banner ads with messages such as "call India for 27¢" on popular community websites such as those of Samachar.com and INDOlink, which targeted NRIs. At the time of its acquisition by Rediff.com, the company had an estimated customer base of forty-five thousand with revenues over $13 million a year.[67] Making clear that its intention was to break into the American telecom market share organized around Indian immigrant clients, Rediff.com displayed a new message while advertising the Value Communications phone cards on its homepage shortly following the acquisition. While Value Communications has historically privileged their rates, which were "cheaper than" those of telecom giants like AT&T, Rediff.com began advertising the same phone cards by stating that the service they provided was "of AT&T quality," a code phrase for fast, easy connections.[68] While acquiring an online portal, an Internet phone company, and the leading print newspaper invested in the NRI community were strategically very important to enable Rediff.com to get a foothold in the United States, it is the company's institutional alliance with another Indian entity, ICICI Bank, starting 2002–2003 that foregrounds how critical the construct of the home was to enable both Rediff.com and its allies such as ICICI Bank to recast themselves as part of the NRI family.

To recall, the supplement of the special issue of *India Abroad* titled "The Day of the Diaspora" was sponsored by ICICI Bank. In 2002–2003, when Rediff.com launched a special channel on its U.S. website relating to NRI finances, ICICI Bank was the principal sponsor. ICICI Bank's parent company, the Industrial Credit and Insurance Corporation of India, was created in 1955, and ICICI Bank (which goes by the acronym and not the expanded name), was a subsidiary created in 1994 to diversify the financial interests of the parent company that historically had focused on project financing. While the parent company created shortly after India became a postcolonial nation was a World Bank–funded initiative steeped in development rhetoric, ICICI Bank has been a symbol of India's economic reforms launched in the 1990s. One of the many goals of ICICI Bank is to offer a diverse range of services and promote what the company calls global and universal banking.

In this new vision for the bank, the NRI in the United States is a prime customer to pursue. ICICI Bank is currently a leading player in NRI banking and money remittance business, a position it has acquired in part through early and strategic incorporation of the Web for its business practices. It is the first Indian bank to have its own website and one of the first Indian corporations to use online media for advertising.[69] The bank's online campaigns are also considered as textbook cases of successful online advertising.

As "The Day of the Diaspora" supplement in *India Abroad* demonstrates, while Rediff.com used its acquisition of an Indian American print newspaper to reconstruct itself as an Indian American company, ICICI Bank was using its virtual identity as *icicibank.com* to create an affinity with nonresident Indians. With its catchy messages, including "It's not that lonely at the top when we're right there with you" and "High Achieving NRIs, we have a lot in common," aimed at NRIs, *icicibank.com* leaves little room for ambiguity. By crossing the country's borders to make a life in a new land and creating history by becoming the first Internet bank in India, the NRI and ICICI Bank, respectively, were being hailed in the sponsor message as the very epitomes of national success in immigrant-virtual spaces.

Preceding the 2003 "The Day of the Diaspora" image articulating the commonalities between Rediff.com, India Abroad, ICICI Bank, and NRI subjects, however, was the institutional alliance between ICICI Bank and Rediff.com on the latter's NRI Finance Channel. During 2002–2003, users of Rediff.com's NRI Finance Channel were treated to an unusual advertisement when they clicked on a link titled "know more about ICICI Bank" on the channel's main page. The advertisement featured an image of Bollywood superstar Amitabh Bachchan, who greeted users with a warm smile and the following words: "You've always been proud of Indian culture, cuisine and heritage. Well, it's time to add banking to the list!"⁷⁰

The advertisement was unusual in part because it was the first time that Amitabh Bachchan was endorsing banking and online banking to the NRI in particular. Although Bachchan is a popular celebrity endorser for many products in India, associating his massive brand value with an emergent form of financial appeal to the NRI segment—namely, online banking—was unique and groundbreaking. The association between Bachchan and ICICI Bank is obviously a successful one, going by the decade-long association they have now had; the Bollywood icon is currently featured in a variety of television campaigns for the bank in the domestic Indian marketplace. Another reason the campaign was unique is because it was one of the first instances when banking, historically a key site for state regulation and therefore not exactly a symbol of flexible citizen rights, was now being pitched as a symbol of national pride, right alongside culture, heritage, and cuisine.⁷¹

A central factor shaping the mobility of home territories in present times is the flexible and innovative pattern of transnational capital flows. These patterns demonstrate the limits of nation-states in controlling economic flows across national borders. At the same time, the new configurations of capital flows are engendering flexible strategies within nation-states as they reinvent themselves in an effort to participate more effectively in the competitive global marketplace. One such strategy used by the Indian nation-state in recent times has been to extend an unprecedented level of financial and investment incentives to NRIs. Given the Web's potential to target transnational users, it is no surprise that highly competitive private banks in India were the first, and arguably the most successful, institutions to target NRIs with e-banking and financial investment opportunities. And no bank has done it better than ICICI Bank.

While a top banner reminded the user of the NRI Services page that the financial services were a joint venture of "Rediff in association with ICICI Bank NRI Services," the key offerings included banking, "money2india" money transfer, and home loans.⁷² The page provided a range of information relating to the Indian government rules regarding taxation of foreign currency, money transfer protocols, banking regulations, and financial rules governing NRI transactions in India; in addition, one could subscribe to the free NRI finance newsletter that was promoted by ICICI Bank. Linking all three services together was the tag line inviting NRIs to "come, be a part of the ICICI bank family!"⁷³

The banking services offered NRIs a variety of options in opening a bank account with ICICI Bank in India; they included logging in online in the United States to create an NRE or Non Resident External Account, where the NRI in the United States could mandate a resident in India to operate the account. Although the NRI was a category that had its institutional roots in the Indian state's attempt to facilitate the inflow of foreign currency and capital generated through NRI labor into the national treasury, there were a series of bureaucratic rules imposed on NRIs' ability to conduct financial transactions in the national space. The creation of new modes of banking such as NRE accounts hence spoke to the desires of the Indian state to rethink its relationship with the NRI, especially in countries like the United States, at the end of the millennium; critical to the rethinking had been the removal of some of the restrictions that had historically been placed on the ability of Indian banks to deal in foreign exchange.[74]

In addition to providing NRIs with the many banking options, ICICI Bank also inaugurated its e-transfer service under the brand name of money2India in November 2002. It described the online service in the following words: "A direct debit facility using ACH (automated clearing house) in USA. A completely online and paperless way of transferring money to India. No branch visits, no posting of cheques. Just issue us your instructions online from your home or office! You can transfer money FREE to any ICICI Bank account or issue a demand draft at more than 670 locations."[75] The promotion ended with the promise that "with ICICI bank, [one can] send money home at express speed." ICICI Bank's "express speed" was advertised as an upgrade from traditional money remittance processes that involve time-consuming paperwork, and the e-transfer service promised unprecedented convenience and speed in transnational financial services.[76] When read in light of the four- to six-week timeframe for earlier transactions, the instantaneity of the online transaction reinvents the very act of repatriating money to one's home. Furthermore, in place of home as "here" and "there" (invoked by the earlier methods), the "express speed" of e-transfer links NRI homes in the United States and India within a narrative of the "here" and "now." It also reinvents the identity of ICICI, India's national bank, within a discourse of the transnational, represented through its cyber home, U.S.-based clientele, and globally competitive financial practices.

ICICI Bank's third service, launched the same year, involved facilitating the entire process of buying real estate in India by NRIs in the United States by migrating all its constituent parts online. Beckoning the NRI with the assurance that "a dream home in your homeland is a definite possibility," ICICI pitched its home loans as "fast to apply and even easier to get!," while its online database of the real estate choices in India made ICICI's Home Search process "the most convenient way of finding your dream home, with access to the entire real estate market under one roof."[77]

Remittances, home buying, and conducting financial transactions have historically been important ways to produce belonging, a sense of ownership of a territory that was once home (India) or is the new home (United States). Buying a home in the United States, as the conversations on the H4 Indian Ladies forum on Indusladies.com (discussed in chapter 2) remind us, is tied to ideas of class, upward mobility, and, more importantly, a sense of feeling more at home in the immigrant landscape.[78] That said, buying property in India has also been a long tradition where the real estate in India could serve multiple functions—a sound financial investment, a symbol of the desire of the NRI to return back home as well as a parental or extended family residence. In that context, ICICI Bank is not inserting a new narrative as much as reframing it within the digital contexts of a national homeland that can be navigated through an online search and a virtual culture where multiple places (households, remittance offices, banks) exist in the same time-space of ICICI Bank's e-service page. Taking note of the remittance culture in the Indian diaspora, Supriya Singh has argued that a "new form of transnational family money is emerging with its own range of valuations vis-à-vis physical care and support."[79] Singh has also noted that the discussion over remittances has often been linked to frames of quantity and financial growth with hardly any attention to the shifting issues of "family, marriage, gender, migration and money."[80] Similarly, V. A. Zelizer has observed that remittances "transform households at both origin and destination."[81]

Over the years while ICICI Bank has used several different images to create an emotional appeal for its ICICI NRI services, the central motif is the NRI son at work or with his family in the United States using the computer to connect with his parental family in India. During its 2002–2003 promotion campaign on Rediff.com the bank used the image of a young father and a child (presumably his son or daughter), both of whom are smiling as they gaze into the computer screen in front of them. The caption at the foot of the image read, "Welcome back to where you belong: Feel at home anywhere in the world with a range of services to meet your every financial requirement."[82] Another version from 2012, seen in ICICI's NRI Facebook page, which shows a young couple presumably in a living room in their U.S. home as they are logged into the NRI services page. The caption reads, "NRIs feel at home even when you are away from home." The visual arrangement of this NRI familial moment is once again significant—the man is shown using the laptop while the woman, semi-reclining on a couch, peers from behind. In the 2012 version of the money2india campaign, we see the NRI son pictured with his parents—seated in the center, he wraps his arms affectionately around them. The relatively comfortable, wired, living space thus always shows the NRI as a male figure and allows for a middle-class, techno-savvy masculinity to be sutured effortlessly to ideologies of familial, national, and migrant identities.

In welcoming NRIs "back" to where they belong, ICICI Bank, a veritable institution in India, conflates its cybernetic space with the national home. Therefore one can feel at home by entering ICICI Bank's virtual space. More importantly, it implies that for the Indian who resides abroad, the act of being at home is mediated through the digital worlds of one of India's leading financial institutions. This idea is reiterated through the series of television advertisements featuring Bollywood superstar Shahrukh Khan. In 2006, ICICI Bank named Khan its global brand ambassador, a move that was not surprising given his popularity among NRIs. Khan's name is synonymous with the NRI cinema genre in Bollywood; starting in the mid-1990s, he has played several memorable NRI characters, and to this day his ability to connect with Bollywood's global NRI fan base is unparalleled. If Khan's films allow audiences to connect with something Indian in some ways, in his ICICI advertisement they are invited to connect with his (and through him their own) experience of being global yet seeking a familiar home. As he states at the end of a very popular ad, "No matter where I am in the world, I know I can bank on ICICI. It's like coming home."[83]

ICICI Bank suggests that fulfillment of the NRI's financial obligations toward his home and family in India is possible only when he enters into a different kind of financial commitment with the ICICI "family." Hence, NRI men can be at home while living in the United States, because they belong through the act of investing in ICICI Bank as well as through their loved ones in India. To fulfill their dreams and obligations, the NRI has to return to where he belongs: the ICICI family (where he is welcomed, of course). Thus home, homeland, and homepage are entangled in the discourse of belonging on Rediff.com's Finance Channel sponsored by ICICI Bank.

By framing NRI familial relationships within a web of financial obligations, Rediff.com's Finance Channel and the ICICI Bank offer an economically reductive discourse of nation, family and the immigrant condition, and the politics of cultural citizenship. The notion of the home, whether that of the bank or the homeland itself (in this instance, India), much like that of the immigrant household, reestablishes its authenticity by mobilizing the virtual. The true value of the immigrant son comes to the fore online, the parents in India maintain their relevance and stature in the new mobile family structure, the Indian nation reclaims the diaspora as "its children," and the bank aspires for a new market identity. And the Web, in all of this, is the key link facilitating these new assemblages. The discourse of home sutures the micro- and macro-level embodiments of space, fusing household and homeland together.

The money transfer narrative reconfigures the transnational Indian immigrant family in patriarchal terms, where the NRI son derives satisfaction in his transnational identity by fulfilling his duty toward his parental family while being in the United States with his nuclear family. In this representation, the son is privileged while his family is marginalized or rendered invisible in this reproduction of immigrant lifestyle. It is men who cross the physical and virtual borders, who authorize the economic restructuring of the Indian family by redefining it within a transnational space (Indian American and online). Such a narrative reproduces masculine privilege but transforms it into a techno-masculine privilege. The online site and the techno-masculine subject are the mediating agents who are able to cross boundaries; they are ones authorized by the nationalist state to cyber-travel.[84]

ICICI Bank's online strategies operate within a broader context where the Indian state's shifting attitudes toward NRIs is opening up a new dimension to the association between the nation and its emigrants, illustrating Aihwa Ong's argument that in the age of globalization, "individuals as well as governments develop a flexible notion of citizenship and sovereignty as strategies to accumulate capital and power."[85] In the early 2000s, ICICI was not the only Indian bank, nor was Rediff.com the only corporate website, to reproduce patriarchal constructions of NRI identity and financial capital. For example, Citibank, the U.S.-based banking giant and a big player in the NRI services market, inaugurated its online service of "wealth management for the global Indian."[86] Like ICICI Bank, Citibank relied on the NRIs' "financial commitments in India" to promote its financial services; not surprisingly, it also deployed the imagery of an elderly couple embracing their youthful son or shots of a young man in an urban professional setting while reassuringly stating to the NRI user that the Rupee Checking Account is "a bridge between you and your family in India." Continuing its address to NRIs, Citibank's promotional text read: "whether it's sending money home to your parents or dependents, fulfilling financial obligations like house rentals, car loans etc., or business related reasons—as an NRI, transferring money to India is one of your important needs."[87]

As with ICICI, Citibank also promised to help the NRI build his dream home by making funds available to him. However, the dream home can be realized only if the NRI has at least two years of work experience in the United States, intends to buy a home in any of the nine city locations selected by Citibank, and, perhaps most important of all, has an annual income of at least $45,000. Citibank's representation of the NRI in the United States as a young, male, professional immigrant living in an urban location reinforces the dominant construction of the Indian immigrant community on many of the corporate websites, including Samachar.com and sify.com, where Citibank made frequent appearance as advertiser or sponsor. By invoking finance as a key factor in the bonding between a son and his parents, and constructing a causal relationship between the fulfillment of a son's financial obligations to his family and enjoying the warmth and affection of his parents in India, Citibank offers a very reductive construction of family life and its obligations. Furthermore, by representing the immigrant labor force through the image of the male, urban professional NRI ensuring the well-being of his family in India, Citibank perpetuates an elitist and patriarchal discourse on the family, nation, and labor.

While Citibank, with its slogan, "wealth management for the global Indian," sought to entice the NRI by privileging his global Indian status, India's largest national bank, State Bank of India, made appeals to national pride, unity, and lineage. The bank framed "investment options in a country of opportunities" as the NRI's "legacy," while reminding the NRI that India is "your country. And Ours." In a climate where NRI investments and banking were beginning to emerge as big business with Indian private sector players such as ICICI Bank and global players such as Citibank, State Bank of India resorts to the familiar national script of common heritage and culture in its statement, "We will see your transaction through better because we speak the same language."[88]

ICICI Bank's advertisements for online banking and money remittances services are now regularly featured in other media spaces, beyond websites, that might appeal to Indian immigrants. In addition to print advertisements in magazines such as *SiliconIndia* and newspapers such as *India Abroad*, the advertisements also appear on Indian satellite channels such as Star TV that are available in the United States through international programming satellite providers such as DISH network and DirecTV. A recent trend noticed within television advertisements is the reinforcement of the "Indian" choice one is making by choosing ICICI Bank as the money remittance service provider. It appears that the tweaking of this message is in part a response to the increasing cooptation of Indian signifiers by internationally managed "global" players in the money transfer business, such as XOOM. The latter roped in Amitabh Bachchan (who previously was the brand ambassador for ICICI's NRI services) as its brand ambassador for 2013; as of January 2014, Bachchan is featured prominently on XOOM's India page.[89] In 2012, XOOM India launched a series of advertising campaigns using the cinematic character of Chulbul Pandey, a Robin Hood–type persona played by Bollywood superstar Salman Khan in his 2010 blockbuster film *Dabangg* (see, for example, "Xoom.com - Bulbul Robinhood Funday" on Youtube, where an actor employs Salman Khan's inimitable style as the no-nonsense Chulbul Pandey to the theme of money exchange rates). XOOM's association with the Dabangg franchise continued when it signed up as an associate sponsor of Dabangg 2 released in late 2012.[90] As the playing field gets more competitive and complex, ICICI Bank is sharpening its message by redefining how nationalist choices can be played out in the online world of capital and commerce.

The ideal of the wired home, as we have seen, is increasingly important in e-commerce websites and on social media. That concept—that we are always online even in (and especially in) the privacy of our own home—performs a diverse set of cultural functions for the Indian immigrant. The economic route to citizenship that many of these representations champion is closely aligned with the websites' own institutional desires to solicit the capital investments of NRIs. While their interests in the NRI market are related to their need to keep themselves relevant in the rapidly changing marketplace of e-commerce, their strategies hinge on using the vision of a transnational Indian family, fully wired and relentlessly mobile, with dual homes and multiple dwellings, to appeal to Indian immigrants in the United States. The companies are also invested in a nationalist vision of transnationalism, one that continues to prioritize a conservative, Hindu, middle-class family regardless of the ongoing shifts in migration, capital flows, and online media. In addition, the commercial advertising of real estate in India, and advertising for money transfers to India in online media (and increasingly on Indian satellite television channels in the United States), position a heteronormative masculine subject at the center of this transnational Indian family structure. The commercial construction of the NRI family reinforces the idea that the ideal Indian family is a network, spread across two nation-states, and that contemporary Indian immigrants can easily navigate the challenges of physical distance and the dispersion of the household.

CHAPTER FOUR

Desi Networks

Linking Race, Class, and Immigration to Homeland

Konrad Aderer's short documentary *Rising Up: The Alams* centers on a Bangladeshi Muslim immigrant couple, Mohammed Alam and Sultana Jahangir, as they fight the U.S. government's effort to deport them. In the shadow of enhanced, post-9/11 security measures, the concept of home figures as a central narrative trope. The film, produced in 2005 by Life or Liberty, a nonprofit multimedia project that supports immigrant rights, begins with scenes of the Alams in their apartment and concludes, eleven minutes later, with them as part of a public community protest, marching alongside thousands of others through the streets of New York City. The narrative highlights the role of the working-class South Asian community organization Desis Rising Up and Moving (DRUM). The group helps the Alams confront their feelings of confinement and isolation and empower themselves through community activism and coalition building with other immigrants and people of color. In a powerful scene in the film, we see Sultana Jahangir addressing a roomful of immigrant activists and community members with the following speech: "I'm a member of DRUM—Desis Rising Up and Moving. And I want to talk to you today about the injustice to immigrants being done in this country. Bush and John Ashcroft have disappeared so many families from all over New York City. We are here today to tell Bush and the Republicans to *go home* [emphasis mine]! We'll never be afraid. We're not going to be afraid. We will continue to fight your unfair laws until we have human rights and justice for all immigrants in the U.S.A. Justice for all!"

While the film was made available for purchase through the DRUM website for a short period following its 2005 release, since 2013 it has been available for free viewing on the YouTube channel DesisRisingUpMoving.

The film's opening sequence begins within the domestic setting of the immigrant household—a backshot shows the silhouette of a young girl looking out of an apartment window onto the world outside, followed by a shot of the young girl writing at a table, squeezed into the tightly organized apartment. The girl reads her narrative aloud. "I am Alisha. I live in New York City. My father's name is Mohammed . . ." She is assisted by her mother, Sultana Jahangir, who attends to household chores while following Alisha's writing. The scene shifts to the public space of a New York City street where we first encounter Mohammed Alam. As a Bangladeshi Muslim immigrant, whose predicament underlies the narrative of the film, the introductory framing of Alam is important. We see Alam at his job, driving a city cab; we are soon told that it has been his sole source of livelihood since he arrived in the United States eleven years ago. As we watch Alam at work, the film encourages us to view the intertwined contexts of the needs of American labor and the needs of immigrants in America.

Mohammed Alam begins to narrate how an event following the 9/11 attacks changed his understanding of the United States as his home, and we return to the Alams' residence. With his wife seated next to him, Alam recounts his participation in the Special Registration Program run by the Department of Homeland Security. Initiated in 2002 as part of the National Security Entry-Exit Registration System (NSEERS), the program included a voluntary domestic registration by noncitizen males over the age of sixteen who had come from one of twenty-five countries (twenty-four of which had predominantly Muslim populations) named by the U.S. government. Registration involved going to the local office of the Immigration and Naturalization Services (INS), getting fingerprinted, photographed, and interrogated.[1] Alam describes what happens at the INS office: his passport is seized, he is searched by an INS official who calls him a "fucking Muslim who is no good," and he is thrown into a holding cell. Alam recounts the horrific moment of recognition. Instead of being considered loyal for participating in an act meant to safeguard the country he considered his home, he was viewed as a threat. He was forced to stay overnight in the cell and denied access to a phone to communicate his whereabouts to his family. As the night unfolded, Alam says, he was shaken by the reality of his vulnerable location as an outsider within the United States. His adopted country had transformed into a threatening presence. Facing the prospect of deportation at the time of filming, the Alams nevertheless communicate their intent to fight for their right to stay.

Rising Up, by moving back and forth between inside and outside, home and street, reminds us of the inevitable interweaving of household and homeland, family and nation, private and public. This dynamic continues in the rest of the film as we see Sultana Jahangir and Mohammed Alam in various private and public settings—an indoor meeting with DRUM members planning a protest, walking down a street flanked by police, riding the subway, doing chores at home. While the confined apartment could be read as a metaphor for the isolation and restrictions experienced by the Alams, more pertinent is the fact that the immigrant home is not represented in a stereotypical way, where the household is bounded by the private culture of the insular immigrant family. Instead, we see Sultana trying to catch a television story about the Special Registration Act as she goes about her chores at home; we are in the Alams' living room as they critique the fact that despite being good immigrants and having no criminal activity on their records, they are being treated like threats to the United States. The film's depiction of the Alams in diverse spaces tactically weaves the threads of belonging and being an outsider into all these spaces, thereby resisting a narrow conceptualization of the private home as an a priori space of belonging and the street as one where many immigrants don't feel welcome.

Although one of the enduring myths about America is that it is shaped by immigration, the nation has just as often defined itself through a lengthy and varied list of anti-immigrant biases.[2] Furthermore, as the H-4 visa restrictions in chapter 2 illustrate, even when it seems like immigrants are being welcomed and included within the new community tapestry of the nation, they are often systematically disempowered and expected to live with restrictions on their human rights and civil liberties. As chapter 3 shows, idealized web representations of nonresident Indians and H-1B immigrants reinforce a techno-nationalist cultural identity that imagines transnational mobility and belonging built upon a hierarchical vision of gender, class, religion, and technological expertise, as well as nation. Here we will push further with our exploration of home and homepage, by narrowing in on the DRUM homepage.

A key category of identification—*desi*—that has historically circulated within the Indian and South Asian diaspora in the United States is being reimagined by the South Asian immigrant community, including Indians.[3] The reuse of this term has encouraged a more critical look at race, class, sexuality, and politics. *Desi* is a term both of self and community identification, derived from the Hindi word *desh*, meaning homeland. Among immigrants it has a pan–South Asian appeal and usage; to be desi in the United States, in the most conventional sense of the term, is to claim a cultural belonging, affiliation, and ancestry to one or more of the countries in South Asia, including Afghanistan, Bangladesh, Sri Lanka, Pakistan, Bhutan, and Nepal; but in its typical usage, to be desi has functioned as a code for all things Indian.[4] Additionally, even within the narrow casting of national connection, the desi-ness claimed by a second- or third-generation South Asian American must be understood as overlapping but also distinct from the claims made by an immigrant who comes to the United States from South Asia. My point here is not to reify chronological and geographical distances between iterations of desi-ness, but rather to emphasize that desi, even in its most narrow but popular understanding of cultural affiliation with a South Asian country, cannot be understood as a homogenous claim in terms of its associations and investments. As we see in *Rising Up*, social justice groups within the South Asian immigrant community are also recasting the category of desi strategically. Desi, in this iteration, highlights how race, capitalism, and neoliberalism affect and are responded to by South Asian immigrants. DRUM and other groups are shifting the very terms of the debate. One cannot be content to simply ask who desis are, a question that assumes clear contours of identity and relies on simplified notions of authenticity; rather, we need to explore how desi-ness is being constructed, imagined, and produced, both by desis themselves and by white America in relation to contemporary aspects of life, work, mobility, and security in transnational, capitalist America.

This chapter explores the intersections of race and class in the re-imagining of desi location and politics in the contemporary United States. By focusing on the DRUM website, drumnyc.org, it shows how online media facilitate and expand the critical project of rethinking the homeland from a particular, and often ignored, immigrant perspective. This particular perspective is attuned to the structural dynamics of a racialized state, the struggles over citizenship, and the possibilities for forming multiracial alliances. The site links desi concerns to issues such as labor conditions of low-wage immigrants; the post 9/11 articulation of immigration with terrorism; the demonization of brown, Muslim bodies; state-sponsored racism; and attacks on the civil rights of immigrants irrespective of their legal status. Desi in this iteration does not simply tell of being from South Asia but rather suggests being brown, networking immigrants in the United States who are marked as deviant bodies by the U.S. state that needs their low-wage labor but denies them access to, in Lisa Lowe's words, "the narrative of American citizenship."[5] Using the term *desi* is also to recognize the processes, structural and ideological, by which their difference—national origins, religious affiliation, cultural and class backgrounds—are threatening and contaminating, effectively casting them as the racial Other that cannot be included in the white nationalist homeland. DRUM's political ideology emphasizes a critical and oppositional stance toward the American nation-state and its ideal, white normative subject.

As we will see, the DRUM website exemplifies the potential of online media: by interrogating the homeland, and its reliance on raced and classed identities, the site reveals the instability of the categories of Indian and Indian American. DRUM pushes past the stereotyped image of the Indian immigrant and focuses instead on the often ignored elements of South Asian immigrant identity: being working class, being a youth, being a woman, and being Muslim.[6]

My central argument in this chapter is that the DRUM website foregrounds a particular vision of citizenship among working-class South Asian immigrants, wherein belonging and rights are articulated to and negotiated through issues of race, immigration, and networking. The site represents its immigrant members as active political participants in their U.S. homeland who cultivate a sense of belonging for themselves by engaging and resisting the disciplinary strategies of the technologized, racial state. In doing so, the activists of DRUM reveal how belonging is produced and enacted through the transnational nature of the Web, and through the immigrant, labor, and racial coalitions that are enriched by online media. Central to the site's politics is the reimagining of South Asian immigrants as a raced, classed, transnational formation in a relationship of struggle and negotiation with the U.S. nation-state.

Race and Class in Rethinking Desi Webs

DRUM's mission, described on its website, includes mobilizing and building, "the leadership of thousands of low-income, South Asian immigrants to lead social and policy change that impacts their own lives—from immigrant rights to education reform, civil rights, and worker's justice."[7] Since the attacks of September 11, 2001, in New York, DRUM, founded in 2000, has been actively involved in critiquing and responding to the U.S. state regimes of terror, anti-immigration, and border control as low-income South Asians in the city have found themselves increasingly targeted through strategies of surveillance, policing, and deportation, all in the guise of security enforcement. While DRUM members are active in the New York area, they also do an equal amount of activist work online. In its early years, DRUM's website, which bore the URL[8] drumnation.org, was heavily text and image-centric, but the site has been revamped in the past few years to include more multimedia features and more interactive, participatory elements. The site has expanded its media coverage section to include video links, introduced an archive feature, produced a national webinar on the topic of community organizing, and introduced a blog section, "DRUM Beats Blog." In March 2013, DRUM further revamped its site by linking a Facebook page and a YouTube channel to its homepage.[9] It also phased out the older URL Drumnation.org and rearranged some of its website content. While much of this chapter focuses on content available at drumnyc.org, it also draws on earlier iterations of the DRUM website and related content. In many instances, such content is not available on a public archive (for example, though Internet Archive gives access to the main page, it has not archived the content posted under the links on the main page), and I draw on my personal archive to support my discussion. While some of the content I cite in my following discussion might no longer exist on the DRUM website, the themes and practices addressed through older web content continue to be very relevant to DRUM social justice activism online.

To begin with, the physical territories that are invoked in the definition of *desi* on the DRUM website indicate the counter-hegemonic politics supported by DRUM. In addition to the seven countries of South Asia, the site states that desis or people of South Asian descent also are part of the populace in Africa, Fiji, Guyana, the United Kingdom, and Trinidad. At the same time, DRUM positions itself as an online space marking the particular concerns faced by the desi community in New York City. The change in the web address from drumnation to drumnyc seems to parallel the intensification of the organization's focus on New York City and is a subtle but important gesture toward a better alignment between the site's web identity and its political ideology.

In addition to signaling its local affiliation through the website address, the specificity of its investment in New York City is also exemplified through the documentation of DRUM's presence in City Hall for the passage of the Community Safety Act in 2013, its monthly membership meetings in Jackson Heights, its community workshops in the Bronx, and its Dignity in Schools Campaign in the Queens public school district in 2012. Drumnyc.org links the assault on the civil and human rights of immigrants, especially Muslim immigrants, to the desi condition in the post-9/11 era, as racism, xenophobia and surveillance, and religious intolerance became touchstones of the desi struggle for dignity and equality.

DRUM, like another local social justice organization, New York Taxi Workers Alliance (NYTWA), created in 1998, reiterates the importance of situating the struggles that face working-class, daily wage earners and immigrants facing poor working conditions in relation to local governance and policy-making bodies. NYTWA, created through the leadership of Bhairavi Desai, a working-class immigrant from New Jersey, is a union representing the interests of New York City cab drivers. The more than forty thousand drivers, who comprise what is considered the world's largest taxi industry, represent a multiethnic community, many of whom are South Asian immigrants.[10] Like NYTWA, DRUM is also founded by a female desi activist; Monami Maulik, who is executive director and founder of DRUM, had previously worked with NYTWA.

DRUM is a membership-based organization, and many of its members (numbering over 1,500 as of January 2014) are desi youth and women from working-class backgrounds.[11] The layout of the website foregrounds affective and embodied representations of South Asian women and youth in public spaces as a collective: We see images of them as they march, hold banners, shout slogans, and conduct rallies at DRUM's Jackson Heights headquarters, the city streets, public square, and outside City Hall (see Figure 4).

The emphasis on women and youth also underlines some of the key community projects undertaken by DRUM, including one titled Youth Power! and another titled South Asian Workers Center. Youth Power! is a youth-only run program that empowers desis between the age of thirteen and twenty-one (covering those who might be in high school, college, or entering the workforce) to

FIGURE 4. DRUM members at a press conference and rally outside of City Hall demanding the passage of the Inspector General Bill for oversight of the New York Police Department in 2013.
Credit: Homepage of DRUM, drumnyc.org 2013

become agents of social justice and speaking truth to power in the areas most connected with their lives, such as school policies, peer behavior, and preparation for college.[12] The South Asian Workers Center more broadly addresses the poor working conditions affecting those in the service and low-wage industries, many of whom are women. Additionally there is a catering cooperative for women that focuses on helping women who possess cooking skills but are not organized or aware of their rights (also linked to their lack of education and resources) to generate income in a manner that builds their community power and dignity.[13]

While *desi* as used above implicates working-class women and youth of South Asian descent living in New York City in the post-9/11 climate at the heart of the organization's membership, the DRUM website articulates the locally produced identity within a transnational context of immigration, racialized citizenship cultures, and global labor and capital flows. The "About Us" section along with the several factoids dispersed through the site (including its previous versions) illustrates this point well. The site and the organization trace their beginning in the year 2000 to an event that on the surface has little to do with Indian or South Asian immigrants.[14] The event was the February 2000 acquittal of four New York Police Department officers in the shooting and killing of Amadou Diallo, a low-income Guinean immigrant in the Bronx in 1999. The acquittal resulted in community outrage as it was reported that the NYPD officers in plain clothes fired forty-one shots at an unarmed Diallo after erroneously identifying him as a criminal they were after. The People's Justice, a grass-roots NYC coalition of community organizations, issued a call for "41 days of Action," wherein a multiracial collective of civil rights and social justice organizations held public rallies, marches, and performances to draw attention to the specific case and the broader issues of racial profiling, police brutality, and community organizing against the injustice.[15]

While DRUM traces its beginnings to a racially charged New York city event revealing unjust state measures against immigrants and racial minorities, the factoids, which were presented in early versions of the site, linked issues of undocumented immigration, deportation, and racial alliances to South Asian immigrant politics. The facts listed included, first, that there are approximately one million undocumented desis in New York City; second, that this figure represents 22 percent of the total undocumented population in the city, making desis the second largest population within the undocumented category following Latinos (who account for 27 percent) and third, that thousands of New York City desis have faced home raids and have been deported since 9/11 as part of Homeland Security's war on terror measures.[16]

This is an important intervention in the utopian narratives about Indian and South Asian Americans and their elite migration cultures. DRUM's efforts in documenting information about the concerns and numbers of undocumented and illegal South Asian migrants are being replicated in other online spaces such as the website of the national organization South Asian Americans Leading Together (SAALT), which works on behalf of immigrant rights. Eschewing the simplified concept of roots as referring to a singular origin, authenticity, and history, DRUM instead envisions its social justice efforts as "rooted in working in solidarity with people of the Global South for just global trade, economic, and foreign policies."[17] Desi, on drumnyc.org, is a counter-hegemonic identity that seeks to interrogate the elitist, racist, and capitalist agendas of the nation-state, particularly the United States, while highlighting the global resonance of oppositional politics.

The typical conservative use of the term *desi* has been a code for Indian, Hindu, middle-class, heteronormative cultural values in South Asian diasporic spaces.[18] On the Web, the Desi Hits! site, desihits.com, exemplifies a normative understanding of desi location, especially those shaped by youth cultures in the United States. The site, currently a very popular multimedia entertainment portal for South Asians in the United States, was created in 2006 by three Indian immigrants. One of the most visible cofounders of the site, featured in magazines and business segments about Indian presence online, is Anjula Acharia-Bath, who was once described in the Indian American magazine *India Currents* as "a shrewd entrepreneur who has aligned DesiHits! with numerous Silicon Valley venture capitalists."[19] Acharia-Bath, who apparently has played a key role in getting angel investors for Desi Hits!, has also shaped the site's partnership with Apple's iTunes to make Desi Hits! a competitive hub for the purchase of Bollywood remix music. The New York–headquartered site describes its target audience, urban desis, as "bilingual, trendy, cosmopolitan and as likely to jive to Madonna as they are to Bollywood." Outlining its emphasis on Bollywood remix cultures, the site asserts that "bi-cultural remixes uniquely represent the next generation (and beyond) South Asian experience."[20] In addition to featuring Bollywood content, the site regularly features desi remix and hip-hop artists including Jay Sean, Tigerstyle, M.I.A., DJ Rekha, DJ Suketu, Nindy Kaur, Culture Shock, and the Bilz and Kashif. With reference to desi remix cultures, Sunaina Maira in her work on second-generation Indian American youth cultures has demonstrated that while India's Bollywood films are immensely popular, they are also regularly "remixed" with Punjabi folk music known as Bhangra and American hip-hop to create a particular Indian American sound.[21] Desi Hits! reiterates that trajectory of mixing "Indian" with "American" to produce a desi sound. While the politics of remix for disrupting conventions cannot be ignored, the institutional framing by Desi Hits! of what the remix implies for the South Asian desi's location in the United States reinforces a traditional and narrow framing. The site employs the jargon of East and West to frame remix, essentially suggesting that remixing Bollywood with Western sound is a popular and profitable enterprise in this age of multiculturalism.

The exclusive focus on Bollywood and Indian Americans to mark the cultural space of desi and the construction of desi as part Indian, part Western, can be understood as a migration of hegemonic tendencies that were present in "older" media such as film. In her study of South Asian diasporic film, Jigna Desai problematizes films such as *American Desi*, *Namaste*, and *ABCD* (American Born Confused Desi) for their exclusive focus on Indian American (instead of South Asian American) identities and their construction of desi identities as shaped by a culture of confusion around belonging. She argues: "These culturally nationalist films that characterize desi identity as being caught between two cultures inadvertently forward a homogenous, normative, and transparent understanding of desi subjectivity. Very few films render the possibility of culture as open and dynamic, instead seeking to define South Asian-America as a space suspended between the Manichean binary of East and West, in lieu of a space that is heterogeneous and hybrid."[22]

In an interview, Acharia-Bath refers to herself as a brown subject keenly aware of the power hierarchies shaping the mainstream and minority order in the United Kingdom, where she grew up, and in her present home, the United States.[23] Yet, her articulation of desis as brown in the context of the website she runs seems more aligned with the commodification of brown as ethnic chic and desi power as financial clout rather than any overt expression of racialization of South Asian immigrants.[24] This is tellingly on display when responding to a question about the Desi Hits! strategy and plans for becoming the one-stop portal for the sale of Bollywood "fusion" music for desis and nondesis alike (the latter referenced on the site's "About us" page as "those curious about desi culture"). Acharia-Bath concludes her answer by suggesting that "if we as desis demonstrate our collective buying power, the mainstream will notice us."[25] The idea that economic clout exercised through consumption will fully open the gates toward integration into the mainstream is undoubtedly problematic in many ways. The notion that the consumption practices of a minority group are what can legitimately be the channel for greater levels of acceptance by the mainstream and maybe into the mainstream seems to be the product of twenty-first-century framings of model minority that have been recalibrated to better resonate with neoliberal capitalist agendas.

Relatedly, problematic though it might be, the incorporation of brown as ethnic chic is a strategy that has easily migrated to the web environment and is exemplified through the presence of the e-clothing company Desi Threads (desithreads.com). As the tagline "clothing for your culture" indicates, Desi Threads makes and markets clothing with the aim of inspiring, in their words, "desi pride."[26] While the Houston-based company describes itself alternately as a "new generation clothing company" and the "hottest urban desi clothing company," the articulation of *desi* as urban, cool, and hip continues with the design and look of the clothes, which are meant to allow desis to "create their own identity." When I first encountered this site in 2009, the framing image that covered almost half of the main page was of a young female wearing a brown-colored T-shirt with the words "Brown is sexy" written across the front; the sexualized pose of the female model was yet another reminder that normative understandings of gender and sexuality also play a crucial role in consolidating the hegemonic discourse of desi identities in the United States.[27]

Other notably worded T-shirts include "Desi Inside" (a rebranding of the famous Intel image by referencing the high-profile as well as prolific contribution of Indian immigrants to the software company's success), "My other T-shirt got outsourced" (a tongue-in-cheek comment on the Indian role in the offshore business industry and the controversies in the United States around it), and "Thank you Come Again" (with an image of Apu, who is credited with that phrase on the animated television show *The Simpsons*). Although Desi Threads contributes to a niche market and employs several youth-centric signifiers of desi cool and to that extent loosens some of the more traditional boundaries of representing desi in the terrain of popular culture, the commodification of desi as cool, sexy, consumptive brown bodies cannot be overlooked. It is pertinent here that as a clothing company, Desi Threads relies heavily on brown bodies to model and sell its products. When the sexualized body of a woman wearing a "Brown is sexy" T-shirt is part of the new appeal of desi cool and desi pride, we must note the overlapping frames of the new hegemony with the old as heteronormative gender and sexual ideologies in the Indian nation and its diaspora are summoned to reposition desi in the age of network capitalism as "ethnicity, inc." and minority culture pride; in the new hegemony, while markers such as language, profession, and cultural taste recur, racial location is elided.

The avoidance of race, or what some have discussed in terms of "racial ambivalence," within the Indian and South Asian diaspora is tied to the privileging of idealized notions of culture and authentic ethnic identities within conservative factions of the community, which in turn are tied to their investment in the model minority image.[28] Focusing on professional and economic successes, middle-class Indian immigrants, more focused on their diasporic roots, oftentimes remain ambiguous with regard to their stance about racial difference, racism, and where they fit in.[29] The ambivalence is underpinned by the simultaneous presence of a desire to be close (or closer than other racial minorities) to the white normative ideal as well as the recognition that they are not "white." Speaking to the desire to be seen as white, Vijay Prashad, in *Karma of Brown Folk*, notes that many Indians participate in a racial fantasy where they are grouped along with whites in a "racial family called Aryan," believing in turn that such a mythology might very well open the doors to their acceptance.[30] Such an investment in whiteness also encourages the antiblack racism that has been observed within the Indian and South Asian communities.[31] Yet they also recognize that no matter their stellar achievements through relentless work and capital accumulation, their cultural status is built on white colonial and imperial epistemologies that relegate racial minorities to a subordinate position. Whether that divide is expressed through overt racism or subtle forms of discrimination, Indians are eventually forced to confront the fact that they will never be considered white. Yet despite such recognition, many immigrants still believe in the promise of the model minority stereotype and strenuously distance themselves from any form of resistance politics that reveal their frustrations with the white American status quo.

A related concern, one to which critical Asian American studies, along with Native American and Latino studies, is increasingly trying to respond, is the analytical and intellectual gaps in polarizing the race debate along white and black; the binary, as Aihwa Ong argues, symbolically whitens or blackens Asian Americans when they are not placed in a position of mediation between the two.[32] The inadequacy within academic debates is itself a symptom of the manner in which race relations are addressed, discussed, and presented in the public sphere. Hence complicating the racial ambivalence of Indian and South Asian immigrants is the racial invisibility with which they have historically had to contend.

The question of race, of course, is not just complex but is also shifting and evolving. As Stuart Hall has observed, it is a shifting signifier, with new contexts and meanings attached to it. Recent studies of desi politics and culture in the United States have foregrounded the decade of the 2000s for rearticulating desi identity and location to resistance of white, Anglo-centric hegemony and solidarity with other subaltern groups and political practices. As the contributors in *Desi Rap: Hip-Hop and South Asian America* illustrate, hip-hop, especially rap and the spoken word, emerged as a legitimate vehicle of cultural expression within U.S. desi communities by the mid-2000s and linked the question of race and class to the political subjectivity of becoming desi.[33] Nitasha Tamar Sharma's work on desi hip-hop and Shalini Shankar's ethnography of desi teen culture in Silicon Valley reinforce the idea that the reconfiguration of desi-ness in the present needs to be understood as an everyday negotiation of questions of race, class, immigration, public presence, and political subjectivity.[34] While shifts in migration, mobility, social class, popular culture, and political ideologies are important aspects shaping the resignification of desi, I would add online media as another crucial feature that is remediating the category of *desi* in contemporary times. In this regard, DRUM exemplifies an appropriation of the ultimate symbol of digital capitalism—the Web—to engender what Monisha Das Gupta has called "space-making politics," where organizations "create structures and resources that transform daily life into an arena of political contest."[35]

As the previous chapters have shown, websites targeting Indian immigrants very often serve up a narrative relating to the deployment of the Web to better serve the needs of the nationally imagined but transnationally located Indian immigrant; whether commercially or community oriented, such sites through their website "origin" stories redraw essentially the lines of the web community in alignment with the elitist and cultural bias of the hegemonic Indian nation-state. DRUM highlights oppositional politics and the racism faced by desis and invites closer alliances with other minority groups because of racial and class identification with them. Instead of transnational alliances that reimagine citizenship in dual or flexible contexts, DRUM's desi locations are routed via a critical political stance towards neoimperial globalization, institutionalized forms of white normativity, and a collaborative stance toward racial and class identification, not bounded by national "origin" or culture.

The DRUM website reframes the contexts of transnationalism, immigration, and citizenship cultures in its "About Us" section by articulating racism toward an African immigrant in New York, xenophobia toward Muslim immigrants since 9/11, neoimperial labor practices toward the people of the Global South, and South Asian ancestry-shaping communities in several areas including Africa, Fiji, and Trinidad to the category of *desi*; in light of my reference in the previous chapter to the Indian state's deliberate exclusion of its diasporic communities in Fiji and Trinidad when unveiling their plans for dual citizenship, DRUM's inclusion of the same communities within its framework of history and context is a profoundly political act. While this tactic ruptures the Indian national as the center of the desi imagination, the insertion of imagery supporting female- and youth-shaped collectivities shifts the representation of "rising" and networking desis away from middle-class, Indian male, techno-wired figures to reveal other formations of minority and immigrant power. By doing so, it recodes the meaning of desi and destabilizes the hegemonic notions of desis as Indian model minority elites, as racially ambivalent or disengaged, and as politically inactive.

CHAPTER FOUR

Desi Links: Online Activism of Immigrants of Color

In this section, I draw on the "Programs" page of the DRUM website, which lists four key initiatives supported by the organization: Global Justice, a program that works toward social justice in the Global South; Racial and Immigrant Justice, a program that is invested in just immigration reform policies and in the ending of raids on low-income, Muslim immigrant homes; Youth Power!, a program that is invested in issues such as student safety, dignity in school, and the DREAM act;[36] and the South Asian Workers Center program, which focuses on labor issues faced by those in the low end of the service industries such as taxi driving, domestic work, restaurant work, and construction; the site lists unpaid wages, poor working conditions, and a lack of knowledge about their rights as key areas of struggle. It also addresses concerns about language barriers, gender politics, and fears about immigration enforcement as obstacles that get in the way of low-wage workers' claims to rights.

Political activism especially around issues of race, class, gender, and sexuality is marginalized within conservative histories of the politics and struggles of South Asian immigrants that reproduce ideologies of nation-centric diaspora, model minority, and ethnic minority in a multicultural society.[37] In this scenario, the potential of online media as a critical space for making visible community agendas and political viewpoints that are counter-hegemonic and in dissonance with mainstreamed representations of the political locations of immigrants cannot be overlooked. Furthermore, when working-class struggles, racialization, immigration policies, state-sponsored policing practices, and transnational politics are constitutive of the activism of a site such as drum-nyc.org, the significance of the online representation extends beyond that of visibility to include the politics of the techno-mediation of discourses of race, class, immigrants, and cultural citizenship.

As websites and online media increasingly become part of our everyday cultural and communication experience, it is imperative to interrogate the practices and politics informing web cultures. Furthermore, when groups such as immigrants rights activists, rarely visible on U.S. national media and communication forms such as television, make their presence and politics visible in online media, it provides us with a ripe opportunity to ponder the implications of the transnational form of the Web for disrupting ideologies of national community and immigrants as cultural noncitizens (in that they are always coded as being from somewhere else and therefore never quite belonging here).

The unhinging of dissent and rights from nation-based conceptualizations of citizenship is key to critical modes of transnational activism, argues Monisha Das Gupta in her provocative analysis of South Asian queer, labor, and feminist organizations in the United States.[38] She writes, "Just as global capital has led to denationalized 'global cities' within national borders ... so the migrant struggles for justice in their homes, workplaces, and communities in the United States have led to new spatial expressions—the creation of transnational social justice organizations."[39] Pointing to a model of immigrant activism within the South Asian community that has been developing since the 1980s, Das Gupta notes that the formulation of a "transnational complex of rights" is at the core of its development and politics.[40] Ideas of model minority or dual citizenship are appealing to many in the immigrant community as a viable location for their marginality to be integrated into the mainstream order; it is what Das Gupta calls "the familiar framework of second-class citizens asking for first-class status."[41] Yet the implicit racism, gender bias, elitism, and heteronormativity in such constructions make them incongruent with the political and cultural ideologies advanced by feminist, labor, and queer organizations. Hence, the latter, Das Gupta argues, "inventively draw on rights regimes that are local, national (laws of more than one nation can be involved), and international in order to claim entitlements for their constituencies, who are otherwise treated as practically without rights in their nation of residence. Within this complex, migrants, not citizens, claim and bear rights."[42]

Against this backdrop, I discuss the DRUM website, drumnyc.org, for its politics in expanding the association of desi activism beyond the South Asian community to include a multiracial working-class and immigrant coalition within the United States and connected to the Global South. While information technologies are imbricated in the politics of transnational economies, global migration, and cultural citizenship, desi critique, as it emerges on the site, forces us to acknowledge the contradictions in the political, economic, and cultural spheres of neoliberal, capitalist America.[43] Drumnyc.org articulates the material, virtual, and ideological contexts of desi belonging and struggle to the social justice movements of immigrants of color and racial minorities in the United States, in turn challenging the "cybertypes," to use Lisa Nakamura's term, associated with racial minorities, (South) Asian Americans, and immigrants online. Nakamura elaborates that cybertypes are "more than just racial stereotypes 'ported' to a new medium ... they reflect the ways that machine-enabled interactivity gives rise to images of race that both stem from a common cultural logic and seek to redress anxieties about the ways that computer-enabled communication can challenge these old logics. They perform a crucial role in the signifying practice of cyberspace; they stabilize a sense of a white self and identity."[44]

Although the cybertyping of Indians that most often bleeds into understandings of middle-class South Asian Americans renders them as a wired, mobile minority comfortably belonging within digital capitalist and neoliberal citizenship formations, DRUM instead mobilizes the online to reveal the force of the U.S. state that regulates racial minorities by creating various checkpoints in the everyday transit of life as students, daily-wage earners, low-income families, homemakers, parents, and young citizens. It is also significant that the site's assertion of a coalition of interests articulated around immigrant rights and social justice is not organized around the notion of a pan–Asian American ethnicity, which, as Yen Le Espiritu has documented, was first forged in the 1960s within the struggle for civil rights.[45] As some of the examples below indicate, the category of Asian American is unsustainable as there are implicit hierarchies of nation and class and religion within its categorization.

The Racial and Immigrant Justice Program is organized along local and national campaigns to end racial profiling and create a just immigration reform through policy changes and community alliances. The page clearly "names" the core issues in each campaign, identifies the problem it seeks to tackle, and subsequently lists an array of local and national campaigns of which DRUM is a part in its efforts to create a solution. For example, in its End Racial Profiling campaign, DRUM offers the following context: "South Asians make up one of the largest undocumented populations in New York City. Large numbers are also well targeted by policies that racially and religiously profile them as immigrants, Muslims, low-wage workers, and youth. All of these factors push community members to live in a state of fear, and become marginalized, criminalized, and easily exploitable."[46] Elaborating on the nature of the problem of racial profiling, the site identifies one key source of the problem as the 2006 published ninety-page NYPD report, "Radicalization in the West: The Homegrown Threat."[47] This quantitative analysis poses the research question: "How do 'unremarkable' people in the domestic national scene emerge as radical terrorists?" It then follows up with a methodological section and offers its conclusion that the solution to the problem of radical domestic terrorism is greater profiling of the "unremarkable" people.

While this report signed by the police commissioner of NYPD is the officially created narrative about the need for racial profiling, DRUM offers a counter-knowledge by locating the report as the (racist) problem and including its retraction within its array of solutions, which include conducting surveys of South Asian immigrants to document their experiences with law enforcement and subsequently create a report that can be used by policy makers. To indicate the feasibility and actualization of these solutions, the site carries links to its local and national allies in this plan of action. Key among them is the School of Law at City University of New York (CUNY); in 2009, the school launched a program called CLEAR (Creating Law Enforcement Accountability and Responsibility) through which senior law students work closely with South Asian, Muslim, and Arab community organizations in New York, aid its members with free legal representation, and help with conducting surveys of immigrants' encounters with law enforcement. One campaign within this program is to conduct "Know your Rights" workshops in mosques, schools, homes, and neighborhoods in NYC to counter the escalation of immigration raids. Another ally linked here is the national advocacy group South Asian Americans Leading Together (SAALT), which works toward inclusion of South Asian voices in the U.S. public sphere. DRUM's activities around immigration reform are in the areas of reduction of detention and deportation, equal labor rights for undocumented workers, and noncompliance with the REAL ID Act, a federal law governing security and authentication procedures for state drivers' licenses and ID cards that has come under sharp criticism from several immigrant and civil rights groups, among others. The SAALT site similarly reveals its predominant address of issues of xenophobia, racial profiling, and targeting of Muslims, thereby reinforcing DRUM's perspective that racism, religion-based discrimination, and efforts to deport "unwanted" migrants are some of the most urgent "desi" issues facing the community. In this context, being desi has less to do with a direct relationship with South Asia and more to do with the reinscription of colonial and imperial tendencies in the contemporary conflicts around globalization, terrorism, foreign policy, and security. While CUNY and SAALT are in New York City, the Washington, D.C.–based Rights Working Group (RWG), a coalition of 340 human rights and justice organizations across the nation, is DRUM's national ally in this program.

The tactical placement of SAALT, CUNY's Clear Program, and RWG web links under the local and national campaigns section signals a relationship of relevance. Linking, as George P. Landow notes, "involves the essence of hypertext technology."[48] While the nonsequential linking of data creates an open, decentered text, the articulation of local and national allies as links generates a new organization of knowledge and establishes a new field of relations where none were visible before; in this new field of political alliances, the institutional knowledge provided by NYPD is reframed through the information produced through another set of institutional alliances of progressive legal voices, student organizations, and social justice nonprofit groups. Relatedly, although DRUM is a recent entrant to social media, it has been referenced in the Twitter feeds and Facebook page of SAALT as well as other non–South Asian immigrants rights groups. Such references to DRUM's work in the social media landscape foreground its relevance across multiple online locations.

While through its program on Racial and Immigrant Justice DRUM highlights the material reality of the desi body subject to racial profiling, immigrant enforcement, deportation, and detention, its program on Youth Power! reveals microsites of belonging, such as New York City public schools as sites of regulation, surveillance, and policing of immigrant youth, which in turn shape the processes of racialization of desis and their sense of identity as brown immigrants.

YouthPower! is a very successful program run by DRUM members aged thirteen to twenty-one with the goal of helping desi youth take charge of the struggles they have in schools, colleges, and the workplace—such as constant surveillance and fear-inducing police actions—and build their power as working-class, brown youth leaders who can work together and effect policy change for themselves and others like them. The program enables young desi students, many of them Muslim and undocumented, to lead a campaign as part of the Urban Youth Collaborative (created in 2004 by high school students for school reform) and Student Safety Coalition to address the practices of the police in New York City schools, especially in low-income neighborhoods.[49] The campaign was spurred by the 2006 groundbreaking report "Education Not Deportation: Impacts of New York City School Safety Policies on South Asian Immigrant Youth," where DRUM members conducted survey research and concluded that almost half of the students interviewed reported being questioned or threatened by police officials in and around the school premises as part of the safety implementation policies in public schools following 9/11.[50] Asserting that such aggressive behavior of the police was generating a fear culture and resulting in greater levels of school dropouts in the community, DRUM youth researchers, however, did not isolate the problem as a distinctly South Asian one. Rather, while noting the specific ways in which South Asian immigrants are prone to profiling, the report concluded that the state's techno-surveillance was a multiracial, working-class issue, because, in their words, "we see that our community's struggles for racial justice are rooted in all low-income communities facing the same issues."[51]

Immigrant activism around race and racism has been recharged especially since the very overt and insidious manner of race-based Othering that has become systemic to post-9/11 America. In a compelling ethnographic study on South Asian teenagers grappling with and responding to the disciplinary power of U.S. state surveillance after the events of 9/11, Sunaina Maira explicitly links questions of race to regimes of globalization, war, and terror. Maira argues that for desi teenagers, racialization, or the process by which a racial subjectivity is produced, is shaped by everyday experiences of work, education, leisure, family life, religion, and mobility even as those experiences are shaped by larger historical and political events.[52] She addresses the incorporation of the racial difference of the Arab, South Asian, and Muslim immigrant figure into the hegemonic reordering of the figure of the terrorist, the enemy, and the deviant Other in post-9/11 United States.[53]

Maira's research on her working-class subjects reveals that race is crucial to the latter's struggles over belonging and meaning in everyday contexts. For example, she notes that the sites where immigrants feel the disciplining moves of the state most acutely are those pertaining to school, labor, and immigration policies affecting work, travel, and family life, where their status as outsiders and culturally different is constantly marked.[54] While desi youth try to negotiate their racialized status in the contemporary United States, they have to struggle with, among other things, the cooptation of their dissent-based citizenship culture by the liberal multicultural ideologies of the American state. This is exemplified in the strategic inclusion of culturally diverse bodies in public demonstrations of the antiwar movement, thereby preempting any discussion of the overlaps in the demonization of the enemies within and outside the nation.[55] Maira's exploration of the politics of cultural citizenship in this framework is useful for my present study, since it opens up a space for thinking about online culture as a site of mediation with regard to the production of citizenship and belonging—for example, drumnyc.org as a site that imagines belonging but also reimagines the sites of work, school, labor, and immigration from the perspective of working-class desis.

As a site representing the activism of South Asian working-class immigrants in the areas of labor, education, political participation, and civil rights, drumnyc.org offers us an insight into the diverse nature of political and social justice work that falls within the category of online activism. The literature on online activism largely suggests that while activists have included the online into their strategies of media use, a more significant phenomenon is the transformation of activism in the wake of current media technologies. Characterizing political activism on the Internet as cyberactivism, Martha McCaughey and Michael D. Ayers note, however, that the use of technology for activism is not in itself "new," since "social-movement groups have historically incorporated new technologies into their social-change struggles ... to circulate information, make statements, raise consciousness, raise hell."[56] What is perhaps distinct about online activism, then, is its ability to represent the multifaceted and complex realities of the political struggle by summoning multiple temporalities and spatialities through links, uploaded documents, online text, images, and video; while each can be considered a discrete text in and of itself, the narrative on the page, as exemplified through its spatialization along the lines of problem and solution, reveals how closely embedded the political is with the economies of the homepage.

By articulating a local and national network of alliances and virtually embedding them in proximity with each other, DRUM enacts its politics of citizenship through hypertextual framing and rendering the homepage as a political space for networking. The site forcefully shifts the focus from diaspora-centric framings of community to transnational contexts of immigration policies, labor issues, state power, racial politics, religious discrimination, and gender bias. It represents DRUM's forging of new affiliations and alliances that disrupt their identity as solely South Asian. Articulating linkages with organizations such as the National Network for Immigrant and Refugee Rights, Rights Working Group, and United for Peace and Justice, DRUM redefines the scope of desi involvement and consciousness, online and within the U.S. nation-space. Finally, in representing the organization's coalition-building efforts through its Global Justice Program, DRUM lists national organizations such as the National Network for Immigrant and Refugee Rights and the United National Anti-War Committee as part of its physical and virtual network.[57] The Resources link includes educational tools such as downloadable rights and campaign brochures, published findings of reports undertaken by DRUM, web-based information sources, articles on immigrants right activism, and DRUM's sole webinar thus far, while the media link functions as an archive of the press coverage of DRUM's activism.

Lisa Nakamura's reflection that the critical study of Asian American new media "centers on the possibility of hybrid and de-essentialized Asian identities that address contemporary narratives of power and difference" is pertinent here.[58] While the DRUM site calls attention to working-class desis, it simultaneously veers away from representing them as a monolithic block; instead, through specific programs and initiatives it foregrounds how gender, age, vocation, race, and religion differently shape the struggles in which desi activists are engaged. Drumnyc.org visually and discursively imagines a multigenerational coalition of alliances in its representation of desi-ness.

Additionally, the visual cultures of representing physical bodies on an activist site add a new layer of meaning to the viewpoint that "a substantial component of political activism has always been the activist's willingness to put her body on the line."[59] While the site has not replaced the street, it has engendered a remediation of the notions of public space, community forms of protest, and activist bodies; drumnyc.org's visual archiving of desi bodies is one such ex-

FIGURE 5. DRUM Youth Power! members at the 2011 Open Mic on "Desi: Undocumented and Unafraid."
Credit: Homepage of DRUM, drumnyc.org 2013

pression of the resignification of the brown, immigrant, politically conscious body. Relatedly, and speaking to the idea of the site as enacting or performing its politics of citizenship, DRUM's deployment of images reveals the embodied and affective nature of this struggle. While the textual discourse on the site references how fear, official power, and legal enforcements oppress desi bodies, the visual narrative privileges the response of desis to such systemic violence (see Figure 5).

The images used include scenes of organized community protests over the abuse of students in a high school in Jamaica, Queens; nationwide demonstrations to urge the Obama administration for immigration reform; supporting the New Orleans Workers' Center for Racial Justice in its campaign to end the "slave-like" conditions for thirty Mexican "guest workers" in the strawberry fields of Amite, Louisiana; and endorsing a protest march in Times Square against the violence toward Palestinians in Gaza.[60] Images of DRUM-led demonstrations in public spaces such as the Brooklyn Bridge, City Hall, the streets of Jackson Heights, and the National Capitol in Washington, D.C., where desis share the space with other immigrant, working-class, and racial minority groups that appropriate the category of desi (and its conventional meaning around ancestry), circulate new meanings about desis' racial consciousness, class and religious identities, and community-based practices of organization and political participation (see Figure 4, p. 121).

In the context of South Asian immigrant rights activism, DRUM's online visibility has a multilayered politics attached to it. Mainstream U.S. media rarely offer any substantive or continual treatment of the complexities of immigrant politics, much less of its activist cultures that sharply critique the status quo of state and civil society.[61] At the same time, the Internet presents certain unique possibilities for social organizing, connection, and participation for immigrants unlike previous communication media such as film or television. Such possibilities revolve around the temporal-spatial complexities of the online environment, such as its virtual cartography of transnational mediations in national territories and its technological and institutional characteristics that enable communities hitherto invisible in mainstream media to be rendered visible.

From Screens to Web Pages: Homeland Politics and Racialized Citizenship

Scholarship on Asian American representations in mainstream U.S. and alternative or independent media has highlighted their relationship to the dynamics of border policing of the American body politic.[62] Employing the phrase "screening Asian Americans," Peter X Feng has argued that *screen* can be understood in three senses of the term: as a veil (which conceals from view), as a filter (which sifts the desirable from the undesirable), and as a process of projecting cinematic images.[63] Several scholars have discussed the relationship between Hollywood's investment in producing the white nationalist imagination of the American homeland and its tradition of representing Asian Americans (often not distinguished from Asians) within formulaic conventions underpinned by racist and sexist ideologies, including, the "yellow peril," the "brown hordes," "Charlie Chan," "Madame Butterfly," and the desexualized "geek," among others.[64] With respect to U.S. network television, Darrell Hamamoto used the concept of "controlling images" to address the objectification and "psychosocial" dominance of Asian Americans through the textual, ideological, and institutional practices of network programming.[65] Shilpa Davé has theorized the notion of "brown voice" to address the role of accent in locating South Asian immigrants in the U.S. (televisual) landscape as "foreign but understandable."[66] One can add here that while in the past few years there have been several examples of mainstream television characters being South Asian, the model minority image, whether a doctor, engineer, or technology professional, is not far removed from such characterizations.[67] Writing about the emergence of the model minority image in Hollywood depictions of "Asians" in the 1960s through films such as the 1961 film *Flower Drum Song*, Gina Marchetti observed that it represented "a new bent on racist representations" of Asian Americans, where the depiction of the minority's model behavior is inextricably intertwined with fears and fantasies of the white, heteronormative American nation.[68] In contemporary representations, one might consider how a show such as NBC's *Outsourced*, where the humor is apparently at the expense of the American protagonist in an Indian setting, might be read against the grain to reveal the underpinnings of white nationalist anxiety about Indian model minorities, especially in the realms of technological and economic capital.[69] If mainstream U.S. film and television, the screens so to speak, are mired in the white nationalist logics that predominantly shape them even in this era of global television and convergence culture, do the differently organized structures and dynamics of the web page enable a reimagining of the racialized South Asian immigrant or Asian American? If they do, how might we understand the iteration of *desi* on drumnyc.org within the contexts of the American body politic and the policing of its material and metaphorical borders?[70]

Here I focus on two specific web pages on the DRUM website, "Media" and "Blog," to elaborate on my argument that the homepage of drumnyc.org interrogates the trope of belonging embedded within the dominant imagination of the U.S. homeland as a geographical territory with borders that outline what lies "outside" its boundaries. While the Blog page no longer exists, its relatively brief appearance on the site in 2011–2012 nevertheless is very significant both for the content of its entry and for signaling the direction DRUM's online activism is taking in the age of social media. I argue that through its blog and the media section, DRUM foregrounds the point that there are continuities and resonances between the regulatory and repressive mechanisms of the American state expressed at the physical boundary marking the end of the national territory and the expressions of disciplinary state power regulating the bodies of immigrants of color, working-class, and Muslim subjects within the nation's schools, workplaces, homes, and public spaces. Not only do the images, voices, and narratives embedded on the media and blog section reframe the hegemonic view of the border and articulate it to boundaries within the nation, but they also resignify the border as a space for fostering alliances that transgress the racial order advanced by the state. By doing so, they simultaneously point to the limits of cultural citizenship within multicultural America and the emergent (and possibly radical) modalities for recasting the racialized politics of inclusion, exclusion, and belonging in the United States within the temporal-spatial logic of the Web.

"DRUM Beats Blog," as the blog page was titled, was intended as a collective blog where the members of the organization could share their views on their "movement building travels, actions and events."⁷¹ The one entry that was featured related to the August 2011 National Border Justice and Solidarity Delegation, a national event that DRUM along with another New York immigrant rights organization, VAMOS Unidos (which organizes and fights for licensing rights for Latino street vendors in the area), helped convene in Tucson, Arizona, to call attention to the twin issues of migrant struggles and border crossings. A link to the Border Justice and Solidarity Blog, dedicated to the U.S.-Mexico border struggles, within DRUM's blog entry connected what on the surface might have appeared as a distinct set of issues, places, and concerns—Mexicans crossing the physical border into the United States at Tucson, Arizona, and working-class desis facing discrimination in New York City—and reproduced this hypertextual alliance as "a semic web of meaningful relations."⁷² A closer examination of the Border Justice and Solidarity Blog revealed that the multiple entries on its featured page related to DRUM's presence and engagement with the August convention it helped organize, and that many of the entries made were by DRUM members as they reflected on the literal as well as conceptual implications of the border in the United States. This attempt to draw on resonances between different spaces of U.S. immigration struggles is captured in the short film *Checkpoint Nation? Building Community across Borders*, which was featured at the top of the blog and, as of 2014, appears as one of the series of videos posted on DRUM's "Media" page. This film is now available on YouTube, and the DRUM website maintains a link to the YouTube link. This effort by DRUM to include YouTube in its social activism reveals a strategy that involves building connections across different media such as documentary films, community videos, and web links. Made by Ishita Srivastava of Breakthrough Films, one of the twenty-five delegates at the National Border Solidarity Convention, the film uses scenes from the convention, along with one-on-one interviews with Monami Maulik, the creator of DRUM, and Rafael Samanez of VAMOS Unidos, along with footage of the surveillance and patrolling along the U.S.-Mexico border wall near Tucson. The documentary begins with Maria, a Mexican immigrant recounting a horrific experience of being stopped by immigration police when she, who was nine months pregnant at the time, had gone out for breakfast with her husband. While her husband was being interrogated for no obvious reason, she was almost forced to deliver her baby in the presence of the immigration agents. The emotionally charged retelling of her experience with racial profiling, which is, as several activists note in the documentary, mandated by the SB-1070 law in Arizona, is broken down, both literally (since it is presented in fragments throughout the duration of the documentary) and conceptually (through the inclusion of several voices from the convention echoing Maria's understanding of the repressive laws to secure the border). While DRUM's Monami Maulik notes that the physical border is "a microcosm of what is happening in the rest of the country," a delegate of the Black Alliance for Just Immigration, Oakland, California, articulates a black-brown alliance when she suggests that for the state, citizenship (in the legal sense) is not the issue, since black "citizens" have faced racial profiling for a long time. As she puts it, "earlier it was just about blacks being stopped while driving, now it is about a lot of us."

The blog posts made in response both to the film and the Tucson border solidarity event, many of them made by DRUM members, reinterpreted the meaning and association of the term *checkpoint nation* to point to virtualized checkpoints within the nation as well as to revisit the border as a space for intervening in the nationalist discourse. For example, an entry made by a DRUM member titled "From Borders to Schools" drew parallels between the militarization of the U.S.-Mexico border and criminalization of migrants with the digital and police surveillance in New York City schools, where metal detectors, NYPD agents, and the criminalization of immigrant youth effectively inscribe the school as site of the state's repressive border control mechanisms.

The border does not emerge solely as a trope for "absolute alterity" within the DRUM blog space.[73] Rather, it was used to enact solidarity that transgresses through its racial alliances the hierarchy of racialized citizenship inscribed by the dominant ideologies of the American nation. Black, brown, Global South, and human rights politics are uplinked together in the same temporal-spatial economy of the blog as images, bodies, and ideologies associated with organizations including the Alliance for Educational Justice, the Black Alliance for Just Immigration, ACLU–Arizona, the Funding Exchange, Breakthrough Medi, and Coalición de Derechos Humanos (Coalition for Human Rights) are articulated together. In her critique of the imperializing tendencies of digital capitalism, Ella Shohat states that "the traveling of information is clearly used against the traveling bodies of refugees, immigrants and border crossers."[74] While information technologies are a key tool in enacting the state's surveillance project, the blog offers a counter-narrative to the relationship between borders, information, travel, and race and immigration. The border in the DRUM blog is neither antiplace nor indeterminate. Here the idea of physical travel of the delegates to the "real" U.S.-Mexico border is significant because albeit virtually articulated on the blog, it foregrounds the point that the multiracial alliance formation and critique of America's homeland politics are embedded within material, affective, historical, and site-specific contexts. It is in the continual mapping of the linkages across distinctly defined "races"—Asian American, Black, Latino, South Asian—exemplified through the DRUM blog that alternatives to the pathways of inclusion or exclusion of immigrant and working-class subjects of color within the model of neoliberal citizenship can be imagined—so seems to be one of the emergent practices of recasting the racialized contexts of belonging and cultural citizenship in the United States.

The media section of the DRUM website consists of hyperlinks of news items featuring DRUM's role in initiating and, more importantly, creating policy change within the areas of its activism. While in 2012 the DRUM website had an archive that listed news coverage of its activities dating back to the early 2000s, its 2013–2014 renovation foregrounds videos and press coverage from 2013 while archiving only news listings from 2012. Drawing on my readings of the previously existing archive as well as the 2014 version of the news listing, I note that the listings provide a glimpse into the localized context within which much of DRUM's activism is operationalized. Hence, unlike the blog, the voices and perspectives that emerge on the media section foreground the place and time-space of New York within which the immediate meanings of the phrase "Desis Rising Up and Moving" are generated. Take, for instance, the news listing for December 2010, when the Student Safety Act was successfully passed by the New York City Council. The act, a step toward school safety reform, proposed a series of steps to make police activity in NYC schools more visible and better account for the cases of disciplinary action, especially against the poor, black, and Muslim immigrants in the guise of "safety" measures. Passed after two failed attempts in 2008 and 2009, the Safety Act was supported through the efforts of DRUM as well as the Urban Youth Collaborative, Sistas and Brothas United, Future of Tomorrow (F.O.T.), Make the Road NY, the NAACP, the NYCLU, and Advocates for Children. Although all the news sites that are linked have a New York connection, they speak to different facets of the "community" imagined through DRUM's perspective. For example, the *Epoch Times*, whose story on the Student Safety Act is linked to DRUM's page, is a Chinese American independent news media outlet based in New York and historically having its beginning with coverage of democratic practices within China. Ed Vox, or "real voices of the people," is an online blog that emphasizes parents as advocates and policy changers vis-à-vis the American education and public school system, while the *Gotham Gazette* is a politics and policy news site run by the public interest group Citizens Union Foundation. Following the revamping of the DRUM website in 2013, there also appears to be a more deliberate attempt to link to global media coverage of DRUM's activities; for example, by including news sources such as Voice of Russia and the Bangkok Post.[75]

Prior to its 2013 revamping, DRUM's media page offered a detailed record of media coverage of DRUM's activism from 2009 onward until 2012 but offered very little by way of media coverage of its activities between 2000 and 2009. Gaps notwithstanding, the media listings in previous and current versions of the site register DRUM's activism through a genealogical narration of its activism whereby the most recent events are placed at the very top of the page. Even as we get a sense of the ongoing desi political work, the temporalities articulated within the page also position it as an archive of particular struggles. For example, for April 28, 2011, one of the news stories listed was "After Nine Years of Pressure, DHS Finally Drops 'SB1070 for Muslims,'" published by *ColorLines*, an online news magazine that covers racial justice issues. The SB1070 in question was the NSEERS (National Security Entry-Exit Registration System, sometimes called Special Registration), the same initiative of the U.S. state that is addressed in the DRUM-supported film *Rising Up*, discussed previously. In the *ColorLines* coverage, Maulik, executive director for DRUM, is quoted as saying: "I think the news surprised a lot of us. But really, we have been meeting with legislators for years about ending this."[76] The sense of despair (that things might not change, hence the surprise) and practical hope (we have been at it for years) that underpin this comment is better understood against the backdrop of the media listings that in chronological time preceded April 28, 2011, but were spatially positioned after it on the web page. The featured stories covered DRUM's response over several years to counter and rally against the anti-Muslim backlash, speak out against immigration enforcement, conduct political awareness building through community workshops, initiate a call to action to generate community involvement, and work toward policy change by meeting with congressional leaders in Washington, D.C.[77] Derrida's observation that " the archivization produces as much as it records the event" is pertinent here since the media page as previously mentioned omits several periods of time in its narrativization (for example, while we see a 2003 digital short DRUM Beats archived, there is no news coverage listed for the same year) and contains only stories that can be accessed in digital format. Following DRUM's increased investment in social media in the past couple of years, the media site features several video clips and short films focused on DRUM's activism, such as DRUM leaders speaking at the United Nation High Level Dialogue on Migration and Development in 2013).[78] Discussing the concept of archivization, Derrida noted that the technical factors such as the archiving process and structure "also determine the structure of the archivable content."[79] Further, invoking Nicholas Burbules's reference to the web link as the "elemental structure" of our hypertextual media worlds, I suggest that this structural logic of the web page is a critical component of the narrativization of DRUM's historical and contemporary role in social justice activism.

As working-class immigrants of color become key targets of America's technosurveillance, the relevance of a site like the DRUM website cannot be overstated.

The neoimperial strategies of the state work to make immigrants of color invisible in as many ways as possible: stripping them of their human rights, policing their movements, deporting them, and inculcating a culture of fear. At its most obvious level, drumnyc.org makes this community visible; no less important is the fact that it is the community members who make themselves visible.

Taking charge of the ways that they are represented, DRUM members offer an alternate narration of America as homeland. A critical component of their political intervention is their tactical employment of the homepage. While the DRUM website is about immigrants from India, among others, it is not invested in the maintenance of culture-based traditions, nor does it imagine an East-West paradigm for Indian American or South Asian American politics. Rather, it uses the homepage to demonstrate how the neoimperial policies are engineered and why and how they must be unpacked and resisted. DRUM members rely on images of public demonstration, but they rely as much on member-led research into their local communities, affiliation with a wide variety of interest groups, and the dissemination of awareness about immigration, labor, civil rights, and state regulation.

While conventional narratives tend to privilege the region of South Asia as the center of immigrants' political work and aspirations, the DRUM website reveals the everyday realities and investments of South Asian immigrants as political and cultural subjects in their contemporary locations; furthermore, it makes working-class subjects, issues, and political agency visible within online constructions of the immigrant community. The website hence testifies to the shifting terrains of identity formation, racial politics, and state regimes in the United States. New media spaces, in turn, can foster new understandings of how complex transnational spaces reconstitute the hegemonic frames of the nation, its citizens, and its immigrants.

DRUM's presence online exemplifies how a category of identity—in this case, the term *desi*—can be reconfigured to engender new meanings and affiliations. Having a web presence is now crucial for an activist organization to facilitate organizing, mobilizing, and creating awareness about its social justice work. But perhaps more important, DRUM's website demonstrates how the racialization of South Asian Americans in relation to the U.S. government is being rearticulated in online media through the emergence of critical collective identities and practices.

Conclusion

Home Matters in the Age of Networks

What is the most fitting way to conclude a book about immigrant belonging and the politics of home online? Rather than embracing the upbeat rhetoric of homecomings or remaking home—in the sense of creating a new, stable location in place of the old—I am emphasizing a deconstructive and critical position. As Rob Shields reminds us, "the Web is not visible from the point of one single webpage. There is no one page at which it all comes together."[1] Although Shields is speaking more generally against totalizing myths of the Web's technologies, the literal and metaphorical insights of his remarks bear particular significance in the context of our effort to interweave the idea of the homepage with that of home.

The online media examined in this book are complex cultural sites where the technological, social, and political dynamics shaping the early twenty-first-century world converge. A highly dynamic and increasingly important aspect of that world is immigration: The movement of people from one place to another continues to be one of the defining features of modern life. And now more than ever, we understand immigration through media, particularly online media. As a result, our physical mobility is increasingly played out via the tools of technological mobility.

In turn, the equations between the physical and the virtual, the national and the transnational, the private household and the public homeland, are being reformulated in myriad ways as immigrants use online media to make sense of their place in the world. Against such a backdrop, this study has attempted to reinvigorate the question of what home means by studying homepages and by considering how online media targeting specific segments of the Indian immigrant community bring various dimensions of belonging, both old and new, to the fore. Yet, notwithstanding the centrality of home to its investigation, this study does not offer a totalizing perspective on the contemporary Indian immigrant home space. Instead, it has tried to emphasize the need to take into consideration multiple realities or ontologies of conceptualizing, engaging, and engendering belonging.

The notion of a "global Web" is tantalizing but is a myth. It is beguiling to think of the Internet as "a landscape before us awaiting our instructions" and the Web as a preexisting, singular network of sites, from which we can summon exactly the individual pages and data we need onto our computer screens.[2] But such a fantasy does us a disservice. Shields argues that when we give websites a static and "singular integrity," we feed into that myth of a total, coherent, and, most importantly, preconstituted online space. To deconstruct websites and their homepages, then, requires us to shift our focus from the tempting idea of a stable page to that of a dynamic hyperlink. The link has a "double function, as a sign that is a seamless part of a page or text and as an indexical sign that flags and indicates."[3] In Shields's vision, then, it is the link, rather than the page, that is the heart of the Web, reminding us of the mobility and movement inherent in online media. *Virtual Homelands* has explored that mobility a bit further for what it indexes, signals, and points to in terms of online media's role in reconfiguring home, and our epistemological frames of engagement with it.

This study, while about migration and movement in multiple senses, is not an uncritical celebration of immigrant sensibilities, practices, or spaces. Rather, much in the spirit of Shields's rhetorical query—"What is the ontology of the mouse click?"—this study has attempted to ask and, to an extent, has offered some avenues for thinking about a related question: Is there an ontology of the Indian immigrant homepage? Of course, rhetorical or otherwise, we cannot claim to pose or seek to arrive at an understanding of the above question without related queries, like "Is there an ontology of the homepage?" and "Is there an ontology of the immigrant home?" Pertinent to this framing is the overwhelming attention that has been given to mobility and deterritorialization in the twenty-first century. David Morley calls attention to similar themes when he writes in *Home Territories* that while "images abound of our supposedly deterritorialized culture of 'homelessness': images of exile, diaspora, time-space compression, migrancy and 'nomadology,' the concept of home often remains as the uninterrogated anchor or alter ego of all this hyper-mobility."[4]

One might say that critiquing the discursive construction of metanarratives about the technological, institutional, and cultural domains of homepages, while essential for the analysis of websites, is less necessary for the wide range of social media, mobile media, and online media that have emerged in the last decade or so. While it is the case that concerns generated about social media, peer-to-peer networks, remix cultures, and Web 2.0 user-generated practices have significantly dented the hyperbole and utopian narratives associated with the Web's origins, histories, and past and present trajectories, it is my view that if anything, the ontology of online media in the present moment requires a careful retracing of the history to contextualize how normative understandings of the Web were constituted and in turn are constitutive of our contemporary ideas about mediated mobility and migration.

I would point to the reemergence of these key themes in three recent books, Gerard Goggin and Mark McLelland's *Internationalizing Internet Studies* (2008), Niels Brügger's *Web History* (2010), and Lisa Nakamura and Peter A. Chow White's *Race After the Internet* (2011), as evidence of the need to reexamine the foundational issues in new media studies in a new light.[5] While the first book takes a sobering look at the uneven and lopsided nature of framing American-centric issues and agendas as the "global" paradigm for Internet and web studies, the second makes a solid case for developing a theoretical framework for doing web historiography, and the third book reworks major theoretical debates on race and ethnicity in relation to contemporary contexts of new media. All three books critically intervene in the rewriting of the meanings assembled about online media by strategically linking old and new themes, older paradigms and emergent ones. Thus, Euro-American centrism in dominant paradigms of new media, transnationalism, race, and ethnicity are revisited and revised in the context of agenda setting and mapping of the so-called digital futures. What kinds of concerns are seen as central to the field and what must be sought after the main storyline has been set? In a similar vein, by paying close attention to historical contexts we may be able apply the brakes on what has come to be known as the presentist approach to new media and insist on a critical framing of the present by including a reflexive approach toward its imbrication with the past. In the presentist approach of the latest is the best, the current moment is the one to understand in all its complexity, and the present is also the most pressing (of things that need our intellectual attention).

While there is nothing problematic about the investment in the present, the presentist approach should be problematized. Charles Ess in his foreword to the *Web History* anthology seeks to do that when he observes that, "in 2010—i.e., towards the end of the second decade of the bewildering phenomenon called 'the World Wide Web'—it is perhaps difficult to recall a time when the web was *not* an increasingly important component of our lives (at least within the developed countries)." Ess goes on to suggest that one of the key reasons for such difficulty is the bias in definitions of "new" media (including the Web) toward "the present and the all-too-imminent future," which, in turn, he argues, shapes the marginal location for questions of history and the past.[6]

Although this book is not a historical account, as it focuses on online media from the mid-1990s to the present, it foregrounds the significance of paying close attention to historical contexts in understanding the emergence of new media. Using a combination of methods—textual, institutional, and discursive analyses—it has moved back and forth in time and space with a specific agenda: to examine, interrogate, and understand how ideologies of home and belonging emerged and were sustained, recast, and contested for and by Indian immigrants in the United States through the textual, institutional, and cultural practices and politics of online media. We have seen how two key temporal-spatial imaginaries associated with the trope of home—the private, familial household and the public, national homeland—have been rerouted through the mediations of the homepage. We have engaged the trope of *home* in the homepages of websites by locating it within a transnational context of identity, community, activism, capital, and citizenship. I believe that online networks of Indian immigrants, typically mobilized across India and the United States, reveal the ongoing shifts in the technological, cultural, and political domains of immigrant life, and in the ways that belonging is engendered online. And hence I have discussed how online media provide unique opportunities for Indian immigrants living in the United States to reimagine their roles, within both the United States and India, in our age of transnational, neoliberal, digital capitalist networks.

To that end, each chapter has grappled with specific sites to explore how ideas of home and homeland are being reconfigured online. A key objective of *Virtual Homelands* has been to contribute to narratives about belonging and citizenship in late capitalist techno-culture. However, a related objective has been to revisit the under-interrogated framing of the homepage as an always-already site of belonging in network culture. The dominant logics of such a framing become particularly visible in the epistemologies and ontologies shaping the understanding of the global dimensions of online media and their ethnic and immigrant "enclaves."

As online media are increasingly mobilized around the transnational timespace, what becomes of the identity of the homepage? What makes a website "Indian" or "Indian American" or "American"? What are the various assumptions about their modes and contexts of production, circulation, and user appeal? What happens when online media businesses and their websites, like their target immigrant subjects, migrate from India to the United States or vice versa? Can their migration from the United States to India be understood not as "return" migration but as the emergence of a new alliance between India and U.S.-based interests? How can the institutional strategies of online media be understood as meshing with the cultural politics of home and homeland that are advanced through their textual strategies?

Chapter 1 addressed the significance of the construction of Silicon Indians as transnational agents in the network era. However, I argued, by reading them only through the frame of national identifications, we miss out on the nuanced and overt ways in which they are raced, gendered bodies. Particularly fascinating here is the circulation and usage of the term *curry* in discussions about Indian presence in the IT corridors of the United States. Reading food as a way to understand how immigrants are perceived by mainstream white America and relatedly how immigrants try to carve a space for belonging through their "ethnic" food can be especially helpful for our (re)theorizations of online media and their politics. Building on that analysis, chapter 1 then explored my formulation of the problematic of homepage nationalisms and through that problematic saw that home and homeland are not predetermined sites of belonging. It connected discussions of the categories of capital and technology within a nebulous framework of the "global Web" to critical analyses of immigration, transnational racial, and ethnic communities and cultures within the framework of a "digital diaspora."[7] It suggested that we focus too much on how those people outside the national framework of the United States (like immigrants) use online media to engender net nationalisms, and we do not focus enough on analyzing how those within the nation (web users, policy bodies, popular and "global" web companies) are, in fact, equally complicit in the ongoing nationalizations of online spaces.

As we encounter the specificity of the politics and presence of online media within particular immigrant groups, we are reminded of the urgency of mobilizing these various accounts, which do no less than force us to reconsider the hegemonic versions of new media histories, cultures, economies, and practices. The reconsideration, I suggest, must be with a view to disrupt the dominant logic whereby discussions about the relationships of diasporic, immigrant, racially and ethnically marked groups with online media are viewed as particularistic minority reports and add-ons that nicely diversify the unmarked, general accounts emerging from dominant centers in the United States and Western Europe without fundamentally questioning the premise and privilege underpinning their dominance. The unmarked space shaped largely by Euro-American centrism and white normativity renders the difference—for instance, how an immigrant community engages the Web—as interesting for its particularity rather than significant for what it can tell us about the modes and processes through which a hegemonic knowledge has been formed around online media, ways of studying it, and, furthermore, the kinds of investments that shape the established, dominant paradigm. Engaging this problematic of homepage nationalisms also implies recasting our debate about home through an interdisciplinary theoretical and conceptual framework.

Chapter 2 examined the online conversations and networking practices of Indian women on the H-4 dependent visa in the United States. It highlighted the ambivalence that surrounds the condition of migration—particularly when class mobility, patriarchal cultures of marriage, and the H-4 woman's own investment in marriage and the NRI life conflict deeply with her desires for financial independence, dignity, and agency. An online forum like H4 Indian Ladies invites us to reconsider the diverse ways in which immigrant women experience and debate the curtailment of their rights. When the women of the forum lament that they left their vibrant, active lives in India to experience the cultural shock of an America shaped by the patriarchal ideologies of immigration policies, their critical viewpoints become a point of entry into understanding the gendered and racial politics shaping the contemporary United States. Furthermore, it makes visible a storyline that is nearly invisible in our public cultures—that the American state and its institutions are very actively involved in the shaping of Indian immigrant homes and their gendered contexts. At the same time, community formations like H4 Indian Ladies, organized around a critique of racial, class, and gender hierarchies, reveal the inadequacy of both the institutionalized and discursive regimes of the nation to contain and maintain such markers of difference.

Chapter 3 critiqued the elitist, techo-centric, and U.S.-centric discourses shaping the Indian state's turn to the ideology of flexible citizenship for its diasporic subjects. It framed the critique through commercialized narratives of NRI home life and agency and showed how those narratives forge an alliance between the state, financial institutions, and the institutionally recognized category of the NRI and his family. Building on the earlier discussion about women's participation online, this chapter reminds us that digital technology produces knowledge about men and women and very often that involves, in the words of Jennifer Terry and Melodie Calvert, creating an ideology that "deploys binary oppositions as a means for structuring hierarchical social relations between men and women."[8] In consumer-oriented narratives about networking Indians who are mobile in a transnational age, women are often positioned in a relationship of passive consumption with new media while immigrant Indian men are depicted as active sons and technological experts who, at heart, are productive Indian nationalists.

In recent years, there has been some talk about the reduced desirability of the United States as the ultimate destination for certain sections of the Indian middle class; pointing to trends such as the rise in the number of U.S.-based NRIs relocating to India and the growth in the Indian corporate sector and consumer market, such conversations indicate that the cultural capital associated with the American dream and the NRI life are vulnerable to fluctuations based on the relative merits associated with work, income, and quality of life in India and the United States.[9] That said, however, two other points need to be stressed here. One, that ongoing debates in the Indian media over whether the United States is trying to officially but subtly push back against H-1B Indian immigration (especially in light of the Comprehensive Immigration Reform Bill of 2013) implicitly suggest that while a shift might be happening, the NRI and in particular the H-1B Indian still continue to figure prominently within discussions of Indian middle-class aspirations and desirable lifestyles.[10] As we saw in chapters 2 and 3, discussions about home life in the United States on the H4 Indian Ladies Forum challenge precisely the idealized re-creation of the NRI household as a middle-class, transnational family made possible by the professional H-1B man. Here online media help H-4 women negotiate the varied degrees of mobility and immobility that are part of their everyday life and that are shaped by the structural logics of labor migration in the United States. In the hegemonic representations of the wired Indian immigrant, digital technologies and online networking are the mechanisms to maintain and sustain the new global Indian family structure. In the alternative rendering of networking immigrant women, we witness the complex of desires, dissatisfactions, and negotiations that shape the actual dynamics of that same household.

These narratives and codes of belonging must be understood as being performed at a time when Indian Americans are increasingly being viewed as successful minorities, when Indian immigrants are also returning to India in great numbers, and when investment in the imagery of home is getting more charged in political, economic, and cultural terms. While mainstream accounts of home ownership by Indian immigrants in the United States or advertising for homes for NRIs in India pose the question of belonging in neoliberal capitalist terms, surveys by organizations such as the PEW report on Asian Americans in 2012 reify categories of identity, membership, and cultural location around hegemonic state-imagined notions of citizenship, labor, work, and lifestyle.

Chapter 4 with its attention to the class and racial positioning of South Asian immigrants illustrated how their identity as desis is being reconfigured in popular and political culture. When we examine the idea of the homeland through the online desi activism of organizations such as DRUM, we can see how hegemonic rearticulations of immigrant belonging expressed through ideas of the transnational, wired household and the virtual, mobile homeland become unstable when critical race and class perspectives are brought to bear upon them. I emphasize the need to see the linkages between these seemingly divergent issues; doing so, I suggest, will allow us to engage the complexities of online cultures in a more thorough and grounded fashion as well as to understand the politics of new media in the making and unmaking of borders, communities, and state regimes today. Furthermore, it reveals that there are a variety of political ideals, social experiences, and cultural ideologies that make up the Indian and South Asian immigrant community formations in the United States. Organizations like DRUM, in using online media to show how desi networks are shaped by race and class, also reframe the racialized notion of Asian Americans as a "wired minority."[11] Further, its significance lies in the fact that the perspectives advanced by the site are those of working-class immigrants—subjects whose cultural and political life is for the most part invisible within mainstream conversations about multicultural America and its present forms of globalism. The few constructions that do exist oftentimes reinforce racist stereotypes of the unethical, illegal, or lazy migrant or lump them as a part of a mass migration, which in turn is one of the unintended consequences of globalization and an "open door" immigration policy.[12] Rarely are working-class immigrants represented in the U.S. mainstream as active political subjects engaging the nation-state and its policies.

Our online explorations have shown that unchanging and stable concepts of the home, homeland, and homepage are fundamentally untenable. Yet this book's argument is that precisely because the very ideas of home and homepages are dynamic, there can be a productive movement toward engaging the stories of origin and myths of arrivals and destinations that underwrite dominant academic and mainstream discourses about the web pages and immigrants. After all, one of the earlier vocabularies to emerge in the technical and institutional characterization of the homepage was that it was "a destination," a virtual place at which to arrive after "traveling" through the network (in the age of Google search, we might say "crawling" instead of "traveling," after the search spiders that crawl over the data-sphere to gather information).

Moving away from destinations (and, for that matter, arrivals), this study foregrounds movement and contingency. That emphasis allows us to illuminate the dynamic iterations of home online in ways that refuse a foreclosing of the questions around home or belonging. Relatedly, while each of the specific web case studies selected invites attention to issues that I argue are central to and constitutive of contemporary renderings of the Indian immigrant identities and cultural location, issues of race, class, gender, immigration, law, state, and nation, I don't make a case for them to be understood as the representative sites or the definitive examples of a given cultural dynamic in the community at large. To do so would suggest that there are some websites, some users, and some practices that can speak for an entire constituency, and that is a suggestion in which this book is not invested by any means.

Virtual Homelands adds to and complicates existing studies of Indian immigrants in the United States by foregrounding constituencies whose identities, politics, and cultural locations are very closely tied to the network era, software technology–related labor migration, immigration regimes, and surveillance and policing strategies of the information state. It deconstructs the Indian immigrant location through considerations of issues of gender, race, and class in the making of as well as unmaking of the hegemonic imaginations around it. The book hence advances the logic that there is no knowable, static Indian immigrant home and homeland culture to be found online; rather, there are temporal-spatial specific renderings of the affective, material, political, and cultural modes of engendering spaces of belonging.

Critical to the ongoing rethinking of the modality of belonging is the technology of the information, digital, hypertextual, and virtual network that remediates both the limitations and the emergent possibilities vis-à-vis Indian immigrants' routes to cultural citizenship in the United States. By exploring specific websites, the chapters complicate the normative understandings of Indian immigrant web cultures—by interrogating the hegemonic power and terrain of the cultural ideologies that produce normative ideas about which Indian immigrants are online, as well as what their interests, concerns, and investments are (or what they should be). At the same time, I have also foregrounded narratives that are usually marginal and often ignored altogether. This book illustrates that spaces that might appear to be marked as elite Indian immigrant spaces, such as the wives of H-1B professionals forum, reveal something more complex and contradictory if issues of gender and nation are brought to bear onto questions of state, law, race, and techno-centric class divisions. And as the discussion of the DRUM website suggests, when questions of race and class are made front and center of the imagination as well as analysis of a community's vision and politics, the picture that emerges puts a familiar take on the national in the South Asian American context (as in it is an "Indian" or "Bangladeshi" website) in the background while foregrounding a perspective about nation that aligns white nationalism, U.S. state agendas, and racialized minorities in America within its purview. Throughout I have tried to move beyond, and thus disrupt, normative expectations about the epistemological frames that should be used to view the network of connections made by and for Indian immigrants through the Web.

To include institutional analysis into our understanding of the online culture of Indian immigrants is thus to think against the grain of dominant codes in the field of new media studies, which usually locate cultural issues of immigrants within textual spaces, and issues of technology and capital within nonimmigrant spaces of (unmarked) American institutions. The book contends that it is fruitful and productive to see how Indian immigrant elites are not just using online media for cultural returns but are in fact strategically investing in a brand of transnational Indian culture and ethnicity for political, economic, and technological leverage in a globally networked society. In other words, online media are not just conduits to return to the same old story of roots and tradition, a story that still dominates our understanding of diasporic cultures. Rather, online media are the "links" that enable a new set of imaginations and agendas to be entrenched around elite desires for the maintenance and consolidation of the status quo. Crucial to that new imagination is a material and symbolic investment in the institutional, technological, and cultural domains of online media.

Virtual Homelands argues for reconsidering the contours of belonging in contemporary contexts of new media and transnationalism through its specific study of Indian immigrant cultures online. It contends that the question of belonging must be applied more thoroughly to the institutional contexts of online media, for not doing so would leave unexamined a very significant alliance between capital and citizenship in the neoliberal, digital age. Furthermore, in the United States, especially since 2001, immigrants, racial and religious minorities, women of color, and the working class have found themselves at the receiving end of the disciplinary practices of neoliberal states and globalization practices. These institutional contexts shape belonging as much as the textual and hypertextual practices that generate categories of exclusion and inclusion in online media.

Notes

Introduction

1. A note on usage of the terms *Web*, *Internet*, and *online*: These terms are often used interchangeably. In some popular definitions, it might appear that the Internet came first, followed by the Web and then social media. However, as is evident from current debates on Web 3.0 or the semantic web (as a postsocial media revolution), the Web is a term that can be applied to technologies that come after social media, as much as to technologies that came before. Moreover, as discussed in books such as *Race after the Internet* (Lisa Nakamura and Peter A. Chow White, eds. [New York: Routledge, 2012]), *Web History* (Niels Brügger, ed. [New York: Peter Lang, 2010]), and *Internationalizing Internet Studies: Beyond Anglophone Paradigms* (Gerald Goggin and Mark McLelland, eds. [New York: Routledge 2008]), there isn't such a clear-cut temporal sequence to the usage of these terms either in academic studies or in industry discourses. However, to maintain clarity in my discussion of the central issue of homepages as it relates to websites, social media, and new media in general, I use the term *online media* instead of the Web as a general term of description. When essential, I use the word *Web* in discussions that refer exclusively or historically to websites that do not include social media. This distinction between the specific term *Web* for discussions of websites and a more general term *online media* to collectively refer to the Web, social media, and mobile technologies is to ensure that the transitions between analyses of websites, discussion forums, social network sites, and social media are more reader-friendly.

2. Nonresident Indian, a category created by the Indian state in the 1970s, refers to Indian citizens who live overseas. I am drawing on Lisa Nakamura's discussion of the

construction of Asian Americans as digital elite and therefore a "wired minority" in *Digitizing Race: Visual Cultures of the Internet* (Minneapolis: University of Minnesota Press, 2008), 173.

3. For recent examples, see Jeremy Quittner, "How Silicon Valley Is Transforming the Immigration Debate," Inc. com., July 9, 2013, http://www.inc.com/jeremy-quittner/silicon-valley-immigration-reform.html, accessed July 11, 2013; Adrianna Gardella, "How the Web and an Attitude of Sharing Helped a Law Firm Take Off," *New York Times*, June 26, 2013, http://www.nytimes.com, accessed July 11, 2013; Stephen Croucher, "Communicating through Social Networks Helps Immigrants," *Communication Currents* 6, no. 5 (October 2011), http://www.natcom.org/CommCurrentsArticle.aspx?id=1792, accessed July 11, 2013.

4. A recent example of this long-standing narrative includes Neesha Bapat, "How Indians Defied Gravity and Achieved Success in Silicon Valley," October 15, 2012, http://venturebeat.com/2012/10/15/how-indians-defied-gravity-and-achieved-success-in-silicon-valley/, accessed November 20, 2012.

5. Adam Turner, "A Place to Call Home: A Social Media Giant Has Reinvented the Smartphone Interface," *Age* (Australia), April 28, 2013, http://www.theage.com.au/digital-life/mobiles/a-place-to-call-home-20130425-2ifn3.html, accessed June 1, 2013.

6. Michael Arrington, "Google Has Acquired YouTube," Tech Crunch, October 9, 2006, http://techcrunch.com/2006/10/09/google-has-acquired-youtube/, accessed January 10, 2012; "Nokia and Microsoft Announce Plans for a Broad Strategic Partnership to Build a New Global Mobile Ecosystem," Microsoft News Center, February 10, 2011, http://www.microsoft.com/en-us/news/press/2011/feb11/02-11partnership.aspx, accessed January 10, 2013; Chris Isidore, "Yahoo Buys Tumblr, Promises to Not 'Screw It Up,'" CNN Money, May 20, 2013, http://money.cnn.com/2013/05/20/technology/yahoo-buys-tumblr/index.html, accessed January 10, 2013.

7. Tim Berners-Lee, *Weaving the Web* (London: Onion Business Books, 1999), 39.

8. Ibid.

9. Ibid.

10. Megan Sapnar Ankerson, "Web Industries, Economies, Aesthetics: Mapping the Look of the Web in the Dot-com Era," in Brügger, *Web History*, 173–195.

11. Martin Lister et al., *New Media: A Critical Introduction* (London: Routledge, 2003), 245.

12. Nakamura, *Digitizing Race*, 2008.

13. Philip Elmer De Witt, "Battle for the Soul of the Internet," *Time*, July 25, 1994, 144, 150.

14. Webindia.com, "About Us." March 2, 2000. Internet Archive, https://archive.org.

15. David Gauntlett, ed., *Web.studies: Rewiring Media Studies for the Digital Age* (London: Arnold, 2000).

16. I am drawing here on my printed pages and some online pages that I briefly collected in the early 2000s.

17. "Geocities Shutting Down Today," Slashdot, October 29, 2009, http://news.slashdot.org/story/09/10/26/1359223/geocities-shutting-down-today, accessed April 12, 2012. The

Internet Archive tried to generate a partial archive of the 38 million pages that were being hosted by Geocities when Yahoo shut it down in 2009.

18. Madhavi Mallapragada, "The Indian Diaspora in the USA and around the Web," in Gauntlett, *Web.studies,* 179–185.

19. Arun A. Aguiar, "Indian Internet Users Multiplying Fast," *NewsIndia-Times,* October 22, 1999, accessed through Proquest December 20, 2013.

20. "Rediff.com Launches New Redesigned Website," *Hindustan Times,* April 29, 2013, http://www.hindustantimes.com, accessed May 13, 2013.

21. See, for example, ICICI bank ad on rediff.com's Money channel, October 27, 2000, Internet Archive, https://archive.org.

22. PEW Research Center, "The Rise of Asian Americans," June 19, 2012, http://www.pewsocialtrends.org/2012/06/19/the-rise-of-asian-americans/, accessed June 20, 2012.

23. Daniel Y. Jang, "How MTV and Other Corporations Are Challenging Asian America: An Examination of the Business Perspective on Asian American Identity," *Asian American Policy Review* 15 (2006): 49–56, accessed through EBSCO host January 25, 2010.

24. PEW Research Center, "Rise of Asian Americans."

25. Ibid.

26. Karthick Ramakrishnan, "When Words Fail: Careful Framing Needed in Research on Asian Americans," *Hyphen,* June 27, 2012, http://www.hyphenmagazine.com/blog/archive/2012/06/when-words-fail-careful-framing-needed-research-asian-americans, accessed June 28, 2012.

27. Gary Y. Okihiro, *Margins and Mainstreams: Asians in American History and Culture* (Seattle: University of Washington Press, 1994).

28. U.S. Census Bureau, "The Asian Population: 2000," February 2002, http://www.census.gov/prod/2002pubs/c2kbr01-16.pdf, accessed May 10, 2011.

29. U.S. Census Bureau, "We the People: Asians in the United States," December 2004, http://www.census.gov/prod/2004pubs/censr-17.pdf, accessed December 19, 2005.

30. Jang, "How MTV and Other Corporations."

31. PEW Research Center, "Rise of Asian Americans."

32. U.S. Census Bureau, "The Asian Population: 2010," March 2012, http://www.census.gov/prod/cen2010/briefs/c2010br-11.pdf, accessed April 10, 2012.

33. Ronald Takaki, *Strangers from a Different Shore: A History of Asian Americans* (New York: Penguin, 1989).

34. Among the others communities in the Asian American population who together account for less than 1 million are Cambodians, Hmongs, Laotians, Bangladeshis, and Pakistanis.

35. U.S. Census Bureau, 2010; PEW Research Center, "Rise of Asian Americans," 2012.

36. Lisa Lowe, *Immigrant Acts: On Asian American Cultural Politics* (Durham, NC: Duke University Press, 1996), 5–6.

37. Darrell Y. Hamamoto, *Monitored Peril: Asian Americans and the Politics of TV Representation* (Minneapolis: University of Minnesota Press, 1994); Peter X Feng, *Identities*

in Motion: Asian American Film and Video (Durham, NC: Duke University Press, 2002); Sucheng Chan, *Asian Americans: An Interpretive History* (New York: Twayne, 1991).

38. U.S. Census Bureau, "Asian Population: 2000"; U.S. Census Bureau, "Asian Population: 2010"; U.S. Census Bureau, "We the People."

39. U.S. Census Bureau, "Asian Population: 2000"; U.S. Census Bureau, "We the People."

40. Madhulika Khandelwal, *Becoming American, Being Indian: An Immigrant Community in New York City* (Ithaca, NY: Cornell University Press, 2002); Vinay Lal, *The Other Indians: A Political and Cultural History of South Asians in America* (Los Angeles: UCLA Asian American Studies Center, 2008); Vijay Prashad, *Karma of Brown Folk* (Minneapolis: University of Minnesota Press, 2000).

41. U.S. Citizenship and Immigration Services, Department of Homeland Security, "H-1B Specialty Occupations, DOD Cooperative Research and Development Project Workers, and Fashion Models," http://www.uscis.gov, accessed September 7, 2011.

42. Ibid.

43. U.S. Department of Labor, Wage and Hour Division, "H-1B Program," http://www.dol.gov/whd/immigration/h1b.htm.

44. Institute of International Education. "Top 25 Places of Origin of International Students, 2011/12–2012/13," *Open Doors Report on International Educational Exchange*, http://www.iie.org/opendoors, accessed December 20, 2013.

45. Ibid.

46. Inderpal Grewal, *Transnational America: Feminisms, Diasporas, Neoliberalisms* (Durham, NC: Duke University Press, 2005); Prema A. Kurien, "To Be or Not to Be South Asian," *Journal of Asian American Studies* 6, no. 3 (October 2003): 261–288; Sharmila Rudrappa, *Ethnic Routes to Becoming American: Indian Immigrants and the Cultures of Citizenship* (New Brunswick, NJ: Rutgers University Press, 2004); Padma Rangaswamy, *Namaste America: Indian Immigrants in an American Metropolis* (University Park: Pennsylvania State University Press, 2000); Anna Lee Saxenian, *Silicon Valley's New Immigrant Entrepreneurs* (San Francisco: Public Policy Institute of California, 1999).

47. Prashad, *Karma of Brown Folk*, 80; Priya Agarwal, *Passage from India: Post-1965 Indian Immigrants and Their Children: Conflicts, Concerns and Solutions* (Palos Verdes, CA: Yuvati, 1991); Arthur Helweg and Usha Helweg, *An Immigrant Success Story: East Indians in America* (Philadelphia: University of Pennsylvania Press, 1990); Kamala Visweswaran, "Diaspora by Design: Flexible Citizenship and South Asians in the U.S. Racial Formations," *Diaspora* 6, no. 1 (1997): 5–39.

48. Biju Mathew, *Taxi! Cabs and Capitalism in New York City* (New York: New Press, 2005).

49. Monisha Das Gupta, *Unruly Immigrants: Rights, Activism, and Transnational South Asian Politics in the United States* (Durham, NC: Duke University Press, 2006); Jigna Desai, *Beyond Bollywood: The Cultural Politics of South Asian Diasporic Film* (New York: Routledge, 2004); Gayatri Gopinath, *Impossible Desires: Queer Diasporas and South Asian Public Cultures* (Durham, NC: Duke University Press, 2005); Sunaina Marr Maira, *Desis in the House: Indian American Youth Culture in New York City* (Philadelphia: Temple

University Press, 2002); Ajay Nair and Murali Balaji, *Desi Rap: Hip-hop and South Asian America* (Lanham, MD: Lexington Books, 2008).

50. P. Pushkar, "India's Brain Drain Persists," *Chronicle of Higher Education*, January 29, 2013, http://chronicle.com/blogs/worldwise/indias-brain-drain-persists/31365, accessed March 10, 2013. The brain drain theory suggests that highly skilled emigrants financially drain the home country while enriching the host country. This theory, widely circulated in India's political and economic circles until the 1990s, is now contested by new theories that suggest a more dynamic relationship between capital, nation, migrants, and labor.

51. Mihir A. Desai, Devesh Kapur, John McHale, and Keith Rogers, "The Fiscal Impact of High-Skilled Emigration: Flows of Indians to the U.S.," *Journal of Economic Development* 88 (2009): 32–44, www.people.hbs.edu/mdesai/fiscalimpact.pdf; Kanta Murali, "The IIT Story: Issues and Concerns," *Frontline* 20, no. 3 (February 1–14, 2003), http://www.frontline.in/static/html/fl2003/stories/20030214007506500.htm, accessed November 24, 2013.

52. The NRI category was created in 1975 by the Indian government to allow persons of Indian origin (POI) in the United States and the United Kingdom to open foreign currency accounts in U.S. dollars or British pounds sterling.

53. World Bank, *Migration and Remittances Factbook, 2011*, 2nd. ed. (Washington, DC: International Bank for Reconstruction and Development, 2011), 19, http://siteresources.worldbank.org/INTLAC/Resources/Factbook2011-Ebook.pdf, accessed November 18, 2011.

54. Rama Lakshmi, "India Reaches Out to Emigrants," *Washington Post*, January 12, 2003, A21.

55. Pravasi Bharatiya Divas, "The Indian Diaspora," http://indiandiaspora.nic.in/pbdivas.htm, accessed January 2004.

56. "Bill Introduced in RS to Merge PIO, OCI Schemes: Eduardo," *Navhind Times*, December 23, 2011, http://www.navhindtimes.in/goa-news/bill-introduced-rs-merge-pio-oci-schemes-eduardo, accessed June 6, 2012.

57. U.S. Citizenship and Immigration Services, "H-1B Specialty Occupations."

58. India Shining was a marketing campaign launched in a series of advertisements by the ruling political party, the Bharatiya Janata Party (BJP), in 2004; the campaign has been criticized for its politically motivated agenda. See, for example, "Sonia Questions 'India Shining' Slogan," in the *Hindu*, January 25, 2004, http://www.hindu.com/2004/01/25/stories/2004012500930300.htm, accessed March 5, 2005.

59. Howard Rheingold, *The Virtual Community: Homesteading on the Electronic Frontier* (New York: Harper Perennial, 1994).

60. Okihiro, *Margins and Mainstreams*.

61. Julie D'Acci, *Defining Women: Television and the Case of Cagney and Lacey* (Chapel Hill: University of North Carolina Press, 1994).

62. In the context of web studies, Steven M. Schneider and Kirsten A. Foot have described their strategy for analyzing websites as a broader semantic object that is thematically oriented and includes multiple, interconnected sites as "web sphere analysis." See "The Web as an Object of Study," *New Media and Society* 6, no. 1 (2004): 114–122. See

also Paul du Gay, Stuart Hall, and Linda Janes, eds. *Doing Cultural Studies: The Story of the Sony Walkman* (London: Sage/Open University Press, 1997).

63. Schneider and Foot, 118.

64. Internet Archive, http://archive.org/index.php.

One. Homepage Nationalisms

1. Mary Douglas, "The Idea of Home: A Kind of Space," *Social Research* 58, no. 1 (1991): 289.

2. David Morley, *Home Territories: Media, Mobility, Identity* (London: Routledge, 2000), 16.

3. James Clifford, "Diasporas," *Cultural Anthropology* 9, no. 3 (1994): 302–338; Yen Espiritu, *Home Bound: Filipino American Lives across Cultures, Communities, and Countries* (Berkeley: University of California Press, 2003).

4. Ien Ang, *On Not Speaking Chinese: Living between Asia and the West* (London: Routledge, 2001), 10–11.

5. Aihwa Ong, *Flexible Citizenship: The Cultural Logics of Transnationality* (Durham, NC: Duke University Press, 1999).

6. The most consistent attempt to examine home comes from studies of homepages, diasporic groups, and feminist online cultures.

7. Benedict Anderson, *Imagined Communities: Reflections on the Origin and Spread of Nationalism* (London: Verso, 1983).

8. See Robin Cohen, *Global Diasporas: An Introduction* (Seattle: University of Washington Press, 1997); Clifford, "Diasporas."

9. Deepika Bahri and Mary Vasudeva, eds., *Between the Lines: South Asians and Postcoloniality* (Philadelphia: Temple University Press, 1996); Annanya Bhattacharjee, "The Habit of Ex-Nomination: Nation, Woman and the Indian Immigrant Bourgeoisie," *Public Culture* 5, no. 1 (1992): 19–44; Sunaina Maira and Rajni Srikanth, eds., *Contours of the Heart: South Asians Map America* (New York: Asian American Writers' Workshop, 1996); Das Gupta, *Unruly Immigrants*; Desai, *Beyond Bollywood*; Sunil Bhatia, *American Karma: Race, Culture, and Identity in the Indian Diaspora* (New York: New York University Press, 2007).

10. See Karim H. Karim, ed., *The Media of Diaspora: Mapping the Globe* (New York: Routledge, 2003).

11. Andrew Herman and Thomas Swiss, eds. *The World Wide Web and Contemporary Cultural Theory* (New York: Routledge, 2000); Ken Hillis, *Digital Sensations: Space, Identity, and Embodiment in Virtual Reality* (Minneapolis: University of Minnesota Press, 1999).

12. Radhika Gajjala and Venkataramana Gajjala, eds., *South Asian Technoscapes* (New York: Peter Lang, 2008).

13. Ella Shohat, "By the Bitstream of Babylon: Cyberfrontiers and Diasporic Vistas," in *Home, Exile, Homeland: Film, Media, and the Politics of Place*, ed. Hamid Naficy (New York: Routledge, 1999), 226–227.

14. Gajjala and Gajjala, *South Asian Technoscapes*.

15. Rachel Lee and Sau-ling Cynthia Wong, preface to *Asian America.Net: Ethnicity, Nationalism, and Cyberspace*, ed. Lee and Wong (New York: Routledge, 2003), ix.

16. Stuart Hall and Paul Gilroy, "British Cultural Studies and the Pitfalls of Identity," in *Black British Cultural Studies: A Reader*, ed. Houston A. Baker Jr., Manthia Diawara, and Ruth H. Lindeborg (Chicago: University of Chicago Press, 1996), 223–239.

17. Chidanand Rajghatta, *The Horse That Flew: How India's Silicon Gurus Spread Their Wings* (New Delhi: HarperCollins, 2001).

18. Anna Lee Saxenian's studies of Indian immigrants in Silicon Valley offer detailed discussions of this phenomenon. See her reports "Silicon Valley's New Immigrant Entrepreneurs," June 1999, and "Local and Global Networks of Immigrant Professionals in Silicon Valley," April 2002. Both reports are available at the Public Policy Institute of California, http://www.ppic.org/main/home.asp (under Publications).

19. Rajghatta, *Horse That Flew*.

20. Editorial, "Grasping the Future," *Little India*, February 1, 1998, 4, accessed through Proquest January 25, 2010.

21. Directory of Indians on the Net6, rec.music.indian.classical, *Google Groups*, January 1, 1998, https://groups.google.com/d/forum/rec.music.indian.classical, accessed May 2012.

22. Editorial, "Grasping the Future."

23. Ibid.

24. Ibid.

25. Po Bronson, "HotMale," *Wired* 6, no. 12 (December 1998), http://www.wired.com/wired/archive/6.12/hotmale.html, accessed March 1, 2002.

26. Ibid.

27. Ibid.

28. Editorial, "Grasping the Future."

29. A derivative of California's Silicon Valley, Silicon Alley refers to the software industry in and around New York City. While the term was coined in the online newsletter @NY, the industry is said to have experienced a resurgence following the downturn on the West Coast.

30. James Heitzman, "Becoming Silicon Valley," *India Seminar*, 2001, http://www.india-seminar.com/2001/503/503%20james%20heitzman.htm, accessed January 10, 2012. And more recently, Naomi Canton, "How the 'Silicon Valley of India' Is Bridging the Digital Divide," December 6, 2012, CNN Le Web, http://edition.cnn.com/2012/12/06/tech/bangalore-india-internet-access, accessed May 12, 2013.

31. For example, see Rajesh Chandramouli's article "Chennai Emerging as India's Silicon Valley?" *Economic Times*, May 1, 2008, accessed online November 25, 2013, at http://timesofindia.indiatimes.com; Hemand Wakode, "Cyberabad: A New Face of Hyderabad," *Water and Megacities*, January 30, 2012, http://www.waterandmegacities.org/cyberabad-a-new-face-of-hyderabad/, accessed August 21, 20110.

32. An early 2000s example at this effort is discussed in Jay Fitzgerald, "New Silicon Valley VC Group Set to Help Indian Tech Firms," *IndUS Business Journal*, June 1, 2002, accessed online September 16, 2011, at http://www.indusbusinessjournal.com.

33. Rajghatta, *Horse That Flew*, 5.

34. Uma Narayan, *Dislocating Cultures: Identities, Traditions, and Third-World Feminism* (New York: Routledge 1997).

35. For example, Robert Ji-Song Ku, Martin F. Manalansan IV, and Anita Mannur, eds., *Eating Asian America: A Food Studies Reader* (New York: New York University Press, 2013).

36. An early excellent critique of the notion of technological neutrality in the field of computer science is Abbe Mowshowitz's paper titled "Computers and the Myth of Neutrality," published in *Proceedings of the ACM 12th Annual Computer Science Conference on SIGCSE Symposium*, 1984, 85–92, Association of Computer Machinery Digital Library, Online Database, accessed February 22, 2013.

37. Wendy Chun, "Race and Software," in *Alien Encounters: Popular Culture in Asian American*, ed. Mimi Thi Nguyen and Thuy Linh Nguyen Tu (Durham, NC: Duke University Press, 2007), 304–333.

38. Ibid.

39. Tim Jordan addresses this issue in the chapter "The Virtual Individual" in his book *Cyberpower: An Introduction to the Politics of Cyberspace* (London: Routledge, 1999), 59–96.

40. Examples include Anna Everett, *Digital Diaspora: A Race for Cyberspace* (Albany: State University of New York Press, 2009); Nakamura, *Digitizing Race*; Chun, "Race and Software"; Lee and Wong, *Asian American.net*; also Beth E. Kolko, Lisa Nakamura, and Gilbert B. Rodman, eds., *Race in Cyberspace* (New York: Routledge, 2000); and Lisa Nakamura and Peter A. Chow-White, eds., *Race After the Internet* (New York: Routledge, 2012).

41. "Stindian," http://www.urbandictionary.com, accessed January 10, 2008.

42. Ibid.

43. Dice, http://techtalk.dice.com/t5/Tech-Nation-Discussion/Groupon-Is-Hiring-An-Army-Of-Engineers-In-Silicon-Valley/m-p/295118/highlight/true#M42481, accessed December 10, 2012. (The current URL for the Dice discussion forums is http://slashdot.org; it appears that the organization of content has changed in the wake of the website change, and this information may no longer be available.)

44. Dice, http://techtalk.dice.com/t5/Tech-Nation-Discussion/H1B-Workers-Virtually-Enslaved-in-Silicon-Valley/td-p/200349/highlight/true/page/2, accessed December 10, 2012. (Here also the current URL is http://slashdot.org.)

45. Annalee Newitz, "The Curry Menace," *AlterNet*, July 14, 2003, http://www.alternet.org/story/16410/the_curry_menace, accessed January 11, 2012.

46. Ibid.

47. Don Bauder, "Comparatively, Tech Workers Haul in Bucks in San Diego," *San Diego Reader*, January 6, 2011, http://www.sandiegoreader.com/weblogs, accessed May 2, 2012.

48. Ibid.

49. "Why do Indian people always smell like curry, without fail?" Yahoo! Answers, n.d., http://answers.yahoo.com/question/index?qid=20101102024723AAQ8pC7, accessed May 12, 2013.

50. "Racist People on Twitter," http://racist-people-on-twitter.com/about/, accessed May 12, 2013.

51. "You are not desi," Tumblr, http://youarenotdesi.tumblr.com/post/39154748324/no-one-ever-stigmatize-white-people-its-bad-and, accessed May 12, 2013.

52. Srikanth Devarajan, *H1Bees*, CD, produced by Srivatsa Srinivasan, 2005.

53. Tracy Wahl, "Techie Immigrants Make 'Curry Rock,'" November 13, 2005, National Public Radio Music, http://www.npr.org/templates/story/story.php?storyId=5010426, accessed August 1, 2011.

54. "Bee Hive Hierarchy and Activities," Big Island Bees, May 10, 2010, http://bigislandbees.com/buzz/2010/05/19/bee-hive-hierarchy, accessed August 1, 2011.

55. "About Us," SiliconIndia, n.d., http://www.siliconindia.com/aboutusnew/index.php, accessed August 1, 2011.

56. Wakode, "Cyberabad."

57. Patricia Wise, "Always Already Virtual: Feminist Politics in Cyberspace," in *Virtual Politics: Identity and Community in Cyberspace*, ed. David Holmes (London: Sage, 1997), 180. Wise deploys this meaning to consider how women in information technology cultures might be seen as "always already virtual," whereby their historical absence from public narratives about technology and their role as symbolically central but culturally marginal is reproduced with the digital realm. That said, the gendering of technology does not happen in a race-neutral context. So, here I tweak Wise's insight to illuminate how race operates virtually.

58. A recent example is Vivek Wadhwa's article, "Racism in Silicon Valley," *India Currents*, March 22, 2012, http://www.indiacurrents.com/articles/2012/03/22/racism-silicon-valley, accessed November 15, 2012.

59. The fictional character Raj, whose full name is Rajesh Ramayan Koothrappali, holds a PhD in astrophysics, works at Caltech University, is a gaming addict, and is a fierce consumer and defender of media culture that is popular among women. He is also shown to be awkward around women and able to talk to them only under the influence of alcohol.

60. Ravi Sambamurthy, "Austin's Power," *SiliconIndia*, June 2000, 58.

61. Anthony Spaeth, "Coming to Amrika," *Time*, March 27, 2000, http://www.time.com/time/world/article/0,8599,2054206,00.html, accessed May 10, 2004.

62. Nisid Hajari, "Indian-Americans Are Reaching Out to Their Roots to Create a Unique Culture," *Time*, March 27, 2000, http://www.time.com/time/world/article/0,8599,2054707,00.html, accessed July 1, 2001.

63. Michael Lewis, *The New New Thing: A Silicon Valley Story* (New York: Norton, 1999).

64. Ibid., 10.

65. Rajghatta, *Horse That Flew*, 27.

66. Ibid.

67. Ibid.

68. Chidanand Rajghatta, "Brain Curry: American Campuses Crave for IIT Glory," *Expressindia.com*, December 7, 1999, http://expressindia.indianexpress.com/ie/daily/20000907/svsaga5.htm, accessed November 26, 2013.

69. I am drawing here on Vijay Prashad's discussion in *Karma of Brown Folk* and Amitava Kumar's discussion of H-1B immigrants described by U.S. politicians as "indentured" labor for software companies. See Amitava Kumar, "Temporary Access: The H1B Worker in the United States," in *Technicolor: Race, Technology, and Everyday Life*, ed. Alondra Nelson and Thuy Linh N. Tu (New York: New York University Press, 2001): 76–88.

70. Andoni Alonso and Pedro J. Oiarzabal, "The Immigrant World's Digital Harbors," in *Diasporas in the New Media Age: Identity, Politics, and Community*, ed. Alonso and Oiarzabal (Reno: University of Nevada Press, 2010), 11. Distinguishing the term from the dominant concept of virtual communities (and its subsidiary, virtual nation), Alonso and Oiarzabal suggest that the wide usage of virtual community makes it not very useful to consider the particularities of history, place, and culture that they consider integral to the formation of diasporas; in turn both scholars emphasize "strong ties with real nations before creating or re-creating the digital community" as a foundational element of digital diasporas. The authors similarly distance digital diasporas from another emergent concept, digital immigrants, noting that the latter concept indicating one's entry into and gradual acquaintance with new media literacies applies more broadly to all online users.

71. However, as Radhika Gajjala notes in her essay, "South Asian Technoscapes and 'Indian' Digital Diaspora?," the phrase *digital diaspora* is sometimes used loosely in a celebratory way that masks the "layered and nuanced identities assembled in the tensions between mobility and immobility." Refer to Gajjala and Gajjala, *South Asian Technospaces*. Also see Jennifer Brinkerhoff, *Digital Diasporas: Identity and Transnational Engagement* (New York: Cambridge University Press, 2009).

72. For example, Vinay Lal, "North American Hindus, the Sense of History, and the Politics of Internet Diasporism," in Lee and Wong, *Asian America.net*, 98–138.

73. For example, Ananda Mitra, "Virtual Commonality: Looking for India on the Internet," in *Virtual Culture: Identity and Communication in Cyberspace*, ed. Steve Jones (Thousand Oaks, CA: Sage, 1997).

74. Refer to Michel S. Laguerre, "Digital Diaspora: Definition and Models," in Alonso and Oiarzabal, *Diasporas in the New Media Age*, 49–64. Critically interrogating the concept of digital diaspora, Laguerre outlines five models to delineate the differences in the interplay between IT technologies and diasporic communities. Organized around the five themes of marginality, empowerment, displacement, technopolis, and globalization, Laguerre's theoretical interventions signal some of the new directions that can be fruitfully pursued to broaden and deepen the terms of engagement with digital diasporas and counter the reductionism to which it might be vulnerable. One such vulnerability that Laguerre identifies is the overemphasis on the issue of digital divide when considering migrant and diasporic subjects. In this context, it is worthwhile to recall Anna Everett's astute observation that the rhetoric of the digital divide "has assumed the form of a potent trope of repressed racial difference in the information age." See Everett, *Digital Diaspora*, 149. In this book-length study of African American and African diasporic participation in the early years of the Internet, Everett argues that narratives of the digital divide played a crucial role in constructing black people as outsiders to the information highway, cyberspace, and technological networks. Her work uncovers how questions of digital divide, while absolutely valid and important,

can be overdetermined by the cultural baggage of imperial and racial ideologies and thereby introduce or insert old scripts into new contexts.

75. For example, even in Laguerre's sophisticated analyses outlined above, the dominant constructs of the homeland and host land go uncontested.

76. Nakamura, *Digitizing Race*, 178.

77. Berners-Lee, *Weaving the Web*, 1–2.

78. Some scholars have used critical perspectives from postcolonial theory and global media studies to evaluate the politics of race, nationalism, and Western imperialism structuring the technical grammar, network protocols, and governing practices of the Internet. An important collection, *Internationalizing Internet Studies: Beyond Anglophone Paradigms* (New York: Routledge, 2009) brings together some provocative and exciting work undertaken in this direction. Editors Gerard Goggin and Mark McLelland, in their chapter "Internationalizing Internet Studies" (3–17), speak of a key contradiction shaping the field of Internet studies, namely that while the Internet is imagined as "global," the theoretical and methodological frameworks that have dominated the field have been "framed upon Anglophone Internet experience, histories and cultures, particularly that of North America."

79. Guillermo Gómez-Peña, "The Virtual Barrio@ the Other Frontier (or the Chicano Internata)," in *Reading Digital Culture*, ed. David Trend (Malden, MA: Blackwell, 2000), 281–286.

80. Lal, "North American Hindus," 99.

81. Wendy Chun, "Orienting Orientalism or How to Map Cyberspace," in Lee and Wong, *Asian America.net*, 3–36.

82. Daniel Schiller, *Digital Capitalism: Networking the Global Market System* (Cambridge: MIT Press, 1999).

83. Lee and Wong, introduction to *Asian America.net*, xxvi.

84. Irina Shklovski and David M. Struthers, "Of States and Borders on the Internet: The Role of Domain Name Extensions in Expressions of Nationalism Online in Kazakhstan," *Policy & Internet*: 2, no. 4 (2010): 107–129, accessed at Internet, Policy and Politics Conferences, Oxford Internet Institute, http://ipp.oii.ox.ac.uk, January 28, 2014.

85. Chun, "Orienting Orientalism"; Jerry Kang, "Cyber-Race," in Lee and Wong, *Asian America.net*, 37–68.

86. Daniel Chandler, "Writing Oneself in Cyberspace." 1997, http://www.aber.ac.uk/media/Documents/short/homepgid.html, accessed June 5, 2011.

87. Turkle, quoted in ibid.

88. Nina Wakeford, "Networking Women and Grrls with Information/Communication Technology: Surfing Tales of the World Wide Web," in *Processed Lives: Gender and Technology in Everyday Life*, ed. Jennifer Terry and Melodie Calvert (London: Routledge.1997), 61.

89. Ibid., 64.

90. Refer to the poststructuralist stance where "every marked category implies its opposite." See Susan Leigh Star, "From Hestia to Homepage: Feminism and the Concept of Home in Cyberspace," in *The Cybercultures Reader*, ed. David Bell and Barbara M. Kennedy, 2nd ed., 627–663; Melissa Gregg, *Work's Intimacy* (Cambridge: Polity Press, 2011).

91. Kyra Landzelius, introduction to *Native on the Net: Indigenous and Diasporic Peoples in the Virtual Age*, ed. Landzelius (London: Routledge, 2006).

92. Emily Noelle Ignacio, *Building Diaspora: Filipino Cultural Community Formation on the Internet* (New Brunswick, NJ: Rutgers University Press, 2005).

93. Morley, *Home Territories*, 4.

94. Myria Georgiou, *Diaspora, Identity and the Media: Diasporic Transnationalism and Mediated Spatialities* (Cresskill, NJ: Hampton Press, 2006), 86.

95. Doreen B. Massey, *Space, Place and Gender* (Minneapolis: University of Minnesota Press, 1994), 168.

96. Kevin Robins and Asu Aksoy, "Thinking Experiences: Transnational Media and Migrants' Minds," in *Media and Cultural Theory*, ed. James Curran and David Morley (New York: Routledge, 2006), 87–93.

97. James Clifford, *The Predicament of Culture* (Cambridge, MA: Harvard University Press, 1998), 338.

Two. Out of Place in the Domestic Space

1. The H4 Indian Ladies forum website has been recently renovated, and the section that was earlier categorized as "regions" is now retitled as "neighborhoods."

2. Since the H-4 category only exists in the United States, this particular thread doesn't apply to Indians in Canada.

3. U.S. Citizenship and Immigration Services, H-1B Specialty.

4. Each year the USCIS releases a fact sheet detailing which countries received the H-1B visa. See, for example, "Characteristics of H1B Specialty Occupation Workers: Fiscal Year 2012 Annual Report to Congress, October 1, 2011–September 30, 2012," June 26, 2013, http://www.uscis.gov, accessed November 26, 2013.

5. S. Uma Devi, "Globalisation, Information Technology and Asian Indian Women in US," *Economic and Political Weekly* 37, no. 43 (October 26–November 1, 2002): 4421–4428.

6. M. D. Riti, "Black and Blue," Rediff India Abroad: India as It Happens, March 8, 2003, http://www.rediff.com/news/2003/mar/08spec.htm, accessed January 13, 2010.

7. See "H1B Wiki," https://www.facebook.com/h1bwiki; H1B Visa Green Card at https://twitter.com/H1BVISGREENCARD; in addition there are countless videos on YouTube that are focused on H-1B and Indian immigration.

8. Blog entries: Poonam Bhakte, "Breaking Free with H4 Possibilities," Poonam Bhakte, Poonam Bhakte Blog, March 10, 2010, http://poonambhakte.wordpress.com/tag/indian-women-on-h4-visa/; "Amreekan Wives and H4 Issues," Apu's World, April 21, 2009, http://apusworld.com/blog/2009/04/amreekan-housewives-and-h4-issues/; "Trapped," http://trappedinh4mess.wordpress.com; Ridhima Suri, "Are You on the H4? Stop Whining," Digvijay and Ridhima's Blog, October 27, 2010, http://blog.dslamba.net/2010/10/27/are-you-on-the-h4-visa-stop-whining/ October 27, 2010, all links accessed February 15, 2011.

9. "H4 visa, a curse," https://www.facebook.com/pages/H4-visa-a-curse/302349796523744.

Notes to Chapter Two

10. "H4 Visa Holders' Distress, Agony and Hardship: Listen to the Live Testimonies," radio show by Shah Peerally, http://www.youtube.com/watch?v=0f2x7t1tgtw, accessed January 10, 2013.

11. In this chapter, I cite from the posts made by the H-4 forum participants but do not identify them by their user names. I have not named the authors of the quoted posts but identify the thread in which they post along with the URL. The main URL for the forum is http://ww.indusladies.com/forums/h4-indian-ladies/151-h4-wife-things-to-do.html.

12. Morley, *Home Territories*.

13. Indusladies General Forum FAQ, http://www.indusladies.com/forums/faq.php?faq=vb3_board_usage#faq_vb3_forums_threads_posts. There is another single entry thread that was added in 2010 by the site's moderator reminding the posters not to use defamatory language while writing about technology companies. Accessed July 21, 2011.

14. "H4 Wife: Things to do?," H4 Indian Ladies forum, Indusladies.com, September 5, 2007.

15. Chandra Talpade Mohanty, *Feminism without Borders: Decolonizing Theory, Practicing Solidarity* (Durham, NC: Duke University Press, 2003), 126.

16. "Daily Routine of H4 Ladies," H4 Indian Ladies forum, Indusladies.com, April 22, 2010.

17. "H4 Wife: Things to do?," February 11, 2008.

18. Ibid., December 9, 2008.

19. U.S. Citizenship and Immigration Services, H-1B Specialty.

20. "H4 Wife: Things to do?," February 10, 2009.

21. "Looking for job in H4 status: Expert opinions needed," H4 Indian Ladies forum, Indusladies.com, January 15, 2008.

22. Ibid., January 15, 2008.

23. Ibid, January 18, 2008.

24. "H4 Visa Preparation," H4 Indian Ladies forum, Indusladies.com, May 17, 2007.

25. "H4 Wife: Things to do?," August 25, 2002.

26. Ibid, August 27, 2002.

27. Ibid., December 19, 2009.

28. Ibid., May 19, 2010.

29. Ibid., September 27, 2010.

30. See Margaret Abraham, *Speaking the Unspeakable: Marital Violence among South Asian Immigrants in the United States* (New Brunswick, NJ: Rutgers University Press, 2002); Sharmila Rudrappa, *Ethnic Routes to Becoming American* (New Brunswick, NJ: Rutgers University Press, 2004).

31. Lakshmi Chaudhry, "Battered Wives Trapped by Their Visas," *Alternet*, October 19, 2000, http://www.alternet.org, accessed November 18, 2011.

32. Department of Homeland Security, Employment Authorization Documentation (EAD) for Certain H-4 Dependent Spouses, RIN-1615-AB92, Reginfo.gov, accessed January 23, 2014.

33. "Campaign to change the law for H4 holders, please participate and spread!" H4 Indian Ladies forum, Indusladies.com, November 21, 2007.

34. In *Unruly Immigrants*, Das Gupta explores the emergence of a transnational culture of migrant rights that actively imagines itself outside the hegemonic complex of the national-citizen-subject but advances the case of rights for immigrants, legal immigrants as well as those deemed by the state as illegal.

35. "H4 Wife: Things to do?," February 8, 2008.

36. See Sandhya Shukla, *India Abroad: Diasporic Cultures of Postwar America* (Princeton, NJ: Princeton University Press, 2003) 5.

37. "H4 Wife: Things to do?," June 8, 2005.

38. The trope of being "boxed in" is common within diasporic cinema, especially around gendered subjectivities. See Desai, *Beyond Bollywood*; Naficy, *Home, Exile, Homeland*.

39. Barbara Ehrenreich and Arlie Russell Hochschild, eds., *Global Woman: Nannies, Maids, and Sex Workers in the New Economy* (New York: Metropolitan Books, 2004); Katherine M. Donato, Donna Gabaccia, Jennifer Holdaway, Martin Manalansan IV, and Patricia R. Pressar, "A Glass Half Full? Gender in Migration Studies," *International Migration Review* 40, no. 1 (February 2006): 3–26.

40. "H4 Wife: Things to do?," March 11, 2008.

41. "H4 visa opportunities," H4 Indian Ladies forum, Indusladies.com, November 20, 2007.

42. "H4 Wife: Things to do?," July 14, 2005.

43. Ibid., September 10, 2005.

44. Ibid., April 22, 2010.

45. Desai, *Beyond Bollywood*, 136.

46. "Voluntary Work on the H4 Status," H4 Indian Ladies forum, Indusladies.com, July 28, 2008.

47. See Khyati Y. Joshi, *New Roots in America's Sacred Ground: Religion, Race, and Ethnicity in Indian America* (New Brunswick, NJ: Rutgers University Press, 2006).

48. See Bhattacharjee, "Habit of Ex-Nomination"; Kurien, "To Be or Not to Be South Asian."

49. Madhavi Mallapragada, "Desktop Deities: Hindu Temples, Online Cultures and the Politics of Remediation," *South Asian Popular Culture* 8, no. 2 (2010): 109–121.

50. Considering that the parent site Indusladies has another forum dedicated to "parenting" (that is, not U.S. centric but a global forum), it is possible that women on the H-4 who are invested in issues of parenting are more active there.

51. "H4 Wife: Things to do?," August 22, 2008.

52. Ibid., May 27, 2006.

53. "H1B ladies vs. H4 homemakers," H4 Indian Ladies forum, Indusladies.com, March 2008.

54. Ibid., March 21, 2008.

55. Ibid.

56. S. Uma Devi, "Globalization, Information Technology and Asian Indian Women in US," *Economic and Political Weekly*, October 26, 2002.

57. Das Gupta, *Unruly Immigrants*, 112–113.

58. Tiziana Terranova, *Network Culture: Politics for the Information Age* (London: Pluto Press, 2004), 73–97.

59. David Morley and Roger Silverstone, "Domestic Communications: Technologies and Meanings," *Media, Culture, Society* 12 (1990): 31–55, http://mcs.sagepub.com/cgi/content/refs/12/1/31, accessed April 20, 2010.

60. Michel de Certeau, *The Practice of Everyday Life* (Berkeley: University of California Press, 1984).

61. B. Ruby Rich, "The Party Line: Gender and Technology in the Home," in *Processed Lives: Gender and Technology in Everyday Life*, ed. Jennifer Terry and Melodie Calvert (London: Routledge, 1997), 229.

62. Lynn Spigel, "Media Homes: Then and Now," *International Journal of Cultural Studies* 4, no. 4 (December 2001), 385–411, 387 (DOI: 10.1177/136787790100400402).

63. Rudrappa, *Ethnic Routes*, 40.

64. "Looking for job in H4 status: Expert opinions needed," April 3, 2005.

65. Henry Jenkins, *Convergence Culture* (New York: New York University Press, 2006).

66. Alondra Nelson and Thuy Linh N. Tu, interview with Vivek Bald, "Appropriating Technology," in *Technicolor: Race, Technology, and Everyday Life*, ed. Nelson and Tu (New York: New York University Press, 2001), 92.

67. "H4 Wife: Things to Do?" September 20, 2008.

68. "Looking for jobs in H4 Status: Expert opinions needed," August 27, 2007.

69. Ibid., November 8, 2007.

70. Ibid., November 2, 2007.

71. Wakeford, "Networking Women."

72. Raymond Williams, *Television: Technology and Cultural Form* (New York: Schocken Books, 1975).

73. Ibid.

74. Spigel, "Media Homes," 392.

75. Morley and Silverstone, "Domestic Communication," 38. Also see A. Gray, "Behind Closed Doors: Women and Video," in *Boxed In: Women and Television*, ed. Helen Baehr and Gillian Dyer (London: Routledge, 1987), 38–54; David Morley, *Family Television: Cultural Power and Domestic Leisure* (London: Comedia, 1986).

76. Martin Lister, Jon Dovey, Seth Giddings, Iain Grant, and Kieran Kelly, *New Media: A Critical Introduction* (London, Routledge, 2003); Spigel, *Media Homes*.

77. Margaret Wiley, "No Place for Women," *Digital Media* 4, no. 8 (January 1995).

78. Ibid.

79. Aihwa Ong, "The Gender and Labor Politics of Postmodernity," *Annual Review of Anthropology* 20 (1991): 279–309.

80. Peirrette Hondagneu-Sotelo, ed., *Gender and U.S. Immigration: Contemporary Trends* (Berkeley: University of California Press, 2003).

81. Rangaswamy, *Namaste America*.

82. Khandelwal, *Becoming American*.

83. Abraham, *Speaking the Unspeakable*.

84. http://www.indusladies.com/about-us/, accessed January 18, 2014.

85. Ibid.

86. http://www.indusladies.com/forum/neigborhoods, accessed January 16, 2014.

87. Anderson, *Imagined Communities*.

88. INDOlink, "Women's corner," INDOlink.com, Internet Archive. https://archive.org.

89. "The H4 Visa," Women's Corner, INDOlink.com, February 11, 1999, available on the INDOlink page dated February 10, 2001, Internet Archive, https://archive.org.

90. Radhika Gajjala, *Cyber Selves: Feminist Ethnographies of South Asian Women* (Walnut Creek, CA: AltaMira Press, 2004), 103.

91. There are an additional 20,000 H-1B visas allotted each year that are exempted from the overall quota because they are given to those with an advanced degree from a U.S. university. See "FY 2012 Annual Report: H-1B Petitions," U.S. Citizenship and Immigration Services (USCIS), http://www.uscis.gov, accessed December 20, 2013.

92. "FY 2006 Annual Report: H-1B Petitions," USCIS, http://www.uscis.gov.

93. For example, see Chloe Albanesius, "H1B Visa Debate Riles Techies, Congress," *PC Magazine*, June 7, 2007, http://www.pcmag.com; for one example of perspectives on the H-1B debate and its role in the ongoing immigration reform see Neil G. Ruiz and Jill H. Wilson, "A Balancing Act for H-1B Visas," Brookings, April 18, 2013, http://www.Brookings.edu.

94. "Bill Gates Written Transcript from Today's Congressional Testimony," Network World, March 12, 2008, http://www.networkworld.com, accessed December 20, 2013.

95. Marianne Kolbasuk McGee, "Who Got H-1B Visa Petitions Approved in 2008? Look at the List," InformationWeek, April 2, 2008, http://www.informationweek.com; Patrick Thibodeau, "Indian Firms Were Largest H1B Users in 2007," *Computerworld*, March 10, 2008, http://www.computerworld.com.

96. While H1Bjobs.com no longer exists, there are multiple other sites that perform the same task of serving the needs of potential H-1B applicants.

97. "The Problems and Hardships of H1B Visa Holding Employees," NRIOL.com, 1999, http://web.archive.org/web/20000914070945/http://www.nriol.com/content/articles/article8.html.

98. H1B Marriages.com, http://www.h1bmarriages.com/contactus.asp, accessed December 21, 2011.

99. Patricia Wise, "Always Already Virtual: Feminist Politics in Cyberspace," in *Virtual Politics: Identity and Community in Cyberspace*, ed. David Holmes (London: Sage, 1997).

100. Grewal, *Transnational America*.

101. I am making a distinction between victims and discursive positioning of immigrant women as victims.

Three. The Wired Home

Early drafts of sections of this chapter have been previously published. See Madhavi Mallapragada, "Home, Homeland, Homepage: Belonging and the Indian-American Web," *New Media and Society* 8, no. 2 (2006): 207–227.

Notes to Chapter Three

1. ICIC Bank–NRI Services, https://www.facebook.com/ICICIBankNriServices?fref=ts, accessed on January 12, 2013.

2. "ICIC Bank NRI Services Wins Asian Banker Award for Excellence in Business Model Innovation," ICIC Bank press release, April 3, 2009, http://www.icicibank.com/aboutus/pdf/AsianBanker1_Apr09.pdf, accessed April 10, 2010.

3. ICIC Bank–NRI Services, https://www.facebook.com/ICICIBankNriServices?fref=ts, accessed June 24, 2013.

4. Ibid.

5. George Lipsitz, "'Home Is Where the Hatred Is': Work, Music, and the Transnational Economy," in Naficy, *Home, Exile, Homeland*, 194.

6. Khandelwal, *Becoming American*, 122.

7. Bandana Purkayastha, *Negotiating Ethnicity: Second-Generation South Asian Americans Transverse a Transnational World* (New Brunswick, NJ: Rutgers University Press, 2005), 59.

8. See Arlene Davila, *Latinos, Inc.: The Marketing and Making of a People* (Berkeley: University of California Press, 2001). I am drawing here on the notion of the commodification and corporatization of ideas of ethnicity and national difference in the age of global markets and digital capital.

9. "About Indiaplaza," FAQs, http://www.indiaplaza.com/StaticPageContainer.aspx?htmlfilename=Faqs, accessed August 15, 2011.

10. Rajghatta, *Horse That Flew*, 267.

11. Namaste.com, page for December 2, 2000, retrieved from Internet Archive, http://archive.org, accessed April 19, 2012.

12. Ibid.

13. Ibid.

14. For example, see the Ustav Fashion website, www.utsavfashion.com, which sells a range of Indian saris and advertises its Kanjeevaram saris as "very traditional" saris that "never go out of fashion."

15. The information is taken from the pages I have stored in my personal archive as well as those retrieved from the Internet Archive, http://web.archive.org/web/20001018173712/http://namaste.com/, October 18, 2000.

16. Namaste.com, FAQ, from Internet Archive, December 2, 2000, accessed April 19, 2012.

17. Jeff Bezos, statement in an interview in the PBS documentary "Networking the Nerds," *Nerds 2.0.1: A Brief History of the Internet*, by Robert X. Cringely, 1998.

18. Jay David Bolter, and Richard Grusin, *Remediation: Understanding New Media* (Cambridge, MA: MIT Press, 1999), 15.

19. Namaste.com, FAQ.

20. Nithya Ramanan, "Desi Dotcom," *India Currents* 15, no. 9 (January 31, 2001): 21, accessed through ProQuest, January 14, 2010.

21. Namaste Raises $34 Million, *SiliconIndia*, 4, no. 10 (October 2000): 18, accessed through EBSCOhost, January 25, 2010.

22. Melanie Warner, "The Most Successful VC Is Not Who You Think," *Fortune* magazine, October 30, 2000, http://money.cnn.com/magazines/fortune/fortune_archive/2000/10/30/290619/index.htm, accessed November 18, 2001.

23. Vinod Khosla, qtd. in Ramanan, "Desi Dotcom."

24. Simon Butler, "Festive Lights," *Adweek Eastern Edition* 41, no. 41 (October 9, 2000): 64, accessed through EBSCOhost, January 25, 2010.

25. Cited in Butler, "Festive Lights."

26. Nancy Coltun Webster, "B4U to Woo Viewers with Big Effort in '01; Satellite Channels Eye South Asians," *Advertising Age*, October 23, 2000, accessed through LexisNexis, January 31, 2010.

27. Maki Becker, "It's Hooray for Bollywood! Bombay's Hot Flicks Are Hot Tix in Astoria," *New York Daily News*, September 19, 2000, 5, accessed through LexisNexis, January 31, 2010.

28. Simon Butler, "Salaam, Namaste.com!" *Adweek Midwest Edition* 41, no. 28 (July 10, 2000): 4, accessed through EBSCOhost, January 25, 2010.

29. Butler, "Festive Lights."

30. The advertisement appeared in *SiliconIndia*, August 2000, 69. The California-based magazine has been targeting Indian immigrants in the technology and business sectors since 1996.

31. Saskia Sassen, *The Global City: New York, London, Tokyo* (Princeton, NJ: Princeton University Press, 2001).

32. Namaste.com advertisement appeared in *Silicon India* 4, no. 7 (2000): 69.

33. Avtar Brah, *Cartographies of Diaspora: Contesting Identities* (London: Routledge, 1996), 208.

34. In their quantitative study of four matrimonial websites popular among the Indian diaspora, namely Shaadi.com, Jeevansaathi.com, Bharatmatrimony.com, and Rediff-Matchmaker.com, Sonara Jha and Mara Adelman note that fair-skinned women were prominently on display on the site and its success stories (while dark-skinned women were almost absent). They conclude that the sites exemplify "technology-abetted intensification of colorism" (65). See Sonora Jha and Mara Adelman, "Looking for Love in All the White Places: A Study of Skin Color Preferences on Indian Matrimonial and Mate-Seeking Websites," *Studies in South Asian Film and Media* 1, no. 1 (2009): 65–83 (DOI: 10.1386/safm.1.1.65/1).

35. The "woman" question, as Partha Chatterjee argues, was key to the imagining of the nation in the anticolonial and postcolonial struggles of India; it posited the middle-class Hindu woman in charge of the cultural reproduction of the nation within the private, familial, domestic, and spiritual sphere. That such ideologies were being remanufactured within conservative Indian immigrant community discourses in the United States has been brought to our attention by the work of scholars such as Annanya Bhattacharjee; see Partha Chatterjee, *The Nation and Its Fragments: Colonial and Postcolonial Histories* (Princeton, NJ: Princeton University Press, 1993); Bhattacharjee, "Habit of Ex-Nomination."

36. Roland Barthes, *Mythologies*, trans. Annette Lavers (New York: Hill and Wang, 1973).

37. Nira Yuval-Davis, *Gender and Nation* (Thousand Oaks, CA: Sage 1997).

38. Barthes, *Mythologies*.

39. Bhattacharjee, "Habit of Ex-Nomination"; Kurien, "To Be or Not to Be South Asian."

40. Amitava Kumar, *Passport Photos* (Berkeley: University of California Press, 2000).

41. See Wise, "Always Already Virtual," and Rob Shields, *The Virtual* (London: Routledge, 2003).

42. I am a little hesitant to push the reading of city as space of alienation since it is marked as the home prior to the interventions of Namaste.com.

43. Sassen, *Global City*; John Urry, *Mobilities* (Cambridge: Polity, 2007).

44. NRI films of the 1990s—for example, the films of Karan Johar—privilege New York, even though it coincides with the rise of the California-bound techie.

45. See "Directory of Indians on the Net7," Google Groups, rec.music.indian.misc, January 1, 1998, accessed December 20, 2013.

46. "Net Gurus Pick: The Best and Brightest Sites; B. G. Mahesh's Picks," *LittleIndia*, February 1, 1998, 24, accessed through Proquest, June 1, 2008.

47. "About Indiaplaza." Bangalore was called the Silicon Valley of India in the 1980s because of its software and engineering culture and in the 1990s because of the start-up culture.

48. Girish Chaddha, "IndiaPlaza on Rs 150cr Expansion Drive," December 10, 1999, http://www.expressindia.com/fe/daily/19991210/fco10051.html, accessed November 23, 2004.

49. Featured on Samachar.com, August 14, 2000, personal archive.

50. "About Indiaplaza."

51. Ramanan, "Desi Dotcom."

52. "Fabmall.com Buys Indiaplaza.com," *Hindu*, January 20, 2007, http://www.hindu.com/2007/01/20/stories/2007012002131800.htm.

53. "About Indiaplaza," FAQs. Indiaplaza.com, accessed June 11, 2013.

54. Indiaplaza, https://www.facebook.com/indiaplaza.

55. "The Day of the Diaspora," *India Abroad*, January 10, 2003, sec. S, 1–4.

56. In summer 2012, Madhuri Dixit entered the club of returning NRIs when she moved back to Mumbai.

57. "Day of the Diaspora."

58. Ibid.

59. Josy Joseph, "Dual Citizenship Likely for People of Indian Origin," *India Abroad*, January 10, 2003, sec. A, 1.

60. The Indian government had chosen January 9 because it was the day Mahatma Gandhi, India's most famous nonresident Indian, returned from South Africa to India.

61. "PIO Scheme," Ministry of Home Affairs, Government of India, http://mha.nic.in/pioscheme, accessed December 28 2013.

62. "Rediff.com Re-launches India Abroad Weekly Publication," *Business Wire*, August 1, 2001, available through LexisNexis, accessed July 14, 2002.

63. Ibid.

64. Internet Archive for information on Rediff.com in combination with my personal archive.

65. "Silicon Valley Portal to Merge with Rediff.com to Create Rediff USA," *Financial News*, October 27, 2000; "Rediff.com Completes Acquisition of Value Communications Corporation: New Entity to Leverage Strengths and Offer Expanded Services to Indian Americans in the U.S." *Business Wire*, April 12, 2001; "Rediff.com Re-Launches *India Abroad* Weekly Publication," *Business Wire*, August 1, 2001.

66. "Silicon Valley Portal."

67. "Rediff.Com Completes Acquisition of Value Communications Corporation: New Entity to Leverage Strengths and Offer Expanded Services to Indian Americans in the U.S," *Business Wire*, April 12, 2001.

68. Ibid.

69. Madanmohan Rao, "Web Explosion: The Corporate Pioneers," *INOMY: Knowledge on Information Economy*, n.d., http://www.inomy.com/topstories6.asp, accessed March 15, 2002 (no longer available).

70. ICICI Bank NRI Services, Rediff.com, 2002, http://nrifinance.rediff.com/, accessed November 6, 2002, personal archive.

71. Nandini Lakshman, "The Money Movers: With a Growing Indian Diaspora, Banks and New-Age Players Are Pulling Out All Stops to Bag the Remittance Business," *India Abroad*, April 11, 2003, B3.

72. ICICI Bank NRI Services.

73. Ibid.

74. Even in the past, NRIs, by virtue of being Indian citizens even while they lived in a foreign country, were allowed to open bank accounts with certain banks that were authorized dealers of foreign exchange. To be authorized, a bank needs to get approval from its bureaucratic head, the Reserve Bank of India (RBI). However, prior to the mid 1990s, the RBI, following the dictates of the Indian state, placed severe restrictions on banks that were authorized to deal in foreign exchange; in turn, they limited the options that banks could make available for their NRI account holders. But since then, with the Indian government having suddenly awakened to the fact that its 20 million–strong global diaspora members are worth more than $510 billion, the RBI, as the Indian state's financial authority, has initiated some changes within the banking system that are potentially meant to attract more NRI accounts and, hence, more foreign exchange. As a result, banks that are authorized dealers can allow NRIs more options in terms of the type of accounts, amount of money invested, maturity rates, money transfers, and the like. Lakshman, "Money Movers."

75. ICICI Bank NRI Services, Rediff.com, http://nrifinance.rediff.com/ accessed August 10, 2003, personal archive.

76. The most common method in use at the time was to send a check in U.S. dollars that was then deposited in an Indian bank. It took approximately four to six weeks for the check to be cleared. A faster though costlier method was to use a wire transfer, where banks would transfer the money internally while charging an exorbitant transfer fee; approx. $40–50 fee for transferring $1,000.

77. ICICI Bank NRI Services *Rediff.com*, http://nrifinance.rediff.com/, accessed November 7, 2002.

78. Scholars of Indian diasporic cultures have noted how buying property has become a way for the middle-class migrant to make a home in the new country of residence, and it is a trend that is currently on the upswing. In May 2012, *India Abroad* carried a cover story on NRIs who are the third largest "foreign" group in the United States to buy homes this past year; the narrative suggests that while the real estate market is in a slump, NRIs are some of the elite immigrants who are investing in property. Ritu Jha, "Indian Resident, House in US," *India Abroad*, May 25, 2012, A9.

79. Supriya Singh, "Towards a Sociology of Money and Family in the Indian Diaspora," *Contributions to Indian Sociology* 40 (2006): 375–398, 393 (DOI 10/1177/006996670604000304).

80. Ibid.

81. V. A. Zelizer, *The Purchase of Intimacy* (Princeton, NJ: Princeton University Press, 2005), 222.

82. ICICI Bank, NRI Services, Rediff.com, http://nrifinance.rediff.com/, accessed August 8, 2003.

83. "ICICI Ropes in Shahrukh Khan," Money Control.com. January 10, 2006, http://www.moneycontrol.com/news/business/icici-bank-ropesshah-rukh-khan_197333.html, accessed May 1, 2009. The TV ad that is discussed is available on YouTube, http://www.youtube.com/watch?v=oXxIa7i-c-o, accessed March 14, 2011.

84. Shohat, "By the Bits of Babylon."

85. Aihwa Ong, *Neoliberalism as Exception: Mutations in Citizenship and Sovereignty* (Durham, NC: Duke University Press, 2006), 6.

86. "NRI Banking," Citibank India, http://www.online.citibank.co.in, accessed August 8, 2003, personal archive.

87. NRI Services, Citibank India, http://www.online.citibank.co.in, accessed August 8, 2003, personal archive.

88. "NRI Banking", State Bank of India, http://www.statebankofindia.com/nribanking/nrimain.asp, accessed August 8, 2003, personal archive.

89. "Amitabh Bachchan, Legendary Bollywood Star Named Brand Ambassador for Xoom—a Digital Money Transfer Provider," XOOM.com, May 20, 2013, accessed December 20, 2013.

90. "Xoom Signs On as an Associate Sponsor of Dabangg 2," XOOM.com December 4, 2012, accessed December 20, 2013.

Four. Desi Networks

An earlier version of some of the sections in this chapter appear in the article "Rethinking Desi: Race, Class, and Online Activism of South Asian Immigrants in the United States," *Television and New Media*, published online before print May 13, 2013 (doi: 10.1177/1527476413487225).

1. The Special Registration Program was implemented between September 2002 and September 2003 before the Department of Homeland Security suspended it following a widespread criticism of the policy from civil and human rights groups. It was reported that

during 2002–2003, over 85,000 individuals were registered and subject to interrogation for potential ties to terrorism. The NSEERS was dismantled in 2011 (after some of its features were carried over into other immigration policies). See Channing Kennedy, "After Nine Years of Pressure DHS Finally Drops 'SB 1070 for Muslims,'" Colorlines.com, April 29, 2011, accessed December 20, 2013. The article extensively draws on DRUM activists' perspectives on this controversial program. Also see Muzaffar Chisthi and Claire Bergenon, "DHS Announces End to Controversial Post-9/11 Immigrant Registration and Tracking Program," Migration Information Source, May 17, 2011, http://www.migrationinformation.org/usfocus/display.cfm?ID=840, accessed December 1, 2012.

2. Kennedy, "After Nine Years"; Chisthi and Bergenon, "DHS Announces End."

3. In the growing body of scholarship on marginalized politics and locations within the Indian and South Asian diasporic communities in the United States, issues such as working-class activism, community organizing against domestic violence, the desi LGBT (lesbian, gay, bisexual, and transgender) movement and multiracial coalitions emerging within the community are being emphasized and in turn are expanding the terms of debate with respect to the ideological positions and lived experiences of South Asians in the United States. See, for example, Sunaina Maira, *Missing: Youth, Citizenship, and Empire after 9/11* (Durham, NC: Duke University Press, 2009); Ajay Nair and Murali Balaji, eds. *Desi Rap: Hip-Hop and South Asian America* (Lanham, MD: Lexington Books, 2008); Shalini Shankar, *Desi Land: Teen Culture, Class, and Success in Silicon Valley* (Durham, NC: Duke University Press, 2008).

4. See Sunaina Maira, *Desis in the House: Indian American Youth Culture in New York City* (Philadelphia: Temple University Press, 2002).

5. Lowe, *Immigrant Acts*, x.

6. The DRUM website (Drumnyc.org) is neither the only nor the first website to articulate South Asian activism. The South Asian Women's Network (Sawnet.org) has been active since 1995 and can be considered one of the earliest online representations of South Asian feminist coalitions.

7. "About us," DRUM, http://www.drumnyc.org/about-us/, accessed January 20, 2014.

8. A URL, as stated in the introduction, is the web designation that locates the website's home in the WWW space. See Berners-Lee, *Weaving the Web*.

9. The YouTube channel is called "Desis Rising Up and Moving;" in addition, there are several YouTube videos that circulate footage revolving around DRUM activism, in effect creating a network of images, texts, and media, around its message; "DRUM Beats Blog," http://www.drumnyc.org/DRUM/Blog/Blog.html, accessed 2012 (URL no longer available).

10. New York Taxi Workers Alliance, http://www.nytwa.org/, accessed March 2012.

11. Author's telephone conversation with Roxana Mun, staff person at DRUM, November 11, 2011.

12. "Youth Power!" DRUM, http://www.drumnyc.org/youthpower/, accessed December 20, 2013.

13. "South Asian Workers Center," DRUM, http://www.drumnyc.org/south-asian-workers-center/, accessed December 20, 2013.

14. "About Us," DRUM; "Amadou Diallo R.I.P. (RESIST on IN POWER)—14 Years Ago Today," n.d. http://www.drumnyc.org/amadou-diallo-r-i-p-resist-on-in-power-14-years-ago-today/, accessed January 17, 2014.

15. "About Us," DRUM; "Amadou Diallo R.I.P"; also see Jane Fritsch, "The Diallo Verdict: The Overview; 4 Officers in Diallo Shooting Are Acquitted of All Charges," *New York Times*, February 26, 2000, http://www.nytimes.com, accessed April 2008.

16. I am here referencing content from older versions of the site. DRUM, Mission, http://www.drumnyc.org/DRUM/Mission.html, accessed March 2010 (URL no longer available).

17. "About Us," DRUM.

18. Scholars including Vijay Prashad, Sunaina Maira, Jigna Desai, and Sandhya Shukla have made this argument.

19. Ragini Tharoor Srinivasan, "On Our Radar," *India Currents*, http://www.indiacurrents.com/articles/2008/12/30/on-our-radar, accessed December 30, 2008.

20. DesiHits.com, About Us, http://www.desihits.com/about, accessed February 2008.

21. Maira, *Desis in the House*.

22. Desai, *Beyond Bollywood*, 52.

23. Khalid Ilhai, "Desi Hits Co-Founder: Anjula Acharia-Bath," 2007, http://www.desiclub.com/community/culture/culture_article.cfm?id=325, accessed February 2008.

24. Maira, *Desis in the House*.

25. Ilhai, "Desi Hits Co-Founder."

26. Desi Threads: Clothing for Your Culture, http://www.desithreads.com/ accessed September 2008.

27. Desai, *Beyond Bollywood*; Gayatri Gopinath, *Impossible Desires: Queer Diasporas and South Asian Public Cultures* (Durham, NC: Duke University Press, 2005).

28. See Sunil Bhatia, *American Karma: Race, Culture, and Identity in the Indian Diaspora* (New York: New York University Press, 2007), especially the discussion on 12–21.

29. Visweswaran, "Diaspora by Design."

30. Prashad, *Karma of Brown Folk*, 93.

31. Ibid.

32. Ong, *Flexible Citizenship*.

33. Nair and Balaji, *Desi Rap*.

34. Nitasha Tamar Sharma, *Hip Hop Desis: South Asian Americans, Blackness, and a Global Race Consciousness* (Durham, ND: Duke University Press, 2010); Shankar, *Desi Land*.

35. Das Gupta, *Unruly Immigrants*, 9.

36. DREAM (Development, Relief and Education for Alien Minors) is a proposal introduced in 2001 to enable illegal immigrants who arrived in the United States as minors to become permanent residents (upon fulfillment of some conditions including "good behavior"). The Obama administration announced its support for the DREAM act in June 2012.

37. See Das Gupta, *Unruly Immigrants*.

38. Ibid.

39. Ibid, 16.

40. Ibid.

41. Ibid., 14.

42. Ibid., 16.

43. Lowe, *Immigrant Acts*; Ong, *Neoliberalism as Exception*.

44. Lisa Nakamura, *Cybertypes: Race, Ethnicity, and Identity on the Internet* (New York: Routledge, 2002), 5.

45. Yen Le Espiritu, *Asian American Panethnicity: Bridging Institutions and Identities* (Philadelphia: Temple University Press, 1993).

46. Racial and Immigrant Justice Program, DRUM, http://www.drumnyc.org/racial-immigrant-justice-program/, accessed December 20, 2013. Also see "Stop-and-Frisk Campaign: About the Issue," New York Civil Liberties Union, http://www.nyclu.org/issues/racial-justice/stop-and-frisk-practices, accessed June 1, 2013.

47. NYPD, "Radicalization in the West: The Homegrown Threat." The report is available at http://www.nypdshield.org/public/SiteFiles/documents/NYPD_Report-Radicalization_in_the_West.pdf, accessed January 17, 2014.

48. George P. Landow, *Hypertext 3.0: Critical Theory and New Media in an Era of Globalization* (Baltimore: Johns Hopkins University Press, 2006).

49. "YouthPower!" DRUM.

50. Education Not Deportation: Impacts of New York City School Safety Policies on South Asian Immigrant Youth, June 2006, http://www.urbanjustice.org/pdf/publications/Education_Not_Deportation_Report_06jun06.pdf, accessed November 27, 2013.

51. Ibid.

52. Maira, *Missing*.

53. Ibid., 37–75.

54. Ibid., 128–189.

55. Ibid., 190–257.

56. Martha McCaughey and Michael D. Ayers, eds., *Cyber Activism: Online Activism in Theory and Practice* (New York: Routledge, 2003), 4.

57. "Global Justice Program," DRUM, http://www.drumnyc.org/global-justice-program/, accessed January 17, 2014.

58. Nakamura, *Digitizing Race*, 85–86. Also relevant here is Kandice Chuh's argument in *Imagine Otherwise: On Asian Americanist Critique* (Durham, NC: Duke University Press, 2003). Turning her attention to Asian American studies and literary studies, Chuh critiques the recurrence of "the uniform ethnic subject" (26) in the multicultural vein of academic discourse. For Chuh, then, an alternative is to constantly foreground the discursive construction of Asian American at various sites (literary studies, the diversity quota in universities, film representations) so that one gets a better sense of what can count as radical or political in a given context. In this context, the book's titular call to "imagine otherwise" is envisioned as an intervention to "undermine persistently the multicultural, positivist narratives of otherness that suggest a concrete knowability" (26).

59. McCaughey and Ayers, *Cyber Activism*, 5.

60. This discussion includes references to images that existed on previous versions of the DRUM site, such as the protest for workers in Louisiana.

61. While South Asian immigrants are rarely represented as political subjects in print or television, there has been some attention paid just recently to Indian Americans participating in political races at the state and federal level. However, such narratives only bolster mythologies of South Asians as model minorities, and of America as a place of happy multiculturalism.

62. Peter X Feng, ed., *Screening Asian Americans* (New Brunswick, NJ: Rutgers University Press, 2002); Gina Marchetti, *Romance and the "Yellow Peril": Race, Sex, and Discursive Hollywood Strategies in Hollywood Fiction* (Berkeley: University of California Press, 1993); Peter X Feng, *Identities in Motion: Asian American Film and Video* (Durham, NC: Duke University Press, 2002); Glen M. Mimura, *Ghostlife of Third Cinema: Asian American Film and Video* (Minneapolis: University of Minnesota Press, 2009); and Jun Xing, *Asian America through the Lens* (Walnut Creek, CA: AltaMira Press, 1998) are a few examples.

63. Feng, *Screening Asian Americans*, 6.

64. See Jun Xing's critical overview of Asian representations in American mass media. Examining the racist and sexist underpinnings of character types such as the docile, suffering, and sacrificing Lotus Blossom, the aggressive, manipulative, and devious Dragon, the sexualized vamp Suzie Wong, and the unfeminine, cold "Connie Chung," Deborah Gee's groundbreaking documentary *Slaying the Dragon* (1988) foregrounds the ways in which the depiction of Asian women on screen bleeds into public perceptions of Asian American women.

65. Darrel Y. Hamamoto, *Monitored Peril: Asian Americans and the Politics of TV Representation* (Minneapolis: University of Minnesota Press, 1994), 2–3.

66. Shilpa Davé, "Apu's Brown Voice: Cultural Inflection and South Asian Accents," in *East Main Street: Asian American Popular Culture*, ed. Shilpa Davé, LeiLani Nishime, and Tasha G. Oren (New York: New York University Press, 2005), 313–337.

67. I am not ignoring by any means the ways in which the presence of South Asian artists like *The Daily Show*'s Asif Mandvi interrupts such hegemonic representations; however, my larger point here is that there is a paradigm of Asian and South Asian representations within discourses of alterity to the white nation that cannot be overlooked.

68. Marchetti, *Romance and the "Yellow Peril,"* 216. A good example of the fears of a heteronormative white nation from the 1960s is the Marlon Brando film *Sayonara*.

69. "*Outsourced*," Wikipedia.org., n.d. The television series originally aired on NBC from September 23, 2010, to May 12, 2011.

70. Kent A. Ono and Vincent N. Pham's chapter "Asian American New Media Practices," in their coauthored book, *Asian Americans and the Media* (Malden, MA: Polity Press, 2009), 140–156, carries a good overview on this topic.

71. "DRUM Beats Blog."

72. Nicholas Burbules, "Rhetorics of the Web: Hyperreading and Critical Literacy," in *Page to Screen: Taking Literacy into the Electronic Age*, ed. Illana Synder (London: Routledge, 1998), 102–122.

73. Rosa Linda Fregoso, "Recycling Colonialist Fantasies on the Texas Borderlands," in Naficy, *Home, Exile, Homeland*, 169–193, 178. Here I am drawing on Fregoso's argument that films made in Hollywood and Mexico about the border present it as site of absolute alterity.

74. Shohat, "By the Bitstream of Babylon," 220.

75. "Previous Years" Media, DRUM, http://www.drumnyc.org/media/previous-years/, accessed January 18, 2014.

76. See Channing Kennedy, "After Nine Years of Pressure DHS Finally Drops 'SB1070 for Muslims.'"

77. I am referring to material that existed on the older version of the DRUM website. As I suggest in my discussion, this material (as hyperlinks but also as news content) is no longer available on DRUM's media archive, but nevertheless their presence in constructing a narrative of DRUM's activism cannot be overlooked. Tram Nguyen, "Detained of Dissapeared [sic]?" June 15, 2002, *ColorLines*, http://colorlines.com/archives/2002/06/detained_of_dissapeared.html; Heather Appel, "'Suspects' Talk Back: Muslims Complain to FBI," *City Limits*, November 2, 2009, http://www.citylimits.org/news/articles/3830/-suspects-talk-back; Kaitlin Kilimentis, "Immigrants Show Solidarity in Arrests," *Queens Tribune*, October 15, 2009, http://www.queenstribune.com/news/1255622718.html, accessed on May 12, 2011; "South Asians Join Marches in DC for Just Immigration Reform and No More War, March 21, 2010," http://www.drumnation.org, February 13, 2011, available on Internet Archive, https: //archive.org.

78. "Videos" Media, DRUM, http://www.drumnyc.org/media/, accessed January 17, 2014.

79. Jacques Derrida, *Archive Fever: A Freudian Impression*, trans. Eric Prenowitz (Chicago: University of Chicago Press, 1998), 17.

Conclusion

1. Rob Shields, "Hypertext Links: The Ethics of the Index and Its Space-Time Effect," in *The World Wide Web and Contemporary Cultural Theory*, ed. Andrew Herman and Thomas Swiss (New York: Routledge, 2000), 148.

2. Ibid.

3. Ibid.

4. Morley, *Home Territories*, 2–3.

5. See Goggin and McLelland, *Internationalizing Internet Studies*; Brügger, *Web History*; Nakamura and Chow White, *Race after the Internet*.

6. Charles Ess, "History—With a Future," foreword to Brügger, *Web History*, vii.

7. Anna Everett, *Digital Diaspora: A Race for Cyberspace* (Albany: State University of New York Press, 2009); Dan Schiller, *Digital Capitalism: Networking the Global Market System* (Cambridge, MA: MIT Press).

8. Terry and Calvert, *Processed Lives*, 6.

9. "Returning NRIs: Best of Both Worlds," *India Today*, January 6, 2013, http://businesstoday.intoday.in/story/nris-return-to-country-on-rise-in-professional-opportunities/1/190737.html, accessed January 10, 2013.

10. Michael Fitzgerald, "H-1B at the Center of Immigration Reform Debate," *Information Week*, May 16, 2013, http://www.informationweek.com/global-cio/h1b/h-1b-at-center-of-immigration-reform-deb/240155054, accessed May 22, 2013.

11. Lisa Nakamura has complicated the concept by exposing how the term *open door* functions to create a techno-elitist vision of Asian American solidarity vis-à-vis consumption of technology and gadgets. See Nakamura, *Digitizing Race* and *Cybertypes*.

12. Leo R. Chavez, *The Latino Threat: Constructing Immigrants, Citizens and the Nation* (Stanford, CA: Stanford University Press 2008); Prashad, *Karma of Brown Folk*.

Index

ABCD *(American Born Confused Desi)*, 124
Acharia-Bath, Anjula, 123, 124
ACLU-Arizona, 139
activism, 14, 133, 140, 156; community, 71, 115, 146; desi, 18, 129, 150; immigrant, 129, 132; for justice, 120, 141; online, 128–36, 137, 139–41, 173; social, 138; transnational, 129. *See also* social justice activism
Aderer, Konrad, 115
Aditya Birla Group, 102
AdmerAsia, 92–93
advertising, 8, 17, 92–96, 110–14
Advocates for Children, 140
Agii.org, 9
Alam, Mohammed, 115–17
Alliance for Educational Justice, 139
Alonso, Andoni, 39
Amazon.com, 89
ambivalence, 39, 52, 125–26, 148; racial, 35–36
American Desi (film), 124
America Online, 26
Amerindo Investment Advisors, 91
Amul, 87–88
Ang, Ien, 21
Apu's World, 47
Ashcroft, John, 115

Asian Americans: consumer market, 10–11; immigration trends, 11–13; media representations of, 136–38; model minority stereotype and, 9–10, 16; online grocery stores targeted at, 90–91; studies of, 126, 176n58
AT&T, 88, 106
Austin, Texas, 26, 35–36, 38, 65, 72, 102–3
Ayers, Michael D., 133

Bachchan, Amitabh, 107–8, 113
Bald, Vivek, 66
Bandhan, Raksha, 101
Bangalore, 25–26, 32, 86, 100, 102–3
Bangladeshi, 115–16, 118, 151, 155
Banker Magazine, 104
banking, 8, 103–14, 172n74, 172n76
Barthes, Roland, 96
bawarchi.com, 7
bayareaindia.com, 9
beauty, idealized, 94–97
Bedi, Subhash, 90
belonging: domestic discontent and lack of, 55–63; in homepage cultures, 5–9; ideal NRI home and, 84–85; Namaste.com's investment in, 99–100
Benchmark Capital, 91

Index

Berners-Lee, Tim, 5, 22, 41
Bezos, Jeff, 89
Bhaji on the Beach (film), 58
Bhangra, 123
Bharat Ek Khoj, 100
Bhatia, Sabeer, 25–26
Bhatke, Poonam, 47
bhelpuri, 93
Big Bang Theory, The (TV show), 35
Bilz and Kashif, 123
Bing, 4
Black Alliance for Just Immigration, 139
blogs and blogging, 2–3, 29, 47–48, 64–65, 72, 139–40
Bollywood, 74, 82, 92, 104, 105, 111, 123, 124
Bolter, Jay David, 89
border security, 138–39
Breakthrough Films, 138, 139
Brügger, Niels, 145
Buffet, Warren, 82–83
Burbules, Nicholas, 141
Bush, George W., 115

cafepharma, 30
capital, venture. *See* venture capital
capitalism, 10, 118; digital, 22, 36, 75, 97, 127; industrial, 35; informational, 99; network, 9–16
Cbazaar.com, 86
Census Bureau, U.S., 10, 11, 12, 17
Chaddha, Gurinder, 58
Chandler, Daniel, 43
Checkpoint Nation? (film), 138
Chennai, 15, 26, 79, 86, 101, 103
Chow-White, Peter A., 145
Chun, Wendy, 28, 41–42, 43
Citibank, 102, 112–13
Citigroup, 102
citizenship: cultural, 2, 22, 66, 95, 133, , 140; dual, 15, 104–5, 127, 129; flexible, 22, 84, 148
Citizenship and Immigration Services, U.S. (USCIS), 46, 53, 76
Citizens Union Foundation, 140
city, global, 94, 98, 129. *See also* entries for specific cities
City University of New York (CUNY), 131–32

Clark, Jim, 37
CLEAR (Creating Law Enforcement Accountability and Responsibility), 131
clothing, desi, 124–25
CNN, 26
Coalición de Derechos Humanos, 139
colonialism, 38, 163n78
ColorLines (magazine), 141
Community Safety Act, 120
country code Top Level Domains (ccTLDs), 42
cricinfo.com, 7
Culture Shock, 123
curry, 27–28; as metaphor for Indian immigrants, 27–38; social media discussions on smelling like, 28–31. *See also* food
curry brigade, 32–35
curry rock, 31–32
"Cyberabad," 26, 34
cyberfeminism, 75
Cyber Selves (Gajjala), 75

Dabangg (film), 113–14
Das Gupta, Monisha, 129
dating and marriage sites, 8, 79, 170n34
Department of Homeland Security, U.S., 116, 173–74n1
Derrida, Jacques, 141
Desai, Jigna, 58, 124
desi: clothing, 124–25; defined, 117–18; music, 123–24, 126–27; online activism, 128–36; race and class, 119–27. *See also* DRUM (Desis Rising Up and Moving)
Desi Hits! (desihits.com), 123–24
Desimart.com, 86
Desi Rap (ed. Nair and Balaji), 126
Desis Rising Up and Moving. *See* DRUM (Desis Rising Up and Moving)
Desi Threads, 124–25
Devarajan, Srikanth, 31–32
Devi, S. Uma, 62–63
Dham, Vinod, 24
Diallo, Amadou, 122
diaspora, 17, 103–5, 107
Dice (job board), 29–30
digital capitalism, 22, 36, 75, 97, 127
digital diaspora, 23, 39–44, 147, 162n74
Dignity in Schools campaign, 120

Index

DIRECTV, 92, 113
DISH network, 92, 113
Diwali, 87, 92
Dixit, Madhuri, 104
DJ Rekha, 123
DJ Suketu, 123
Domain Name System, 42
dot-com boom, 7, 26
Douglas, Mary, 21
DREAM act, 128
DRUM (Desis Rising Up and Moving), 2, 18, 115; *desi* term and, 117–19; importance of, 141–42; media coverage and, 136–41; membership, 121–22; mission of, 119–20; political activism, 129–31, 133–36, 139–41; *Rising Up* movie and, 115–17; webpage (drumnyc.org), 119–20
dual citizenship, 15, 104–5, 127, 129
Dunkin' Donuts, 68

e-commerce, 1, 3, 7–8, 18, 24, 38, 75, 84–86, 90, 100–103, 114
educational attainment of Indian Americans, 25, 56–57
Ed Vox (blog), 140
emoticons, 57–58
Epoch Times (news outlet), 140
Espiritu, Yen Le, 130
Ess, Charles, 145–46
ethnicgrocer.com, 38, 86–87, 90–91, 92, 97, 103

Fabmall.com (also Fabmart), 102
Facebook, 3–4, 8, 47–48, 55, 82, 103, 110, 120, 132
Federation of Indian Associations (FIA), 104
Feng, Peter X., 136
fiacona.org (Federation of Indian American Christian Organizations in North America), 9
flexible citizenship, 22, 84, 148
Flower Drum Song (film), 136–37
food, 7, 27–30, 64, 87–88, 93, 95, 99–100, 102, 147; ethnic, 27, 90–91, 147; imperialism and, 27; Indian, 27, 29, 83, 88, 96; Indian American, 27–28
Fortune (magazine), 91

Funding Exchange, 139
Future of Tomorrow (F.O.T.), 140

Gajjala, Radhika, 23, 75
Gajjala, Venkataramana, 23
garamchai.com, 8
Gates, Bill, 25–26, 76
geekgrrrls, 44
GeoCities, 7
Georgiou, Myria, 45
Gilroy, Paul, 23
global city, 94, 98, 129
Global Finance Magazine, 104
Global Justice (program), 128, 134
Global South, 123, 127, 128, 129, 139
global Web, 17–18, 39–43, 144, 147
Goggin, Gerard, 145
Gomez-Peña, Guillermo, 41
Gonzalez, Vernadette V., 42
Google, 4, 150; Project Loon, 41
Gotham Gazette, 140
"Grasping the Future," 25
green card, 12, 13, 50, 53–54, 59, 62, 67, 78–79. *See also* permanent residents
Gregg, Melissa, 44
grocery stores, 89–90, 99; ethnic, 87, 89, 90; Indian, 87, 93; online, 89–91
Groupon, 29
Grusin, Richard, 89

H1Bees, 31, 32, 38
H1Bjobs.com, 78, 80, 168n96
H1Bmarriages.com, 8, 79, 80
H-1B visas, 13, 16, 18, 24, 29, 46–47; coded as primary, 76–81; curry rock and, 31–32; eligibility for, 52; stereotypes about, 80
H4 Indian Ladies Forum, 46–49; and the "American Dream," 49–50; educational attainment and, 56–57; and gendered spaces, 72–76
H-4 visas, 18, 46–48, 50–51, 62, 69, 73, 117; gender and, 53–55; ineligibility to work under, 51–53, 66–68
Hajari, Nisid, 37
Haldiram, 87–88, 112
Hall, Stuart, 23, 126
heteronormativity, 9, 59, 80, 96, 114, 123, 125, 137, 177n68

Hindu: festivals, 87, 101; men, 26–27, 48; middle class, 16, 83–84, 95–96, 114, 123; mythology, 92; nation, 96; women, 60, 73, 96, 170n35

Hinduism, 60

Hindunet.org, 9

Hispanic immigrants, 10–11, 138–39

home and homeland, 1–6, 17, 21, 44–45; metaphors in online media, 68–72; online narratives of, 83–85; time-space, 59–61; transnationalism and, 97–100. *See also* household; NRI home/household; virtual home

homegrrls, 44

homelessness, 144

homemakers, 61, 130

homepages, 1, 4, 143–45; cultures of, 5–9; concept of home in, 4–5, 43–44; nationalisms, 39–43; personal, 7–8; possibilities offered by, 22

home screen, 4

home shopping sites, 8, 85–103. *See also* e-commerce; Indiaplaza.com; Namaste.com

homesickness, 58, 59

Home Territories (Morley), 45, 144

Horse That Flew, The (Rajghatta), 27, 37

Hotmail, 25–26

household, 22–23, 44–45. *See also* home and homeland; NRI home/household

HuanYin.com, 90

Hyderabad, 26, 34

Hyderabad Information Technology Engineering Consultancy (HITEC) City, 34

hypermobility, 144

hyperreal, 98, 99

Hypertext Markup Language (HTML), 5

Hypertext Transfer Protocol (HTTP), 5

iacfpa.org, 9

ICICI Bank, 8, 82–83, 104, 106–14; advertising by, 110–11

"imagined community," 22

immaterial labor, 63

immigrants, concepts of home and homeland for, 21–22

Immigration and Nationality Act, 11

Immigration and Naturalization Services (INS), 116

India: brain drain to the United States, 14–15, 157n50; diaspora, 22–23, 110, 144; science- and technology-related labor force in, 14–15; Silicon Valley of, 26

India Abroad (newspaper), 17, 78, 83, 92, 103–6, 107, 113

India Book House, 102

India Central, 100

India Currents (magazine), 123

India Day Parade, 102

Indian American marketplace, 83

Indian Americans: advertising targeted at, 92–96, 110–14; in age of network capitalism, 9–16; banking and, 8, 103–14, 172n74, 172n76; brain drain from India, 14–15, 157n50; concepts of home and homeland, 21, 44–45; curry as metaphor for, 27–38; demographic terms applied to, 12; directories of, 24–25; diversity of, 2–3; dual citizenship of, 15, 104–5; early online presence of, 6; economic clout of, 11; educational attainment of, 25; and food, 27–28; idea of monolithic, 1–2; immigration trends, 11–13; masculinity and, 32–35; model minority stereotype and, 9–10, 16, 26, 129; networking among, 32–33; personal webpages and, 7–8; popular music and, 124; racism toward, 28–30; stereotypes of "wired," 3, 80, 130; transnationalism, 97–100, 101–2, 127, 146–47; visas obtained by, 13–14, 16, 24, 29, 31–32, 76–81; websites targeted at, 8–9. *See also* consumer goods; *desi*; H4 Indian Ladies Forum

indiandating.com, 8

Indian diaspora, 27, 39, 60, 77, 104, 110

Indian Express (newspaper), 93

Indian Institute of Technology (IIT), 14–15, 76

indianmatrimonials.com, 7

indiaplaza.com, 8, 83, 86–87, 100–103

"India Shining," 16, 157

India Today (magazine), 93

Indigo Monsoon Group (IMG), 103

INDOlink.com, 74–76, 79, 101, 106

IndoUS Venture Partners (IUVP), 103

Indusladies.com, 18, 46, 58–59, 69, 72–75, 110

Industrial Credit and Insurance Corporation of India, 107

information technology, 33. *See also* Silicon Indian
Infosys Technologies, 77
Integral Capital Partners, 91
Internationalizing Internet Studies (Goggin and McLelland), 145
Internet, 153n1; country codes, 42; domain names, 42; dot-com boom, 7, 26; global Web, 41–43, 144, 147; growth of Indian Americans involvement in, 6; origins of, 5, 22, 41. *See also* online media
Internet Archive, 17, 130
IT industry, 33. *See also* Silicon Indian

Jahangir, Sultana, 115–17
Jay Sean, 123
Jey, Malathy, 58, 72

Kang, Jerry, 43
Kanjeevaram saris, 87–88
Karma of Brown Folk (Prashad), 126
Karnik, Satwik, 83
Kaur, Nindy, 123
KB Partners, 91
Khan, Shahrukh, 111
Khandelwal, Madhulika, 71, 85
Khosla, Vinod, 24, 91
Kleiner Perkins Caufield & Byers, 91

L-1 visas, 53
L-2 visas, 53
Lal, Vinay, 41
Landow, George P., 131
Landzelius, Kyra, 44
Latino stereotypes, 36
Life or Liberty, 115
Lee, Rachel, 23
LinkedIn, 4
Lipsitz, George, 85
Lister, Martin, 6
Little India (magazine), 24–25, 26, 100
Lowe, Lisa, 12, 118

Mahesh, B. G., 100
Maira, Sunaina, 133
Make the Road NY, 140
Mamidipudi, Annapurna, 75
Manavi, 54

Marchetti, Gina, 136–37
masculinity, 27, 32–36, 38, 96, 99, 111
Massey, Doreen, 45
Maulik, Monami, 138–39, 141
McCaughey, Martha, 133
MCI, 88
McLelland, Mark, 145
media. *See* mobile media; old media; online media; social media
Merrill Lynch, 91
M.I.A., 123
Microsoft, 4, 26, 76
middle class, 24, 68, 95; transnational, 66, 68, 75
mobile media, 2, 4, 8, 99–100, 145
mobile privatization, 69
MobileRediff, 8. *See also* Rediff.com
model minority stereotype, 9–10, 16, 26, 51, 124–29, 136
Mohanty, Chandra Talpade, 49
Morley, David, 45, 144
music, popular, 123–24
Muslim immigrants, 115–17, 127, 128, 141

NAACP, 140
Naidu, Chandrababu, 34
Nakamura, Lisa, 6, 40, 129, 134, 145
Namaste (film), 124
Namaste.com, 8, 38, 83; advertising by, 92–96; customer service, 88–90; founding of, 86–87; goods sold by, 87–88; groceries sold by, 89–91; idealized beauty and, 94–97; intertwining of virtual with mobile, 99–100; role in home narrative of Indian immigrants, 97–98
National Border Justice and Solidarity Delegation, 138
National Border Solidarity Convention, 138
National Global Justice Program, 134
nationalisms, homepage, 39–43
National Network for Immigrant and Refugee Rights, 134
National Public Radio (NPR), 31
National Security Entry-Exit Registration System (NSEERS) program, 116, 141
NBC, 137
netchicks, 44
Netscape Navigator, 5

Index

network capitalism, 9–16
New New Thing, The (Lewis), 37
New Orleans Workers' Center for Racial Justice, 135
Newsweek (magazine), 17
New York Police Department, 122, 130–31
New York Taxi Workers Alliance (NYTWA), 120–21
Nokia, 4
Non Resident External (NRE) account, 108–9
Nonresident Indian Day, 15
nonresident Indians (NRIs), 2, 6, 12, 15, 153–54n2; banking services and, 82–83, 107–14, 172n74, 172n76; home life narratives of, 83–85; idealized life, 53; ideological recasting of, 77–78. *See also* H4 Indian Ladies Forum
Notta, Amritpal Singh, 100
NRI home/household, 18, 50, 55–56, 66, 80–81, 84–85, 109, 148–49
NRIOL.com, 80
nriworld.com, 47
NYCLU, 140

Obama, Barack, 135
Oiarzabal, Pedro J., 39
old media, 41; representations of Asian Americans in, 136–37
Ong, Aihwa, 70–71, 112, 126
online media: activism and, 128–36, 139–41; as break from old media, 41; cultural and racial bias built into, 42; dating and marriage sites, 8, 79, 170n34; digital diaspora and, 22–23, 39–43; feminism and, 44; global Web of, 41–43, 144; H4 women's use of, 63–65; homepage nationalisms and, 39–43; homepages, 1, 4–5, 43–44; home shopping sites, 85–103; Internet architecture and, 5; metaphors of home in, 68–72; recasting home, 16–19, 143–45; study of, 145–52; targeted at different Indian communities, 2–3, 8–9; transnationalism and, 97–100, 101–2, 127, 146–47; virtual and mobile, 99–100; as women's space, 72–76
On Not Speaking Chinese (Ang), 21
Other, racial, 38, 118
Outsourced (TV show), 137

Overseas Citizen of India card, 15
Overseas Indian Citizenship (OCI), 15

Pakistani, 30, 118
Pandey, Chulbul, 113
People's Justice, The, 122
permanent residents, 12–13, 54–55, 175n36. *See also* green card
personal web pages, 7
Persons of Indian Origin (PIO), 15, 104–5
PEW Research, 10, 11, 12
political activism, 128–36. *See also* activism
post-9/11 security measures, 115–17, 122, 132–33, 173–74n1
postcolonial, 73, 107
postsocial media revolution, 153
Pradesh, Andhra, 34, 38
Prashad, Vijay, 126
Pravasi Bhartiya Divas, 15, 104–5
presentist approach, 145
privatized mobility, 69
profiling, racial, 122, 130–31, 138–39
Project Loon, 41
Purkayastha, Bandana, 85

QueRico.com, 90

Race after the Internet (ed. Nakamura and Chow-White), 145
racial ambivalence, 35–36
Racial and Immigrant Justice Program, 128, 130
racial Other, 38, 118
racial profiling, 122, 130–31, 138–39
racism, 38–39; built into online media, 42; curry metaphor and, 27–38; curry rock and, 31–32; masculinity and, 32–35; in media representations of Asian Americans, 136–37; New York Police Department and, 122, 130–31; racial ambivalence and, 35–36; racial profiling and, 122, 130–31, 138–39; stereotypes and, 28–30
Rajghatta, Chidanand, 27, 37–38
Raksha Bandhan, 101
Ramakrishnan, Karthick, 10
Rangaswamy, Padma, 71
Rediff.com, 7, 8, 47, 83, 88, 102, 105–8, 110–12
Rekhi, Kanwal, 24
remediation, 23, 89–90, 99, 134

Rich, B. Ruby, 64
Rights Working Group (RWG), 131, 134
"Rise of Asian Americans, The" (report), 10
Rising Up: The Alams (film), 115–17, 118, 141
Rodriguez, Robyn Magalit, 42
Rudrappa, Sharmila, 64

SAALT (South Asian Americans Leading Together), 2, 131–32
sakhi.org, 9, 54
salganyc.org, 9
samachar.com, 8, 78, 79, 101, 106, 113
Samanez, Rafael, 138
Sassen, Saskia, 98
Satyam Computer Services, 77
SAWNET (South Asian Women's NETwork), 2, 74
Seinfeld (TV show), 26
semantic web, 5, 153
shaadi.com, 8, 79
Shah, Sheila, 100–101
Shah, Vijay, 100–101
Shankar, Shalini, 126
Sharma, Nitasha Tamar, 126
Shields, Rob, 143, 144
Shklovski, Irina, 42
Shohat, Ella, 23, 139
shopping sites. *See* home shopping sites
shrines, virtual, 60
Shrivastava, Sandeep, 106
sify.com, 8, 113
Silicon Alley, 36, 159n29
Silicon Hills, 26, 35
SiliconIndia, 17, 32–35, 78, 93, 95, 96, 113
Silicon Indian: in Austin, Texas, 35–36; characteristics of, 24–27; networking among, 32–33; in the racialized U.S. landscape, 27–28; racist stereotypes of, 28–30; techno-militarism and, 32–35
Silicon Valley, 24, 26, 37
Singh, Arvind J., 106
Singh, Parry, 90
Singh, Supriya, 110
Sistas and Brothas United, 140
smart home, 69
social justice activism, 53–55, 118, 120, 122–23, 128–36, 139–42
social media, 2–3, 8, 39, 47–48, 114, 132, 137, 141, 145, 153–54; platforms, 4, 82

Sony, 92
South, Global, 123, 127, 128, 129, 139
South Asian Americans, 2, 6, 30, 115, 122, 129–30, 142; *desi* term and, 117–19. *See also* DRUM (Desis Rising Up and Moving); Indian Americans
South Asian Americans Leading Together (SAALT), 2, 131–32
South Asian Workers Center, 122, 128
Special Registration Act, 117
Spigel, Lynn, 64, 69
Srivastava, Ishita, 138
Star, Susan Leigh, 44
Star TV, 113
"stindian," 28–29
"Strange New World of the Internet, The," 6
Struthers, David, 42
Student Safety Act, 140
subway, 117
Subway (restaurant), 68
sulekha.com, 8, 9, 48, 65
Sumeet Center, 102
Sunshine Groceries, 100
surfing, 64

TANA.org, 9
"tech-coolies," 38
techno-feminism, 66
techno-masculinity, 38, 79, 99
techno-migrant, 24
techno-militarism, 32–35
techno-Orientalism, 41–42
Terranova, Tiziana, 63
TiE.org, 9
Tigerstyle, 123
Time (magazine), 6, 17, 29, 37
Times of India (newspaper), 17
time-space, 57–59
Times Square, 93–94, 96, 98, 135
Titan watches, 87–88
transnationalism, 97, 99, 127, 145
travel, virtual, 42
Trikone.org, 9
Tumblr, 4, 30, 31
Turkle, Sherry, 43
TV Asia, 92
T visa, 54
Twitter, 3, 4, 8, 30, 47, 132

un-belonging, 2
Uniform Resource Locator (URL), 5, 44, 64, 87, 102–3, 119–20
United for Peace and Justice, 134
United National Anti-War Committee, 134
Urban Dictionary (site), 28–29
Urban Youth Collaborative, 132, 140
URLs, 5, 44, 64, 87, 102–3, 119–20
USCIS (United States Citizenship and Immigration Services), 46, 53, 76

Vaitheeswaran, K., 102
Value Communications Corporation, 106
VAMOS Unidos, 138
venture capital, 7, 86, 91, 103
venture capitalists (VCs), 16, 24, 91
Violence Against Women Act, 54
virtual barrio, 41–42
virtual community, 72–73
Virtual Community, The (Rheingold), 16
virtual diaspora, 23, 40
virtual home, 44, 60, 83
virtual India, 7, 77
virtual network, 18, 41, 77, 91, 97
virtual reality, 34
virtual shrines, 60
virtual signifier, 38
virtual travel, 42
virtual work, 66–67
visas, immigration: curry rock and, 31–32; eligibility for, 52; gender and, 53–55; H-1B, 13–14, 16, 24, 29, 46–47; H-4, 18, 46–48; ineligibility to work and, 51–53, 66–67; L-1 and L-2, 53; primary coding of H-1, 76–81

Wakeford, Nina, 44, 68

Web, global, 17–18, 39–43, 144, 147
Web 1.0, 5
Web 2.0, 4, 47
Web 3.0, 5, 153
Web History (Brügger), 145
webindia.com, 6–7
Wiley, Margaret, 70
Williams, Raymond, 69
Wipro, 77
Wired (magazine), 26
wired Indian, 3, 149
wired minority, 150
Wise, Patricia, 34, 80
women, Indian immigrant: cyberspace as women's space and, 72–76; *desi* term and, 121–22; domestic discontent among, 55–63; DRUM and, 121–22; educational attainment of, 56–57; feminism and, 44, 45, 53–54, 66, 70; Hinduism and, 60; idealized beauty and, 94–97; ineligibility to work, 51–53, 66–68; stereotypes of, 73. *See also* H4 Indian Ladies Forum
Wong, Sau-ling Cynthia, 23
Wordpress, 46
work, virtual, 66–67
World Bank, 15
World Wide Web, 5, 8, 146

XOOM, 113–14

Yahoo!, 4, 6; GeoCities, 7
Youth Power!, 121–22, 128, 132, 135
YouTube, 3, 4, 8, 113, 116, 120, 138

Zee TV, 92
Zelizer, V. A., 110

MADHAVI MALLAPRAGADA is an assistant professor in the Department of Radio-TV-Film at the University of Texas at Austin.

THE ASIAN AMERICAN EXPERIENCE

The Hood River Issei: An Oral History of Japanese Settlers
    in Oregon's Hood River Valley   *Linda Tamura*
Americanization, Acculturation, and Ethnic Identity: The Nisei Generation
    in Hawaii   *Eileen H. Tamura*
Sui Sin Far/Edith Maude Eaton: A Literary Biography   *Annette White-Parks*
Mrs. Spring Fragrance and Other Writings   *Sui Sin Far; edited by Amy Ling
    and Annette White-Parks*
The Golden Mountain: The Autobiography of a Korean Immigrant, 1895–1960
    Easurk Emsen Charr; edited and with an introduction by Wayne Patterson
Race and Politics: Asian Americans, Latinos, and Whites in a Los Angeles Suburb
    Leland T. Saito
Achieving the Impossible Dream: How Japanese Americans Obtained Redress
    Mitchell T. Maki, Harry H. L. Kitano, and S. Megan Berthold
If They Don't Bring Their Women Here: Chinese Female Immigration
    before Exclusion   *George Anthony Peffer*
Growing Up Nisei: Race, Generation, and Culture among Japanese Americans
    of California, 1924–49   *David K. Yoo*
Chinese American Literature since the 1850s   *Xiao-huang Yin*
Pacific Pioneers: Japanese Journeys to America and Hawaii, 1850–80   *John E. Van Sant*
Holding Up More Than Half the Sky: Chinese Women Garment Workers
    in New York City, 1948–92   *Xiaolan Bao*
Onoto Watanna: The Story of Winnifred Eaton   *Diana Birchall*
Edith and Winnifred Eaton: Chinatown Missions and Japanese Romances
    Dominika Ferens
Being Chinese, Becoming Chinese American   *Shehong Chen*
"A Half Caste" and Other Writings   *Onoto Watanna; edited by Linda Trinh Moser
    and Elizabeth Rooney*
Chinese Immigrants, African Americans, and Racial Anxiety in the United States,
    1848–82   *Najia Aarim-Heriot*
Not Just Victims: Conversations with Cambodian Community Leaders in the United
    States   *Edited and with an introduction by Sucheng Chan; interviews conducted
    by Audrey U. Kim*
The Japanese in Latin America   *Daniel M. Masterson with Sayaka Funada-Classen*
Survivors: Cambodian Refugees in the United States   *Sucheng Chan*
From Concentration Camp to Campus: Japanese American Students
    and World War II   *Allan W. Austin*
Japanese American Midwives: Culture, Community, and Health Politics   *Susan L. Smith*
In Defense of Asian American Studies: The Politics of Teaching
    and Program Building   *Sucheng Chan*
Lost and Found: Reclaiming the Japanese American Incarceration   *Karen L. Ishizuka*
Religion and Spirituality in Korean America   *Edited by David K. Yoo and Ruth H. Chung*

Moving Images: Photography and the Japanese American Incarceration   *Jasmine Alinder*
Camp Harmony: Seattle's Japanese Americans and the Puyallup Assembly Center
    Louis Fiset
Chinese American Transnational Politics   *Him Mark Lai, edited and with an introduction
    by Madeline Y. Hsu*
Issei Buddhism in the Americas   *Edited by Duncan Ryûken Williams and Tomoe Moriya*
Hmong America: Reconstructing Community in Diaspora   *Chia Youyee Vang*
In Pursuit of Gold: Chinese American Miners in the American West   *Sue Fawn Chung*
Pacific Citizens: Larry and Guyo Tajiri and Japanese American Journalism
    in the World War II Era   *Edited by Greg Robinson*
Indian Accents: Brown Voice and Racial Performance in American Television
    and Film   *Shilpa S. Davé*
Yellow Power, Yellow Soul: The Radical Art of Fred Ho   *Edited by Roger N. Buckley
    and Tamara Roberts*
Fighting from a Distance: How Filipino Exiles Helped Topple a Dictator
    Jose V. Fuentecilla
In Defense of Justice: Joseph Kurihara and the Japanese American Struggle for
    Equality   *Eileen H. Tamura*
Asian Americans in Dixie: Race and Migration in the South   *Edited by Jigna Desai
    and Khyati Y. Joshi*
Undercover Asian: Multiracial Asian Americans in Visual Culture   *Leilani Nishime*
Islanders in the Empire: Filipino and Puerto Rican Laborers in Hawai'i   *JoAnna Poblete*
Virtual Homelands: Indian Immigrants and Online Cultures
    in the United States   *Madhavi Mallapragada*

The University of Illinois Press
is a founding member of the
Association of American University Presses.

Composed in 10.75/13 Arno Pro
by Lisa Connery
at the University of Illinois Press
Manufactured by Sheridan Books, Inc.

University of Illinois Press
1325 South Oak Street
Champaign, IL 61820-6903
www.press.uillinois.edu